Russian Nationalism and Ukraine
The Nationality Policy of the Volunteer Army
during the Civil War

Russian Nationalism and Ukraine

The Nationality Policy of the Volunteer Army during the Civil War

Anna Procyk

Canadian Institute of Ukrainian Studies Press
Edmonton   1995   Toronto

Canadian Institute of Ukrainian Studies Press
University of Alberta
Edmonton, Alberta
T6G 2E8 CANADA

University of Toronto
Toronto, Ontario
M5S 1A1 CANADA

Copyright © 1995 Canadian Institute of Ukrainian Studies
ISBN 1-895571-04-9

Canadian Cataloguing in Publication Data

Procyk, Anna, 1937-
  Russian nationalism and Ukraine : the nationality policy of the volunteer army during the Civil War

Includes bibliographical references and index.
ISBN 1-895571-04-9

1. Soviet Union - History - Revolution, 1917-1921.
2. Soviet Union, Southern - History - Revolution, 1917-1921. 3. Nationalism - Soviet Union.
4. Minorities - Soviet Union. 5. Ukraine - History - Revolution, 1917-1921. I. Title.

DK265.2.P76 1995   947.084'1   C95-930467-3

Publication of this volume is made possible in part by a grant from the Cosbild Club Endowment Fund.

All rights reserved.

No part of this publication may be reproduced, stored in a retrieval system, or transmitted in any form or by any means, electronic, mechanical, photocopying, recording or otherwise without the prior permission of the copyright owner.

Printed in Canada

To Volodymyr and Motria Procyk

Contents

Preface		ix
Introduction		xiii
I.	**The Question of a Separate Peace with Germany, and the Birth of the White Idea**	1
	National Rebirth during the Revolution	11
	The Nationality Question from the Perspective of the High Command	17
	Developments in Ukraine up to the Separate Peace	19
	The Nationality Question in Russian Liberal Thought	27
	Nationalism and Federalism in Ukraine	31
II.	**"Russia One and Indivisible" and Ukraine**	35
	The Political Objectives of the Volunteer Army	39
	Developments in Kyiv and the Volunteer Army	44
	Russian Interpretations of the Ukrainian Question	49
	Russian Anti-Bolshevik Organizations in Kyiv	52
III.	**An Indivisible or a Democratic Russia: The Root of the White Dilemma**	57
	A White General in a Liberal Saddle	58
	A Black Knight in the White Army	66
	"Bolsheviks of the Right" in the Civil War	72

IV.	The Questions of Russia's Indivisibility and Ukraine at the Paris Peace Conference	83
	Divided at Home, United Abroad	88
	The Nationality Question in International Politics	93
	The Ukrainian Question and the Entente Intervention	105
V.	A Divided or a Bolshevik Russia: Which Was the Lesser Evil?	119
	Denikin and the UNR Directory	125
	Denikin and the Ukrainian Galician Army: An Unholy Alliance	134
VI.	The Crimean Experiment: Wrangel and the Nationality Question	145
	Nationality Policy in the Rightists' Hands	149
	The Polish-Ukrainian Alliance	152
	The Implementation of the Nationality Program	156
VII.	Conclusions	165
Bibliography		177
Index		193

Preface

This is a book about history's losers and about lost opportunities. The losers are the Russian military and political elites who tied their fates to the anti-Bolshevik Volunteer Army (VA), and the Ukrainian federalists and separatists who tried desperately and ultimately in vain to carve out a place for an independent state on the territory of the former Russian Empire. The lost opportunities are a multiethnic, democratic republic that would have replaced the autocratic Russian Empire with a genuinely federal or confederal arrangement and a more equal relationship between the two dominant nations in the squandered federalist alternative, namely, the Russians and Ukrainians. Instead, the Bolshevik victory that ended the fierce years of civil war and social upheaval imposed a unitary arrangement on a Soviet Union that gathered in most of the lands of the former empire; the ruthless, centralizing Stalinist bureaucracy quashed all hopes of national autonomy and democratic rule under the slogans of Soviet federalism and the brotherhood of Soviet peoples.

Thus, in many senses, the conflict between Russia and Ukraine that characterizes post-Soviet politics is a legacy of these earlier developments. The difficulties of transforming the unequal relations of the Soviet multiethnic political economy into a more meaningful sharing of power along federal lines parallel the confrontations of the years 1917–20. Anna Procyk has reconstructed the dynamics of the relationship between the various Ukrainian governments and the leadership of the White movement in the South, the VA, during the civil war years. The conflict between Ukrainian federalists and Russian centralists has its origins, in turn, in an earlier confrontation during the State Duma period of the last years of the autocracy, when the Ukrainian political movement made its first demands on its largely unresponsive and occasionally hostile Russian liberal and socialist counterparts. But the revolutions of 1917 brought the former oppositionists into power and transformed their largely intellectual disagreements into seemingly irreconcilable national interests.

Dr. Procyk revises our understanding of the politics of this critical period in several fundamental ways. By focusing on the nationality policy of the VA and the Kadet leaders who dominated its politics, she challenges the widespread understanding of the White movement's aims as primarily anti-Bolshevik or even restorationist (a view persuasively argued by Peter Kenez in his pioneering *Civil War in South Russia, 1918: The First Year of the Volunteer Army* [1971] and *Civil War in South Russia, 1919–20: The Defeat of the Whites* [1977]) in favor of an interpretation that highlights the nationalist aims encapsulated in the slogan "Russia One and Indivisible" *(Edinaia i nedelimaia Rossiia)*. The White movement was preoccupied with maintaining Russia's position as a great power in the international arena, its unitary state order, and the predominance of the Russian element in any future Russia. Indeed, this study is unique in taking the rich literature about Russian nationalism from the domain of largely intellectual historians to its consequences for real-life political and military conflict; furthermore, the attitudes of the VA toward the issues of autonomy for non-Russian nations may to a considerable degree explain the motives of the many thousands of former imperial officers who joined the Red Army during its war with Poland, a war that was fought largely on territory claimed by the Ukrainian governments.

Dr. Procyk challenges a second commonly held view of the White movement and its failures that has assigned primary blame to the military men and has stigmatized those men as largely reactionary and monarchist in their political orientation. (This interpretation has its roots in the memoirs of the surviving Kadet collaborators with the White movement, whose self-vindicating views have profoundly shaped our perceptions.) In contrast, the author persuasively demonstrates that the Political Center, whose core was dominated by Kadets who had played a prominent role in the Russian Provisional Government, provided the primary ideological and political support during the Denikin period and reinforced Denikin's intransigence in refusing to deal with the various Ukrainian governments that appeared during the course of the civil war, but also with other competing groups such as the Cossacks and Tatars, who also were claiming more autonomy and self-rule in a future Russia. Dr. Procyk's characterization of the Kadets thereby complements and reinforces the collective portrait of their evolution in William Rosenberg's *Liberals in the Russian Revolution: The Constitutional Democratic Party, 1917–1921* (1974).

Finally, the author implicitly challenges another widely shared explanation for the Bolshevik triumph in the civil war, an explanation that is viewed differently by émigré Russian nationalists and liberals on one side and émigré Ukrainian nationalists and separatists on the other. Here the prevailing interpretation is that the Ukrainians were in large measure responsible for the White defeat and/or Bolshevik victory because of their unwillingness to compromise. What Dr. Procyk describes is a series of Ukrainian governments reaching out to the VA, among other contending parties, with federalist schemes for the rebuilding of a democratic Russia, and the Whites rebuffing all such moderate efforts to rebuild from below in favor of reestablishing Russia from above through military conquest (until, of course, the very end when their cause was virtually lost). These episodes highlight the strong federalist trend in Ukrainian political thought, one that is given little attention by Ukrainian historians, except to suggest that it was a stage in the ineluctable development toward national separatism. Although federalist thinking has been described as alien to Russian political thought (and this is clearly the case for the politicians associated with the VA), that description was far less appropriate for political thought on the peripheries of the Russian Empire, particularly in Siberia and Ukraine. The tragic confrontation of Ukrainian federalism with Russian great-power centralism ruled out a united anti-Bolshevik front and thereby rendered both sides in the conflict more vulnerable to the threats of foreign interventionists and Red Army legions.

Of course, thanks to a generation of revisionist scholarship on the revolution and civil war that has focused on its social history, we are now rethinking the major outlines and meaning of that momentous and protracted struggle. But social historians as well have too often focused on a geographically and ethnically Russocentric conflict (see, for example, the conference volume edited by Diane P. Koenker, William G. Rosenberg, and Ronald Grigor Suny, *Party, State, and Society in the Russian Civil War: Explorations in Social History* [1989]) and have accepted the aforementioned characterization of the White movement as primarily one dedicated to the restoration of the autocratic social and political hierarchies. That social history is gradually being expanded to the non-Russian peripheries and enclaves of the collapsed empire, where social conflicts overlapped tragically with ethnic struggles and where foreign intervention was a more genuine threat and constant reality. It is here that Anna Procyk's solidly researched study effectively unravels several historical clichés and compels future historians to redefine and rethink the central characters and ideas that figured prominently at various stages of the conflict.

Mark von Hagen
Columbia University

Introduction

In the historiography of the Russian revolution and civil war, the origins of the White movement appear to be inextricably linked with the Bolshevik seizure of power in November 1917. Indeed, the establishment of the Bolshevik regime in the heart of the Russian Empire is considered as the raison d'être of the White movement. According to this line of reasoning, the movement emerged as a counterforce to the victory of radical socialism in Russia, and consequently the White centers have habitually been linked exclusively with the forces of reaction, restoration, and conservatism. Yet, a closer examination of the White struggle reveals that its roots reached far deeper than the appearance of the Bolsheviks as a political force to be reckoned with. Moreover, one would look in vain for staunch monarchists and reactionaries among the founders of the White cause. In fact, the nucleus of the White movement—its most prominent political and military leaders—consisted of men directly involved in the welter of events that led to the fall of tsarism—the very force they purportedly wanted to put back in power, according to Soviet and most Western writings.

Many factors are responsible for perpetuating the myth that the principal task of the White movement was to resurrect the old order in Russia. Perhaps none is as important as the movement's rigid adherence to the widely publicized slogan of "Russia One and Indivisible." The chief task of this inquiry is to unravel the meaning behind this well-known yet never seriously investigated objective by focusing on the nationality program of the Whites. The study will examine the rights and privileges that were envisaged for the nationalities within the framework of an "indivisible" Russia and attempt to explain why a movement the White leaders founded on the periphery of the empire, where the support of the nationalities was crucial for the successful conduct of the war, adhered so tenaciously to the idea of an undivided Russia.

While pursuing these objectives, the study will attempt to answer these questions: What fundamental principles guided the White movement's nationality policy? What ideological foundations did they have? Were the basic principles consistently adhered to? If so, what accounted for the rigidity and inflexibility of the policy? If changes were introduced in the course of time, what were the reasons for their adoption?

To provide satisfactory answers to the above queries, the study first examines the origins of the White movement and the nationality question in the tsarist empire on the eve of 1917 and during the first turbulent months of the March revolution. It then proceeds to consider the political views and outlook of the White leaders. This, in turn, requires an analysis of the programs of the principal parties involved in the anti-Bolshevik struggle and a thorough investigation of the nationality program and policies of the White movement itself. Finally, it evaluates the role the nationality question played in the intricate relationship between the intervening Entente forces and the White armies. An attempt has been made to explain not only what was happening and why, but also to point out what people thought was happening and why.

Considering the large number of White centers that sprang up during the civil war and the multitude of nationalities in the tsarist empire, definite restrictions on the scope of this study were inevitable. As its title indicates, it focuses on the nationality policy of the VA as reflected in its relations with Ukraine.

These limits have been set on the assumption that a clear exposition of the nationality policy of anti-Bolshevik Russia could best be presented if the research concentrated on one important stronghold of the White movement that preserved the following elements throughout the civil strife: continuity in leadership; immediate proximity to the borderland governments; ties—even if tenuous—with the other Russian anti-Bolshevik centers; and uninterrupted relations with the intervening Entente forces.

The White movement centered in the VA best fulfills these requirements. It was the only stronghold of the White cause that was able to maintain its existence from the beginning to the end of the civil war. Founded almost immediately after the Bolshevik coup in November 1917 by two prominent generals of the Russian Army, the VA was led for two years by one of the ablest White leaders, Gen. Anton I. Denikin. The VA emerged in the Don Cossack region, a territory with strong autonomous tendencies. Shortly after its creation, it ran into serious difficulties in the neighboring Kuban, where not only autonomist but also separatist demands were openly voiced. In Ukraine it was confronted with the existence of independent governments of various political complexions—sometimes conservative, sometimes socialist, pro-Russian federalist, or uncompromisingly separatist—during the tortuous course of the civil war.

From the start the White leaders were confronted with a variety of claims, demands, and aspirations expressed by the nationalities. Their relations with the borderland governments were strained and in most instances ended in open military conflict. This forced the leaders of the VA to devote considerable attention to the nationality question, no matter how hard they tried—outwardly at least—to minimize the question's importance. The documents in the archives of the General Headquarters of the VA in the P. N. Wrangel Military Archives at the Hoover Institution on War, Revolution and Peace, on which this study relies heavily, provide ample evidence of the concern of the White movement with the nationality question in general and the Ukrainian problem in particular.

The VA showed an uninterrupted and intense concern with developments in Ukraine because of (1) Ukraine's economic and strategic importance; (2) the significant strides toward independence made by the Ukrainian leaders at home and especially abroad; and (3) the interest that Ukraine attracted among the West European and neighboring states. Only for Ukraine, of all the major nationalities comprising imperial Russia, did the VA prepare a program and attempt to implement it, in the summer and fall of 1919.

Although this study concentrates on the VA's nationality policy, it also considers the fact that the White forces in the southwest constituted only a part of a general movement for Russia's reunification. Satisfactory cooperation between the various Russian anti-Bolshevik centers was never achieved, but concrete steps were taken in this direction. Denikin, in the spring of 1919, actually subordinated the VA to Adm. Aleksandr V. Kolchak, who headed the White movement in Siberia. At the Paris Peace Conference, where the nationality question of the Russian Empire occupied an important place on the agenda of informal conferences between Allied and Russian representatives, the VA and the Kolchak government in Omsk were represented by the same plenipotentiaries. Therefore, the VA's nationality policy will not be treated in isolation, and comparisons with the attitudes toward the nationalities of other Russian anti-Bolshevik centers and circles is inevitable if one intends to provide a thorough examination of the main problems. For this purpose the N. N. Giers Archives, the V. A. Maklakov Archive of the Russian Embassy in Paris in 1918–23, and the V. A. Maklakov Personal Archive in the Hoover Institution have been used.

To provide a deeper insight into the VA's nationality program, the political objectives pursued during the civil war by parties in a position to exert the strongest influence on the formulation of the White movement's policies in the South have also been examined. Here especially valuable have been the Wrangel Military Archives cited above and the S. V. Panina Papers, P. N. Miliukov Personal Archive, Miliukov's "Dnevnik," and A. I. and K. V. Denikin Papers in the Bakhmeteff Archive of Russian and East European History and Culture at Columbia University. Pertinent information has been drawn from the A. V. Cheriachukin Papers, D. G. Shcherbachev Papers, B. I. Nikolaevsky Collection, and P. Dratsenko Documents at the Hoover Institution.

I wish to acknowledge all those who helped to make this study possible. Foremost among those to whom I am indebted is Prof. Edward Allworth, under whose guidance I prepared my dissertation at Columbia University on which this study is based. I am also grateful to Profs. Loren Graham, Leopold Haimson, Alexander Erlich, George Shevelov, and Andrzej Kamiński, who read the manuscript and made many valuable suggestions. While preparing this study, I received financial support from several institutions. I wish to thank the Program on Soviet Nationality Problems at Columbia University, the Ukrainian Research Institute at Harvard University, and the Hoover Institution for their generous research grants. I also owe special thanks to Lev F. Magerovsky, Dr. Witold Sworakowski, and Prof. Wacław Jędrzejewicz, the former curators of archives at Columbia University, the Hoover Institution, and the Piłsudski Institute of America respectively.

All dates are given according to the Gregorian calendar, except as noted in a few quotations. The Library of Congress transliteration system has been followed.

I

The Question of a Separate Peace with Germany, and the Birth of the White Idea

> Treason ... this frightful word, was spreading in the army and in the rear. It was implicating those at the very top ... like an infectious disease. People who, it would seem, were in command of their senses were going mad.
>
> V. V. Shul'gin, *Dni,* 138.

The overthrow of tsarism in March 1917, according to Pavel N. Miliukov, the eminent historian and prominent political leader of the Russian liberals, had all the attributes of a truly national upheaval because "all parts of the nation and all political groups ... united in one common effort to defeat the common enemy—the autocracy."[1] The conservatives of the State Duma,[2] the moderates of the Progressive Bloc,[3] and the military of the General Staff together endorsed the revolutionary movement in early 1917, after it became obvious that no victory in war was possible as long as autocracy existed in Russia. For Miliukov the spark of the first revolution was ignited not with the bread riots and workers' strikes in the capital in the second week of March 1917, but

---

1. P. N. Miliukov, *Russia Today and Tomorrow* (New York: Macmillan, 1922), 23.
2. The lower legislative chamber introduced by the Constitution of 1906.
3. The military setbacks of 1915 and the growing discontent of the Duma's leaders with the government's conduct of the war led to the formation in August 1915 of a coalition of opposition groups, the Progressive Bloc, to give unified expression to the demands for reform. In its appeal to the tsar and his advisors, it insisted on the formation of a government responsible to the Duma. Ibid., 19. See also N. Lapin, "Progressivnyi blok v 1915–17 gg.," *Krasnyi arkhiv* 50–1 (1932): 117–60; Michael F. Hamm, "Liberal Politics in Wartime Russia: An Analysis of the Progressive Bloc," *Slavic Review,* September 1974, 453–68; Thomas Riha, "Miliukov and the Progressive Bloc in 1915: A Study in Last Chance Politics," *Journal of Modern History,* March 1960, 16–24; and V. V. Shul'gin, "Glavy iz knigi 'Gody,'" *Istoriia SSSR,* 1967, no. 1, 123–44.

four months earlier, when from the tribune of the Duma he delivered his famous speech (14 November 1916). While boldly criticizing the policies of the tsarist regime, he asked the audience "What is this? Stupidity or treason?"[4]

Miliukov obviously exaggerated the impact of his speech on the course of the Russian revolution. Yet it is true that it was in the winter months of 1916–17 that growing discontent with the existing regime solidified into an all-embracing national opposition to autocracy. During those months discontent rapidly spread in the most reliable pillar of the Russian monarchy—the Russian army. Even though the censors did not allow the text of Miliukov's speech to appear in the press, copies of it were clandestinely disseminated among the military. Rumors of a coup d'état were rampant, and officers of the frontline armies were mentioned among the conspirators.[5]

Close ties between the army and the Duma—especially those deputies who participated in the Volunteer organization set up to aid the war effort—existed before November 1916.[6] Most military leaders sympathized with civilian endeavors to reform the government. Nonetheless, they were reluctant to pledge their support because a palace coup was being prepared by political circles in the capital, and it was feared that a radical change in Russia during wartime could have fatal consequences for the army.[7]

By the end of 1916 it had become obvious that all efforts at curbing government mismanagement were futile. Even letters from the grand dukes to the tsar protesting the influence wielded by irresponsible individuals, and such drastic measures as the assassination of Rasputin, failed to improve the situation. The empress's interference not only in domestic but also foreign policy incensed the High Command. Her stubborn insistence on a separate peace and her purported treason were widely discussed in the army. Prominent political leaders and high-ranking military men, including the tsar's chief of staff, Gen. Mikhail V. Alekseev, suspected the empress of treason.[8]

These developments must have had a profound effect on the military, and they undoubtedly weakened the generals' reluctance to lend their active

---

4. P. N. Miliukov, *Istoriia vtoroi russkoi revoliutsii*, vol. 1 (Sofia: Rossiisko-bolgarskoe knigoizdatel'stvo, 1921), 9, 34. "Public opinion," notes Miliukov, "has unanimously recognized 1 [14] November 1916 as the beginning of the Russian Revolution."
5. A. I. Denikin, *Ocherki russkoi smuty*, vol. 1, pt. 1 (Berlin: Russkoe natsional'noe knigoizdatel'stvo), 36; P. N. Wrangel, *Memoirs* (London: William and Norgate, 1929), 5.
6. See George Katkov, *Russia, 1917: The February Revolution* (New York: Harper, 1966), chapters 1–3.
7. Denikin, *Ocherki*, 1, pt. 1, 31–7; S. P. Mel'gunov, *Na putiakh k dvortsovomu perevorotu* (Paris: Rodnik, 1931), esp. 94–102, 143–64.
8. Denikin, *Ocherki*, 1, pt. 1, 17–18; Miliukov, *Russia*, p. 21. See also S. P. Mel'gunov, *Legenda o separatnom mire* (Paris, 1957), 121; and his *Na putiakh*, 96–7.

support to the civilian opposition. When, in the second week of March 1917, unrest erupted in the capital and the tsar still refused to name a responsible government, pressure exerted by the General Staff led by Alekseev[9] proved decisive in the events that led to the tsar's abdication.[10]

The relatively peaceful March revolution awakened a variety of hopes, desires, and expectations. For members of the Progressive Bloc and the generals—the two groups from which the leaders of the White movement were drawn—the primary purpose of the revolution was to assure Russia's effective participation in the war against the Central Powers. For them the primary task of the government established after the fall of the monarchy was to conduct the war more successfully, in compliance with commitments made to the Entente, and to prevent Russia's ignominious withdrawal from the war and the conclusion of a separate peace with all the disastrous consequences that this step would entail. The possibility of a separate peace was frequently discussed by the generals. In view of Russia's weak military position, the military foresaw that this would lead to the dismemberment of the empire and the country's complete economic ruin.[11] The liberal intelligentsia also opposed a separate peace with Germany: for them it would mean the triumph of conservatism in Russia and thus the abandonment of all hopes for any meaningful reforms in the country for many years to come.[12]

The new authority failed to live up to the expectation that it would inject fresh life into the Russian army. During the first days of the revolution the Provisional Government proved powerless to arrest the rapid deterioration of discipline in the rank and file resulting from new military regulations

---

9. The commanders of the five fronts, Grand Duke Nikolai Nikolaevich and Gens. Aleksei E. Evert, Vladimir V. Sakharov, Nikolai V. Ruzskii, and Aleksei A. Brusilov were in favor of the tsar's abdication. Only two generals, Count Fedor Keller and Khan Nakhichevanskii, used their troops to support the monarchy. Keller resigned rather than swear loyalty to the Provisional Government. Neither he nor the khan participated in the White movement. See A. S. Lukomskii, *Vospominaniia*, 2 vols. (Berlin: Otto Kirchner, 1922).
10. The Duma representatives departed for Pskov to demand the tsar's abdication were Aleksandr I. Guchkov and Vasilii V. Shul'gin, the leader of the Progressive (Independent) Nationalists in the Fourth Duma. Shul'gin joined the Progressive Bloc and played an important role therein. Even though a monarchist by conviction, he agreed to accompany Guchkov in his difficult mission. This caused him great anguish even though he was confident that the tsar's abdication would save the monarchy. During the civil war Shul'gin played an active role in the White movement, especially in the intelligence department of the VA. V. V. Shul'gin, *Dni* (Leningrad: Priboi, 1925), 135, 150–1, 194–227; D. O. Zaslavskii, *Rytsar Chernoi sotni: V. V. Shul'gin* (Leningrad: Byloe, 1925), 39–72.
11. Denikin, *Ocherki*, 1, pt. 1, 17; pt. 2, 236.
12. Mel'gunov, *Legenda*, 264, 279–86.

introduced by its rival in the capital, the Petrograd Soviet.[13] Within days of the tsar's abdication, Alekseev, the commander in chief appointed by the Provisional Government, telegraphed a plea to the minister of war to do everything in his power to prevent the disease of disintegration from penetrating the army at the front.[14] The reply Alekseev received from the capital was a shocking revelation of the new authority's weakness. The minister of war admitted frankly that "the Provisional Government exists only so long as the Soviet permits this. Especially in the military sphere it is possible now to give out only such orders as do not definitely conflict with the orders of the ... Soviet."[15] Considering this state of affairs, it is not surprising that the first signs of opposition to the revolutionary government appeared not in the milieu of the reactionary bureaucrats and court circles, but among the frontline officers—the same element that had sided with the revolution at the crucial moment of history.

The military did not criticize the government directly, at least not in the first stage of the revolution. To them the Provisional Government was a legitimate heir to the authority it replaced.[16] The Petrograd Soviet, on the other hand, was seen as the very negation of the state system, destroying by its influence the healthy foundations of Russian statehood.[17] It was not, however, the leftist complexion of the Soviet or its predilection for radical solutions for Russia's economic and social ills that aroused the ire of the military. It was principally the Soviet's role in the disintegration of the army and its agitation for peace that prompted the generals to oppose it most resolutely.

A ready-made explanation for the Soviet's gravitation toward pacifist policies, which the frontline officers considered to be tantamount to treason, was found in the fact that the Soviet's policy-making body, the Central Executive Committee, was composed almost exclusively of non-Russians.[18]

---

13. The Soviet appeared on the political scene before the establishment of the PG. On 14 March it issued a controversial order that called soldiers to obey the Military Commission formed by the Temporary Committee of the State Duma only insofar as it did not contradict the policies of the Soviet. Soldiers were to have complete civic freedom and were given the right to elect committees to supervise routine matters and internal administration of the barracks. Robert P. Browder and Alexander F. Kerensky, eds., *The Russian Provisional Government, 1917*, vol. 1 (Stanford: Stanford University Press, 1961), 848–9; on the impact of the revolution at the front, see Allan K. Wildman, *The End of the Russian Imperial Army: The Old Army and the Soldiers' Revolt (March–April 1917)* (Princeton: Princeton University Press, 1980), 202–45.
14. A. A. Sergeev, ed., "Fevral'skaia revoliutsiia 1917 goda," *Krasnyi arkhiv* 22 (1927): 51.
15. A. G. Shliapnikov, *Semnadtsatii god*, vol. 2 (Moscow and Petrograd: Gosizdat, 1925), 236.
16. Denikin, *Ocherki*, 1, pt. 1, 110.
17. Ibid.
18. Denikin most likely refers to the provisional Central Executive Committee. Of its nine members, only one was an ethnic Russian, and even his origin was in doubt. Ibid., 109.

A member of the General Staff and the future leader of the VA stresses this fact: "the exclusive predominance of foreign elements [in the Soviet's Central Executive Committee], [who are] alien to the Russian national idea, naturally could not fail to influence the entire course of the Soviet's activities in a spirit detrimental to Russian statehood."[19]

Unlike the Provisional Government, which in its foreign-policy statements pledged to keep Russia in the war until the conclusion of a general peace, the Petrograd Soviet earnestly appealed in its first message to the world for an immediate peace.[20] Even though in theory the Soviet was promoting the idea of a general peace "without annexations and indemnities," in practice its policies and slogans appeared to be leading to Russia's withdrawal from the war. The Soviet's chairman, the Georgian Menshevik Nikolai S. Chkheidze, explained somewhat apologetically that because socialists always spoke out against the war, "how can I now ask the soldiers to continue the war, to stay at the front?"[21] Thus deep-seated hostility toward the Soviet existed in the General Staff from the very beginning. As for the Provisional Government, sympathy that was evident among the military during the first days of the revolution turned into indignation and subsequently into direct opposition when the government proved incapable of freeing itself from the Soviet's "captivity."

Initially, military opposition expressed itself indirectly through a spontaneous appearance of officers' organizations at the front and in the rear under strikingly patriotic names such as Union of Military Duty, Union of the Honor of the Motherland, and Union of Volunteers for National Defense.[22] The chief objective of these numerous but widely scattered and loosely organized officers' circles was the restoration of discipline and fighting ability in the army. Somewhat different from these amorphous groups of disgruntled officers was Gen. Aleksandr M. Krymov's organization at the Southwestern Front drawn mainly from officers of the Third Cavalry Corps. Krymov was convinced that the Russian army was on the verge of complete disintegration in the spring of 1917, and he expected the collapse of the front at any moment. Accordingly, he began preparing his men to raise the banner of the salvation of Russia in the event this disaster occurred. The patriotic general was confident that all nationally conscious elements of Russian society would rally to the banner and continue resisting the enemy.[23]

19. Ibid.
20. Ibid., 111.
21. Quoted in V. B. Stankevich, *Vospominaniia, 1914–1919* (Berlin: I. P. Ladyshnikov, 1920), 98.
22. Denikin, *Ocherki*, vol. 2 (Berlin, 1922), 27.
23. Ibid., 1, pt. 2, 107–8.

The military opposition acquired a more organized form when in the early days of May, under the aegis of Gen. Alekseev, an officers' congress was convened at the military headquarters in Mahileu. In his opening speech to the assembled officers, the commander in chief gloomily warned that "Russia is perishing; it is on the brink of an abyss; another push or two and it will go over completely."[24] Therefore he called upon Russian patriots to unite around one broad platform to save the country from disaster. The speeches that followed were addressed in a similar highly patriotic key. They were delivered by three prominent leaders of the Constitutional Democratic party, Fedor I. Rodichev, Andrei I. Shingarev, and Miliukov, who exhorted their countrymen "to sacrifice all, even life" for the defense of the motherland. The three civilians—the most outstanding representatives of Russian liberalism—were also instrumental in the drafting of the resolutions adopted at the congress, which resolved to establish an Officers' Union whose main objective was to strengthen the military might of Russia in order to save the country. The officers disavowed all political objectives and demanded only authority to govern themselves and the army.[25]

The apolitical character of the resolutions adopted at the congress was striking in the highly politicized atmosphere of 1917. It reflected rather clearly, however, the frontline officers' disinterest in social and economic issues, a fact they assert repeatedly in their memoirs. Gen. Denikin, who was an active participant in the congress, observed: "the entire internal social class struggle, which was becoming more and more intensive in the country, was alien to the frontline officers, who were immersed in their work and in their misfortune ... the [class] struggle attracted the officers' attention only when its effects were clearly undermining the life of the army."[26]

The Officers' Union did not attract particular attention because it did not show any signs of becoming a potential opposition to the political authority in Petrograd. It was viewed as merely another group established for the defense of officers' interests. The Provisional Government even sent the union its blessing.[27] The union's activities were initially limited to organizing branches in various sections of the army, investigating complaints directed to it, and providing material aid to officers relieved of their duties by the soldiers' committees.[28]

---

24. Ibid., 110–11.
25. Ibid.
26. Ibid., 111.
27. Alexander Kerensky, *Russia and History's Turning Point* (New York: Duell Sloan and Pearce, 1965), 361.
28. Denikin, *Ocherki*, 1, pt. 2, 114.

Until the ill-fated June offensive, the officers and the High Command appeared to be loyal, and the majority was favorably disposed toward the Provisional Government; they were "patiently enduring in tight-lipped silence all experiments the Provisional Government ... was introducing in the country and in the army, [and were] living by one hope only—the possibility of the regeneration of the army, an offensive, [and] a victory."[29] The dismal failure of the June offensive dispelled this hope. Furthermore, the appearance of the Bolsheviks on the political scene, their demonstration of strength in the middle of July with the slogan of "peace without annexation and indemnities" emblazoned on their banners, and the subsequent alleged unmasking of their leader Lenin as a German agent revealed the full scope of the danger lurking from the left. The specter of a separate peace, as in the last months of the monarchy, seemed to be again hovering over Russia.[30]

In view of the pathetic weakness of the new government, the presence of a radical militant organization believed to be sponsored by the enemy and openly advocating peace naturally alarmed the military and prompted them to abandon purely passive opposition to the Provisional Government. The first step the Officers' Union took against the government was to establish contact with civilian groups, primarily business and financial circles, that were equally concerned with the disintegration of the front. This step laid the foundations for what became known as the Kornilov Affair.[31]

The intricacies of the Kornilov plot are still subject to dispute in view of the conflicting information presented in the accounts of its participants.[32] For

---

29. Ibid .

30. In the spring of 1917 the German government twice attempted to push Russia into separate peace talks under the pretext of a truce. Both attempts were ignored by the Provisional Government. It appeared that now the Germans wanted to achieve their objective—a separate peace with Russia—through the Bolsheviks. General Headquarters considered the Bolsheviks German agents whose principal objective was to take Russia out of the war. Browder and Kerensky, 2: 1158, 1180–81; Kerensky, *Russia*, 301–23.

31. For the part played by the civilian business and political circles in the Kornilov Affair, see Browder and Kerensky, 3: 1527–1613; James D. White, "The Kornilov Affair—A Study in Counterrevolution," *Soviet Studies*, October 1968, 187–205; V. I. Laverychev, "Russkie monopolisty i zagovor Kornilova," *Voprosy istorii*, 1964, no. 4, 32–41; Kerensky, *Russia*, chaps. 20–21; N. Ukraintsev, "A Document in the Kornilov Affair," *Soviet Studies*, October 1973, 283–98; A. Dumova, "Maloizvestnye materialy po istorii kornilovshchiny," *Voprosy istorii*, 1968, no. 11, 69–93; and N. Ia. Ivanov, *Kornilovshchina i ee razgrom: Iz istorii bor'by s kontrrevoliutsiei v 1917 g.* (Leningrad: Izdatel'stvo Leningradskogo universiteta, 1965).

32. For conflicting interpretations, see Abraham Ascher, "The Kornilov Affair," *The Russian Review*, October 1953, 235–52; Leonid Strakhovsky, "Was There a Kornilof Affair?—A Reappraisal of the Evidence," *Slavonic and East European Review* 35 (1953): 372–95; A. Kerensky, *The Prelude to Bolshevism: The Kornilov Rebellion* (New York: Dodd, Mead and Co., 1919); George Katkov, *Russia 1917: The Kornilov Affair: Kerensky and the Breakup of the*

our purposes, it is sufficient to state that the primary objective of the movement headed by the commander in chief and future founder of the VA, Gen. Lavr G. Kornilov,[33] supported by Gens. Krymov, Aleksandr S. Lukomskii, Ivan P. Romanovskii, Sergei L. Markov, Denikin, and Aleksei M. Kaledin, subsidized by the Petrograd financiers Aleksei I. Putilov and Aleksandr I. Vyshnegradskii, endorsed by the Kadet party, and favored by Entente diplomatic circles, was to institute firm authority in the capital in order to forestall the Bolshevik seizure of power, which was expected in September, and its direct consequence—the conclusion of a separate peace. The movement, at least as far as the military leadership is concerned, appears to have had no other political objective. This is one point on which the conflicting interpretations agree. Kornilov, whose outstanding characteristic, according to all accounts, was his straightforward honesty, made the following statement shortly before his march on Petrograd:

> As you know ... all the reports of our intelligence [service] show that a new Bolshevik uprising may be expected to take place on 28 or 29 August [OS]. Germany urgently needs to sign a separate peace treaty with Russia so that it can deploy [its] armies on our front against the French and the English. The German Bolshevik agents, both those who have already established themselves here and those who were sent to us in sealed railway carriages by the Germans, will do everything in their power to organize a coup d'état and take over supreme authority in the country.... I have no personal ambitions; I only want the salvation of Russia.[34]

An editorial for the Kadet paper *Rech*, prepared for the 13 August 1917 (OS) issue but not published because of the failure of the Kornilov coup, contained the following statement:

> Gen. Kornilov is not a reactionary; his aims have nothing in common with

---

Russian Army (London and New York: Longman, 1980); G. Z. Ioffe, *"Beloe delo": General Kornilov* (Moscow: Nauka, 1989); and M. I. Kapustin, *Zagovor generalov (Iz istorii kornilovshchiny i ee razgroma)* (Moscow: Mysl', 1968).

33. Kornilov was appointed commander in chief on 1 August 1917. Alekseev was relieved of his post as the supreme commander shortly after the Officers' Congress in May. Denikin, *Ocherki*, 2: 35.

34. Lukomskii, 1: 227–28. It should be noted that the members of financial and industrial circles involved in the Kornilov Affair did not play an active role in the White movement. The VA's leaders were bitterly disappointed by the meager support they received from them. M. A. Nesterovich-Berg, *V bor'be s bol'shevikami* (Paris: Navarre, 1931), 67; N. Astrov, "Moskovskiia organizatsii, 1917–18," S. V. Panina Papers, box 5, supp. 2, file 2, Bakhmeteff Archive of Russian and East European History and Culture, Columbia University.

the aims of counterrevolution. Kornilov is seeking a path leading toward Russia's victory ... [and] he is not predetermining the people's wishes with respect to the future structure of the Constituent Assembly. It is especially easy for us to support this formula of the national idea because we had voted the same views before Gen. Kornilov. Yes, we are not afraid to say that Kornilov pursued the same objectives that we have considered necessary for the salvation of the motherland.[35]

The Kornilov plot was liquidated within a matter of days by the arrest of the generals and officers directly or indirectly implicated in the mutiny.[36] Yet, the idea that guided the Kornilov movement was not extinguished with their incarceration. Within the walls of the Bykhau prison, where the officers were awaiting their trial, the idea was developing and crystallizing into a new concept for the salvation of Russia during the daily discussions the prisoners were able to hold thanks to the relative freedom they enjoyed. Their common misfortune and humiliation reinforced their ideological bonds, strengthened their patriotism, and confirmed their conviction of the righteousness of their cause. One of the younger generals at Bykhau, Romanovskii, wrote: "Kornilov may be executed, his sympathizers may be exiled to penal servitude, but the 'Kornilov idea' will not die in Russia because the 'Kornilov idea' means love of the motherland and the desire to save Russia."[37]

Considering the political and military realities of 1917, the generals and leaders of Russian liberalism conceived that the salvation of Russia could occur only through its continued participation in the war and fulfillment at least of a modicum of its obligations to the Entente by keeping the German forces tied down on the Eastern Front. If Russian troops were incapable of repulsing the enemy from their territory—this became obvious after the collapse of the June offensive—Russia's integrity and political power could be restored if the Entente proved victorious in the war. It was on this victory that the generals pinned their hope Russia's salvation. To them Russia's withdrawal from the war and the conclusion of a separate peace meant the future dismemberment of the empire and the state's economic collapse. There

---

35. Quoted in S. P. Mel'gunov, *Grazhdanskaia voina v osveshchenii P. N. Miliukova* (Paris: Rapid-Imprimerie, 1929), 27–8.

36. The generals and officers gave themselves up voluntarily when, through the mediation of Alekseev, they were assured by Kerensky that their case would be submitted to a fair and open trial. Alekseev sympathized with the Kornilov plan but was not directly implicated in it. When it became obvious that the plan had misfired, he agreed to cooperate with Kerensky, undoubtedly in order to mitigate the fate of the hapless generals. A. S. Loukomsky [Lukomskii], *Memoirs of the Russian Revolution* (London: T. F. Unwin, 1922), 116–17.

37. Denikin, *Ocherki*, 2: 92. In spite of their uncertain fate, the generals were future-oriented. "We seldom discussed the past," notes Denikin, 93.

was no question in the generals' minds that Germany desired Russia's dismemberment. This theme is restated repeatedly in the memoirs of the White leaders: "One could advance many suppositions on the question of the possibility of a separate peace [in 1917]," wrote Denikin, "would it have been the 'Brest-Litovsk' [peace] or one less onerous for the state and our national dignity. One should assume, however, that this peace ... would have led to Russia's dismemberment and its economic destruction."[38] The generals considered it their moral obligation and military duty to do everything in their power to prevent this disaster. Though most were monarchists by conviction, they turned against the tsar when the dynasty's interests seemed to conflict with the state's interests. Though participating directly in the events of March 1917, the military turned against the authority they helped to establish when it proved too weak to bolster Russia's war effort.

These basic principles—continuation of the war, loyalty to the Entente, prevention of a separate peace, and the preservation of Russia's territorial integrity—guided the men who persuaded the tsar to abdicate. They also provided the driving force for the movement that culminated in the Kornilov revolt, and became the guidelines for the political program of the White cause during the civil war. Thus the basic concept for the movement that emerged in the autumn of 1917 as the VA was born before the Bolsheviks established themselves on the political arena in Petrograd. It first came into being at the end of 1916 in the atmosphere of heightened nationalism, when corruption, ineptitude, or what was interpreted as betrayal of the tsarist regime seemed to have been driving the country to destruction. It emerged again during the revolution, when from the vantage point of General Headquarters it appeared that treason stamped the activities of the extreme left. It crystallized into a fighting force when the Bolsheviks brought their pacifist activities to their logical conclusion by initiating negotiations for peace immediately after their seizure of power in November 1917. Thus the White movement centered in the VA was first and foremost a Russian national movement led by the liberal, strongly pro-Entente intelligentsia and by generals, many of whom differed socially and politically little from their civilian counterparts. To both groups a separate peace and treason appeared synonymous. The movement that emerged in response to the corruption, ineptitude, and irresponsibility of the extreme right became anti-Bolshevik in 1917 because at this time the Bolsheviks were considered the principal architects of the destruction and disintegration of the vast, multinational empire. Being principally a movement for the preservation of the territorial integrity of the state, it opposed and fought with equal vehemence all forces, whether monarchist, socialist, or

---

38. Denikin, *Ocherki*, 1, pt. 2, 236. Denikin is referring to the peace concluded between the Bolsheviks and the Central Powers in March 1918.

separatist-nationalist, whose activities threatened to violate the empire's territorial integrity. Viewing the White movement as basically a drive for the salvation of the unity of the state is the key to understanding the VA's nationality policy.

National Rebirth during the Revolution

The men who found themselves at the helm of the Russian Empire after the fall of the autocratic regime were not insensitive to the problems stemming from the multinational character of the former tsarist state. They were not unaware that the repressive policies of Russification and discrimination against the non-Russians conducted by the old regime engendered deep-seated hostility toward the center among the people of the outlying gubernias. Therefore the Provisional Government decided to act with speed and determination to remove the most glaring injustices suffered by the nationalities under tsarism. Soon after the new authority assumed power, it issued decrees that abolished all restrictive legislation previously imposed on the nationalities and established full equality of all citizens regardless of religion, race, or nationality. On 29 March the Polish people were promised, subject to approval by the Constituent Assembly, "an independent Polish state comprising all territories inhabited predominantly by Poles" that would be "united with Russia by a free military alliance."[39] While the liberal leaders of the Provisional Government were aware that the question of Polish independence was something the new government would have to deal with immediately, they did not foresee the speed and intensity with which aroused national consciousness would assert itself among the other national minorities.[40]

The leaders of the new government were not alone in underestimating the hidden forces of nationalism. Only the more perceptive political observers at the beginning of the twentieth century were evincing concern that the empire had ceased to be predominantly Russian in its ethnic composition.[41]

---

39. Browder and Kerensky, 1, 321–3; P. Galuzo, "Iz istorii natsional'noi politiki Vremennogo Pravitel'stva (Ukraina, Finlandiia, Khiva)," *Krasnyi arkhiv* 30 (1928): 46–79.

40. Because all of Russian-ruled Poland was held by German forces and the Central Powers had announced their own plans regarding Poland's independence, the Russian liberals were forced to act decisively on this question. A. Lednitskii [Lednicki], "P. N. Miliukov i pol'skii vopros," in *P. N. Miliukov: Sbornik materialov*, ed. S. A. Smirnov et al (Paris, 1929), 212–17; M. Benediktov, "P. N. Miliukov i natsional'nyi vopros," in *P. N. Miliukov*, 207–11; C. J. Smith, Jr., "Miliukov and the Russian National Question," *Harvard Slavic Studies* 4 (1957): 395–419.

41. See infra, 27–33.

Although according to the census of 1897, Russians constituted only forty-four percent of the empire's population (excluding Finland),[42] their dominant position appeared to be unchallenged throughout the state. Russian culture seemed to enjoy uncontested supremacy. It alone had the opportunity to develop and enrich itself, and it was assumed that with the progress of industrialization, education, and urbanization, all other cultures—which were of local significance only—would be absorbed and become part of the Russian cultural heritage. Russian political and cultural subjugation of the non-Russians was so well established by the twentieth century because it was ingrained in the very nature of Russian imperial expansion.[43]

Yet, not all of the conquered territories were absorbed into the cultural and political fabric of the empire with equal ease. Some nationalities stubbornly resisted amalgamation and were able to retain, at least for some time, political and cultural autonomy. Ukraine, from 1654 to 1764, and Livonia and Estonia, from 1710 to 1783 and again from 1795 to the 1880s, enjoyed extensive self-rule. Poland, from 1815 to 1831, and Finland, from 1809 to 1899, were constitutional monarchies linked with Russia only through the person of the monarch.[44] Nonetheless, in spite of the great racial, religious, cultural, and economic diversity of the annexed territories, by the end of the nineteenth century the Russian Empire was treated, with some minor variations, as a constitutionally and administratively homogeneous unit.[45]

Russian socialist and liberal leaders criticized the restrictive legislation the regime imposed on the nationalities. When the government forbade public celebrations of the centenary of the birth of the Ukrainian poet Taras Shevchenko in February 1914, the Kadets in the Duma rose to defend the Ukrainians. Miliukov protested the government's order, stating "The [Ukrainian] movement exists, and you can neither suppress it nor alter its significance; the sole question is whether you wish to see this movement as inimical or friendly. That will depend on whether the movement will regard you as friends or enemies."[46] When the war broke out, the Progressive Bloc in the Duma continued to defend, though not as vigorously as in peacetime, the rights of the nationalities.

---

42. N. A. Troinitskii, ed., *Pervaia perepis' naseleniia Rossiiskoi Imperii, 1897 g.: Obshchii svod*, vol. 2 (St. Petersburg: Tsentral'nyi statisticheskii komitet Ministerstva vnutrennykh del, 1905), 2.
43. Marc Raeff, "Patterns of Russian Imperial Policy toward the Nationalities," in Edward Allworth, ed., *Soviet Nationality Problems* (New York and London: Columbia University Press, 1971), 30.
44. Richard Pipes, *The Formation of the Soviet Union: Communism and Nationalism, 1917–1923* (Cambridge: Harvard University Press, 1953), 3.
45. Ibid.
46. O. Lotots'kyi, *Storinky mynuloho*, pt. 2 (Warsaw: Ukraïns'kyi naukovyi instytut, 1933), 422.

Discriminatory policies against Jews, compulsory Russification of Poles, Ukrainians, and Belarusians, persecution of the Armenian church, and violation of the Finnish constitution conflicted sharply with the universal principles of equality, freedom, and legality that were championed by the Russian liberals and socialists. No ethnic Russian political group, however, questioned the justice of the absorption of the non-Russian territories into the swelling empire or *advocated* in its party program the right of secession of the border nationalities.[47] Although they recognized the need to give the Poles and Finns a special status, Russian liberal and socialist leaders were confident that the remaining nationalities would, or rather should, be content with cultural autonomy in a free and democratic Russia.[48]

When the war broke out, the attacks on the government in the Duma subsided considerably. In fact the Kadets were the first political party to issue an appeal calling upon the people to unite for the defense of the country. The appeal explained that in spite of the Constitutional Democratic party's critical attitude toward the government, its first obligation was to see to it that the state was preserved as a single and undivided entity and to maintain Russia's place among the Great Powers.[49] Criticism of the government's policies in general and of the nationality policy in particular was resumed only after Russia's disastrous military defeats in the summer of 1915. This criticism, however, was never as vigorous and consistent as on the eve of the war.

After the fall of the tsarist regime the liberals in the Provisional Government were taken aback somewhat when the new authority's first legislative measures did not immediately satisfy the nationalities' demands. When, on 20 March, the Finnish constitution was restored, the Finns

---

47. The Bolsheviks did not *advocate* secession. Lenin was very emphatic in asserting that his party only recognized the right of secession; it did not advocate or encourage separation. Likewise, the Russian Socialist Revolutionaries, in their party program of 1905, only recognized the right of the nationalities to self-determination. V. I. Lenin, *Sochineniia*, 3d. ed. (Moscow: Gosudarstvennoe izdatel'stvo, 1935), 27: 90, 448–49, 439; *Protokoly Pervago s"ezda Partii sotsialistov-revoliutsionerov* (1906), 361–2.

48. In their 1906 party program the Kadets advocated equality before the law of all Russian citizens regardless of sex, religion, and nationality; free cultural self-determination—full freedom to use different languages and dialects in public life, freedom to use the native tongue in local elementary schools; autonomy for Poland; and reestablishment of the Finnish constitution. The Kadets opposed federalism and insisted most resolutely on the preservation of the empire's unity. B. Nol'de, *Natsional'nyi vopros v Rossii* (Petrograd: "Novoe Vremia," 1917); B. Nol'de, *Avtonomiia Ukraïny z istorychnoho pohliadu,* trans. M. Zalizniak (Lviv: Ivan Aikhel'berger, 1912); F. F. Kokoshkin, *Avtonomiia i federatsiia* (St. Petersburg, 1917); *Zakonodatel'nyia proekty i predlozheniia Partii narodnoi svobody, 1904–1907 gg.* (St. Petersburg, 1907), XI-XIX; Smith, "Miliukov and the Russian National Question"; N. G. Dumova, *Kadetskaia partiia v period Pervoi mirovoi voiny i Fevral'skoi revoliutsii* (Moscow: Nauka, 1988), 139.

49. Panina Papers, box 2, file 1.

responded with a demand for a complete revision of relations with Russia, arguing that the abolition of the monarchy severed the dynastic union of the Duchy of Finland with Russia. The Provisional Government, considering itself a temporary trustee of state sovereignty, insisted that it had assumed the authority and prerogatives of the tsar as the grand duke of Finland until the convocation of the Constituent Assembly.[50] The question of Finland's status was never fully resolved, and relations between the Finnish Diet and the Provisional Government remained strained until the Bolshevik coup in October.[51]

None of the other nationalities were prepared to follow Finland's bold example, at least not in the spring of 1917. As noted above, in the western gubernias most traces of local autonomous institutions had been removed by the end of the nineteenth century. Tsarist repressive measures had stifled even cultural activities within the nationalities.[52] Yet despite these drawbacks, the salient features of the national revivals during the revolution were their vigor and vitality.

The manner in which the nationalities organized themselves for the defense of their rights followed a similar pattern throughout the empire.[53] First, a national council was established (the Radas in Ukraine and Belarus, the Shura among the Turkic peoples). In time these councils established executive committees that soon began challenging the authority of the Provisional Government in their territories. Although the Provisional Government was willing to recognize the nationalities' cultural rights, on the question of political autonomy, as in the case of Finland's independence and all other matters that involved constitutional changes, it held that only the future Constituent Assembly was competent to make the appropriate decision. But no matter how hard the Provisional Government tried to preserve the structure of the empire until the convocation of the Constituent Assembly, it proved powerless to arrest the strong pull of the centrifugal forces loosed by the revolution. In June 1917 the Ukrainian Central Rada proclaimed the autonomy of Ukraine. This so alarmed the Provisional Government that it sent three ministers to Kyiv to investigate the Ukrainian question. After lengthy deliberations the ministers became convinced that it was necessary to recognize the jurisdiction of the Rada's executive committee, the General

50. Browder and Kerensky, 1: 155, 334–5.
51. Galuzo., op. cit., 56–71.
52. See, for example, F. Savchenko, *Zaborona ukraïnstva 1876 r.: Do istoriï hromads'kykh rukhiv na Ukraïni 1860–1870-kh rr.* (Kyiv: Derzhavne vydavnytstvo Ukraïny, 1930; reprint, Munich: Wilhelm Fink, 1970).
53. For a concise review of the developments in the outlying regions of the empire in 1917, see Pipes, op.cit., chap. 2.

Secretariat, in over five Ukrainian gubernias, which in effect meant recognizing Ukrainian autonomy.

This concession to the Rada precipitated a crisis in the Provisional Government. Four Kadet ministers indignantly resigned from the Cabinet. In their resignation note they explained that although the Central Committee of the People's Freedom party[54] acknowledged the necessity of preparing a plan for the regional autonomy of Ukraine, it considered the government's recognition of political autonomy "an inadmissible and highly dangerous precedent, predetermining ... the will of the Constituent Assembly and the future organization of the Russian state."[55] What the Kadet ministers feared most was that the Ukrainian victory would embolden the other nationalities of the empire to pursue their drive toward political autonomy. This would inevitably lead, the leaders of Russian liberalism thought, toward domestic strife, which would undermine Russia's war effort and thus endanger the future of Russia as a unified entity.

The Kadets' concern with the state interests of Russia could be detected already in 1905, when revolutionary turmoil revealed the full scope of the dangers inherent in a general upheaval once elemental revolutionary currents loosened themselves from the control of the leadership.[56] Awareness that a revolution could get out of hand and thus bring about the destruction not only of autocracy but also the state forced the Russian liberals in 1917 to try to reconcile, or at least find some form of a compromise between, the idea of personal freedom they championed and the state interests of Russia. The shift of emphasis in Russian liberal thought from individual freedom—which encompassed the rights and liberties of the nationalities as well—to Russia's state interests, and the transformation of the Kadets from defenders of personal freedom against the encroachments of a despotic state into state-conscious *(gosudarstvenno mysliashchie)*, responsible citizens with statesman-like concern for Russia's imperial interests, was manifested most vividly

---

54. During the revolution the Constitutional Democratic party, popularly known as the Kadet party, was officially renamed the People's Freedom party. For the history of Russian liberalism, see George Fischer, *Russian Liberalism* (Cambridge: Harvard University Press, 1958); Viktor Leontovitsch, *Geschichte des Liberalismus in Russland* (Frankfurt am Main: V. S. Klosterman, 1959); and Jacob Walkin, *The Rise of Democracy in Pre-Revolutionary Russia* (New York: Praeger, 1962). For a detailed study of the Constitutional Democrats during the period under consideration, see William G. Rosenberg, *Liberals in the Russian Revolution: The Constitutional Democratic Party, 1917–1921* (Princeton: Princeton University Press, 1974); for a recent Soviet interpretation, see Dumova, op. cit., and her *Kadetskaia kontrrevoliutsiia i ee razgrom: Oktiabr 1917–1920.* (Moscow: Nauka, 1982).

55. Browder and Kerensky, 3: 1383.

56. See, for example, P. Struve's collection of essays *Patriotika: Politika, kul'tura, religiia, sotsializm; sbornik statei za piat' let, 1905–1910 gg.* (St. Petersburg: D. E. Zhukovskii, 1911).

during the events of 1917–21, when the leading Russian liberals formed the political backbone of the White movement.

The recognition of Ukrainian autonomy and the resignation of the Kadets from the Cabinet did not signal the adoption of a new, more liberal policy toward the nationalities by the Provisional Government. On the contrary, in the summer of 1917 the central authority in Petrograd attempted to tighten its control over the outlying regions. In the opening speech at the Moscow State Conference, Alexander Kerensky, the socialist prime minister who had replaced Prince Georgii E. L'vov in July, strongly admonished the nationalities for what he considered to be exorbitant demands; he warned the Finns especially that if they proceeded to take advantage of Russia's difficulties and "bring about by physical force the triumph of objectives which are at this time impossible and which would spell ruin to the entire state," the Provisional Government would "give appropriate instructions."[57] Similarly, when in September a delegation from Central Asia requested Kerensky to grant concessions to the local people in view of the tense situation in the region, Kerensky replied bluntly, "I do not believe that there will be an anti-Russian uprising in Central Asia, but were that to happen, I would take the most rigorous measures to crush it."[58]

In spite of its own obvious weakness and the growing impatience of the nationalities,[59] the Provisional Government remained adamant on the question of autonomy and federation. When Russia was formally proclaimed a republic on 27 September 1917, the government did not issue a precise declaration regarding the structure of the state. In one of its last policy statements on the nationality question, the Provisional Government merely reiterated its willingness to "recognize for all nationalities the right of self-determination on such principles as the Constituent Assembly shall determine."[60]

---

57. Browder and Kerensky, 3: 1456. Kerensky's threats were of little practical significance. When the Don Cossacks were ordered to dispatch their units to Finland and Khiva, they refused to carry out this order. Ibid., 1623.
58. Quoted in Edward Allworth, ed., *Central Asia: A Century of Russian Rule* (New York: Columbia University Press, 1967), 220.
59. On 21 September a Congress of Nationalities convened in Kyiv. Nearly twenty national and religious groups either sent representatives or pledged their support. The congress outlined a program of reorganizing Russia on federal principles. It also elected a permanent body to guide the struggle of all the nationalities of the empire for the establishment of a Russian federal republic. Under the auspices of this permanent body, the Council of Nationalities, a journal was published for the propagation of the federal program throughout the empire. Pavlo Khrystiuk, *Zamitky i materiialy do istoriï ukraïns'koï revoliutsiï: 1917–1920*, vol. 2 (Vienna: Ukraïns'kyi sotsiol'ogichnyi instytut, 1921), 20–3.
60. Browder and Kerensky, 2: 1716.

The Provisional Government's ambivalent, inconsistent, and at times arrogant attitude toward the nationalities frustrated the efforts of the more moderate Russians and opened the way toward the radicalization of the national movements throughout the empire: the nationalities began organizing their lives independently of the central authority in Petrograd. The lightening speed with which the nationality movements became politicized in the course of the revolution made it clear that the solution of the nationality question could not be left exclusively to socioeconomic forces in the empire if Russian cultural and political dominance was to prevail.

The Nationality Question from the Perspective of the High Command

For the Russian High Command, prior to the revolution the nationality question appeared to be virtually nonexistent in the empire. It was not that the military were unaware of the state's multinational character. The imperial army, after all, represented in microcosm the mosaic of the empire's nationalities. The military leaders minimized or dismissed the empire's heterogeneous character as a potential threat to the stability of the state primarily because of the absence of any overt signs of hostility among the enlisted men of the various nationalities and the ease with which non-Russians seemed to assimilate into both the officer corps and the rank and file.[61] The officer corps, although by the twentieth century composed of the most diverse social and national elements,[62] was distinguished by its highly developed sense of solidarity and *esprit de corps*. Long years of training and hardships suffered on the battlefields seemed to erase national distinctions.[63] From the vantage point of the High Command, the national factor was less significant in the rank and file. The common soldier appeared little distinguishable from the masses and was as ignorant and apathetic, "meekly taking up arms, yet without any inspiration and with no clear awareness of the necessity of the

---

61. Denikin, *Ocherki,* 1, pt. 2, 127.
62. The army reforms of 1874 introduced universal conscription, without regard to social status. About the reforms and the Russian army, see A. I. Denikin, *Staraia armiia,* 2 vols. (Paris: Knizhnoe delo, 1929, 1931); N. N. Golovine, *The Russian Army in the World War* (New Haven: Yale University Press, 1931), 100–1; P. A. Zaionchkovskii, *Voennye reformy 1860–1870 godov v Rossii* (Moscow: Moskovskii universitet, 1952); and Wildman, op. cit. The nationality question in the Russian army is discussed in Denikin's lengthy essay "Natsional'nyi vopros v armii," A. I. and K. V. Denikin Papers, box 10, Bakhmeteff Archive of Russian and East European History and Culture, Columbia University.
63. Denikin, *Ocherki,* 1, pt. 2, 127.

great sacrifice."[64] Irrespective of whether he was Russian or not, the common man's outlook was assumed to be too narrow to comprehend such abstract concepts as nation, state, and national interest. The pathetic naïveté and provincialism of the Russian soldier was epitomized in the phrase often repeated during the war, "We are from Tambov, the Germans will not get there."[65]

Finding no signs of national animosity among the soldiers and considering the army one of the most effective instruments of assimilation, the generals were naturally surprised when, during the revolution, the most active and vociferous elements among the nationalities turned out to be serving in the army. Being preoccupied with the conduct of the war, the military leaders would probably have overlooked this unexpected phenomenon had not one of the demands most urgently made by the non-Russians, especially the military, been the division of Russia's armed forces into national units.[66] As this demand affected the basic structure of Russia's army, the High Command could not avoid turning its attention to the nationality question.

Small national units, such as the Polish Riflemen's Brigade, Lettish rifle regiments, and the Caucasian Savage Division, did exist prior to the revolution, but they were too small to disturb the High Command. The demand for reconstructing the entire army along ethnic lines was a revolutionary innovation and was therefore not viewed with equanimity by the High Command. What is surprising, however, is that the opinion of members of the General Headquarters was divided.[67] While Gens. Alekseev and Denikin were resolutely opposed to this reform and made every effort to hinder its implementation, Gens. Kornilov, Dmitrii G. Shcherbachev, and Brusilov favored it, possibly in the hope that the formation of national units would bolster the fighting spirit of the soldiers and that at least part of the army would thus be removed from under the influence of the Soviet. Kornilov, who in the initial stages of the army's reorganization was the commander in chief of the Southwestern Front, was favorably impressed with the morale of the newly organized Ukrainian units. This prompted him to take the initiative for the formation of a separate Ukrainian corps under the command of Gen. Pavlo Skoropads'kyi, the future hetman of the conservative Ukrainian State of 1918. In fact, it was Kornilov who personally issued orders for the transfer of

64. Ibid., 1, pt. 1, 19.
65. Ibid.
66. Khrystiuk, 1, 48–55; Denikin, *Ocherki*, 1, pt. 2, 129.
67. The Provisional Government was resolutely opposed to the reorganization of the army. Kerensky accepted this demand only when he was faced with a fait accompli: the nationality units came into being as a result of local initiatives. Dmytro Doroshenko, *Istoriia Ukraïny 1917–1923 rr.*, vol. 1, *Doba Tsentral'noï Rady* (Uzhhorod: Osyp Tsiupka, 1930), 326–63; Denikin, *Ocherki*, 1, pt. 2, 131–2; Khrystiuk, 1: 48–55.

Ukrainian officers to units that were designated for reorganization according to the national principle. On the other hand Denikin, who succeeded Kornilov as commander in chief of the Southwestern Front, tried to hinder the process of "nationalization." He failed to detect any improvement in morale and fighting capacity in the new national formations. On the contrary, he detected signs of "an unhealthy spirit of intolerance and alienation" between the Ukrainians and those Russians who remained in the new formations.[68] Regardless of whether the formation of new national units awakened new hope for the regeneration of the army or whether they evoked, as in Denikin, "a piercing pain and awareness that the end of the army is near,"[69] the reorganization of the army produced a profound impression on the military. Neither in the political nor economic life of the country did the sudden resurgence of national aspirations have such immediate and direct impact as it had on the army during that period. Irrespective of whether the generals were favorably disposed toward the demands of the nationalities or whether they passionately opposed all manifestations of independence among the non-Russians, they could no longer remain indifferent to the nationality question.

Developments in Ukraine up to the Separate Peace

In the autumn of 1917, the parliament of the Ukrainian People's Republic (UNR), the Ukrainian Central Rada, was well aware of the discouraging state of affairs at the front. But after the Bolshevik seizure of power in Petrograd in November 1917, it gave no indication that it was willing to join the Bolsheviks in their determined drive for peace. It failed to do so even though conditions in Ukraine were no more favorable for continuing the war than they were in other parts of the disintegrating empire. The people of Ukraine were as war-weary as their northern neighbors, and the Ukrainian soldiers, both those organized in separate units and those serving under various Russian commands, were no more willing to fight than the soldiers of other nationalities. The First All-Ukrainian Military Congress, which met in May, denounced all wars in general, declaring that every war was carried on only to promote the "imperialist politics of the ruling classes."[70] Subsequently a conference of the Ukrainian Party of Socialist Revolutionaries (UPSR) also declared itself in favor of peace and, furthermore, demanded the resignation of Prince L'vov's government in Petrograd because it had failed to bring the

---

68. Denikin, *Ocherki*, 1, pt. 2, 130–3; Doroshenko, 1: 369–70; Khrystiuk, 1: 48–55.
69. Denikin, *Ocherki*, 1, pt. 2, 130–3.
70. Khrystiuk, 1: 54.

long and devastating war to an end.[71] A resolution that alluded to the possibility of a separate peace for the first time was adopted by the First All-Ukrainian Workers' Congress in July.[72] A separate peace concluded independently not only of the Allies but also of Russia, i.e., directly between Ukraine and the Central Powers, was advocated by the Third All-Ukrainian Military Congress, which convened in Kyiv during the eventful days of November 1917. The rationale was that the prolongation of the war "brings closer the total annihilation of the vital economic and cultural power of the toiling people of all nations ... causes hunger and anarchy in the territory, and destroys all the achievements of the revolution."[73]

The Rada could not and did not ignore this almost unanimous cry for peace in the country. On several occasions between March and November 1917 it urged the Provisional Government to take concrete steps toward the cessation of hostilities. Sometime in October 1917 the Ukrainian representative in Petrograd threatened that the Rada might find it necessary to open direct negotiations with the Germans unless the Provisional Government did so itself.[74] But as soon as the Provisional Government disappeared from the political scene after the Bolshevik coup of 7 November 1917, the Rada's eagerness for peace began to wane, and in its Third Universal proclaiming the UNR two weeks later, it merely issued a vague promise to make a resolute effort to compel both the Allied and Central Powers to begin peace negotiations at once.

Two factors primarily made the Rada hesitant to embark on the road of a separate peace independently of both the Allies and Russia. The first stemmed from Ukraine's undetermined political status and its remaining ambiguous ties with the former Russian Empire. Even though the Third Universal proclaimed the UNR, Ukraine's ties with Russia were not yet considered completely severed; the universal stated that "Without separating from the Russian Republic and destroying its unity, we shall firmly establish ourselves on our own land in order that with our strength we may help the rest of Russia ... to become a federation of free and equal peoples."[75]

For the predominantly socialist leaders of the Ukrainian government, the desired polity that should emerge from the ruins of the defunct empire was a federated Russia comprised of autonomous states and held together by an

---

71. Ibid., 102.
72. Ibid., 102–3.
73. Ibid., 2: 48–9.
74. Riezler (Stockholm) to Hertling (Berlin). Telegram no. 9, 19 November 1917, German Foreign Office Archives, microfilm no. 110, Archives of the United States of America, Washington, DC.
75. James Bunyan and Harold H. Fisher, eds. *The Bolshevik Revolution 1917–1918* (Stanford: Stanford University Press, 1934), 435.

All-Russian socialist-coalition authority. This view was succinctly expressed in an article that appeared in a UPSR organ shortly after the publication of the Third Universal. Although the proclamation of the UNR was hailed as the realization of a dream for which the Ukrainian people had struggled for centuries, the article stated that the UPSR "never regarded the idea of a Ukrainian state, or statehood in general, as sufficient in itself, as an idea to which all else should be subordinated ... [and that] federation is a higher form of international collaboration than the existence of separate states."[76]

In the Rada's opinion, an all-Russian government had ceased to exist with the fall of the Kerensky government. Although the Rada was willing to recognize the Bolshevik government in Petrograd—the Council of People's Commissars—as the authority in the Russian Republic, it categorically refused to accept it as an all-Russian authority. Such an authority could be formed, according to the Rada's socialist leaders, only by the unified efforts of all socialist parties and nationalities of the former empire. In the Rada's judgement, only a future all-Russian socialist government would have the authority to conduct negotiations for peace. Neither the government in Petrograd nor the government in Kyiv, therefore, had the right to initiate peace talks. Although confidence in the possibility of creating an all-Russian socialist authority had been seriously undermined during Kerensky's premiership, the highly idealistic, politically inexperienced Ukrainian socialists in the Rada were still reluctant to acknowledge that a true and just federal authority created from below—not from above, as had been tried by the Provisional Government—was a naïve invention of nineteenth-century utopian dreamers.

Scrupulous adherence to the pursuit of this socialist ideal by the Rada placed the UNR government in an extremely difficult position. On the one hand, in view of the collapse of the former imperial army at the front and a growing demand for peace at home, a speedy termination of the war was imperative; on the other hand, a quick end was doubtful, since there was no one government on the territory of the former empire with enough authority to undertake peace negotiations.

The Rada's unwillingness to take definite action toward arranging a separate peace was also the result of its reluctance to antagonize the representatives of the Entente, who were just beginning to evince interest in the new national republics on the periphery of the disintegrating empire. During the existence of the Provisional Government the Entente representatives in Petrograd tended to be hostile toward the Rada's demands for territorial autonomy in Ukraine. In the difficult year of 1917 the Entente

---

76. Doroshenko, 186–7.

looked with dismay at any movement that appeared to weaken their ally Russia. The strivings of the various nationalities in the empire for self-government were, in their opinion, a dangerous step toward Russia's disintegration. But even though the Entente diplomats in Petrograd were not in sympathy with the Ukrainian movement, they could not ignore it, especially after the "Ukrainian question" precipitated a crisis in the Provisional Government in the summer of 1917.

The first Entente representatives came to Kyiv with the aim of gathering information on developments in Ukraine. For this purpose an attaché of the Japanese embassy in Petrograd, Ashida, arrived in Kyiv shortly after the cabinet crisis in the Petrograd government.[77] Similarly, in August the French ambassador in Petrograd, Joseph Noulens, sent the well-known French journalist Jean Pélissier to Ukraine. Pélissier met the leading figures of the Rada, among them Volodymyr Vynnychenko, the chairman of the General Secretariat,[78] and Mykhailo Hrushevs'kyi, the president of the Rada. The question that interested Pélissier most was the relation of the Ukrainian movement to the Central Powers. Evidently developments in Ukraine had made a strong impression on Pélissier, as he reported to his superiors that the time was very near when the Rada would assume all power in Ukraine.[79] Sometime in September a French Military Sanitary Mission arrived in Kyiv and presented itself officially to the General Secretariat in the company of the French consul in Kyiv, Balakhovskii.[80] In the autumn of 1917 various Entente military missions visited leading members of the Rada to establish a closer rapport with the Ukrainian military.[81]

The task of the Entente agents sent to Kyiv—whether their assignment came from the various embassies in Petrograd or from the foreign military missions in Russia—was to gather first-hand information on political and military developments in Kyiv, because their superiors in Petrograd did not consider it propitious at that time to establish official contact with the government of autonomous Ukraine. The attitude of the Entente toward the Rada, however, changed significantly after the Bolshevik coup. As soon as the Bolshevik government demonstrated that it was determined to conclude a separate peace, the Entente hoped to salvage at least a portion of the Eastern Front by supporting the Ukrainian government and thus assure its participation in the war on the Allied side.

At the end of November Gen. Georges Marie Tabouis, the head of the

---

77. Ibid., 232.
78. A position equivalent to prime minister.
79. Elie Borschak, "La paix ukrainienne de Brest-Litovsk," *Le Monde Slave*, 1929, no. 4, 53.
80. Doroshenko, 232.
81. Alexandre Choulguine, *L'Ukraine contre Moscou* (Paris: F. Alcan, 1935), 159.

French Military Mission in Kyiv, accompanied by Maj. Fitzwilliams of the British Military Mission, paid a visit to the secretary of foreign affairs, Oleksander Shul'hyn. Tabouis declared that the Allies in general and France in particular had great sympathy for the cultural and political rebirth of Ukraine. He further stated that as the Entente states were well aware that the building of a new republic, especially under existing circumstances, was not an easy task, they were ready to extend their aid to the newly proclaimed UNR. Therefore Tabouis requested information as to "what Ukraine required and how they [the Entente] could be useful."[82] Shul'hyn, following the decision of the General Secretariat, did not hasten to accept this offer, although the republic was in dire need of outside aid. He merely replied that before these matters could be discussed between the Ukrainian government and the Allied states, the latter must first recognize the UNR by an official declaration or, at least, establishing formal diplomatic relations.[83] Tabouis renewed his offer on 18 December, stating that he had been instructed by his government to extend to the Rada Allied sympathy "for the effort made by the Ukrainian government to reestablish order and to reorganize the forces of resistance and remain faithful to the Allies."[84] In return for aid in the form of large loans, military supplies, and technical help, the Entente expected the Rada to act energetically in reorganizing Ukrainian regiments, which could, together with the Czecho-Slovak and Polish legions, gain control of the strategic areas on the Romanian and Southwestern fronts and thus pin down at least a portion of the German army.[85]

Many high-ranking officials of the Rada and General Secretariat were avowed supporters of the Entente, and some of them even entertained hopes that the UNR Army could actually be reorganized with the aid of the Entente into an effective military force so that the war could be continued until the conclusion of a general peace. A contemporary Ukrainian source observed that these "Ententophiles" were rewarded handsomely by their Western friends for their efforts to promote the Entente cause in Ukraine.[86] It is estimated that the French alone turned over to the UNR government approximately fifty million rubles.[87]

The loans, promises, and sympathies extended by the Entente were insufficient to counter the pressure for peace stemming from two simultaneous

---

82. Doroshenko, 233–4.
83. Ibid.
84. Ibid.
85. Khrystiuk, 2: 92.
86. Ibid., 92–3.
87. George F. Kennan, *Russia Leaves the War* (Princeton: Princeton University Press, 1956), 184.

developments in early December. On 3 December, a telegram was received in Kyiv from the Russian commander of the Romanian Front, Gen. Shcherbachev, which informed the Rada that he was obliged to open peace negotiations with the enemy and asked the Ukrainian governmnet to send its representatives to the negotiations.[88] On the same day formal armistice negotiations were opened at Brest-Litovsk between the Central Powers and the Bolsheviks, the latter conducting them in the name of all territories of the former Russian Empire.

A special meeting to discuss the question of peace was held by the Little Rada[89] early in December. Of the Ukrainian parties represented there only the moderate conservatives, the Socialist Federalists, were opposed to the idea of a separate peace. Their spokesmen merely recommended that the government appeal to the West European democracies to hasten a general peace.[90] The representatives of the national minorities also argued against a separate peace or any step in its direction. They reminded their compatriots that peace could be concluded only by an all-Russian government.[91]

The resolution finally adopted by the Little Rada reflected the views of the Ukrainian Social Democrats and Socialist Revolutionaries, the two most influential parties in the Rada. Representatives of the UNR government were to be sent to the Romanian and Southwestern fronts to participate in the armistice talks, and an appeal was to be sent to the Allies and Central Powers urging peace negotiations at once. The Rada was to prepare a program of peace to be submitted on behalf of the UNR to all the belligerent states.[92] In accordance with this resolution, on the following day the General Secretariat appointed delegates to the fronts, and subsequently, sometime in the second week of December, the government announced its decision to send a separate delegation to Brest-Litovsk, where negotiations between the Soviet Russia and the Central Powers were already in progress.[93] This was to be a special delegation, since its purpose, as explained by Vynnychenko, was merely to influence and control the acts of the Bolsheviks.[94]

The presence of the Rada representatives at Brest-Litovsk was not yet an indication that the UNR government was fully committed to a separate peace. The decision to send a delegation to Brest-Litovsk was reached only at the

---

88. Khrystiuk, 2: 93.
89. The executive committee of the Central Rada, consisting of forty-five members representing the various parties united in the Rada. It performed legislative functions when the Rada was not in session.
90. Khrystiuk, 2: 93.
91. Ibid.
92. Ibid., 94.
93. Ibid., 95.
94. Ibid., 83.

end of December, six days after the peace conference there was formally opened. This decision was the direct result of the outbreak of hostilities between the UNR and Soviet Russia.

To the Bolsheviks, the Central Rada, though dominated by socialists, was a hostile government, and their main objective, once they established their power in Petrograd, was to set up in Ukraine a Soviet regime fully subordinated to the center. Their unsuccessful attempt in November to seize power in Kyiv convinced them that it was impossible to install the power of the soviets by the force of local Bolsheviks alone. Yet an outright invasion of Ukraine was inconvenient for the leaders in Petrograd; this step would openly violate the principle of self-determination that the Bolsheviks recognized for all peoples in their decree of 15 November 1917.[95] Therefore, in the weeks immediately following the November coup, the Soviet Council of People's Commissars adopted a conciliatory attitude toward the Rada, hoping that it would not interfere in matters directly affecting the revolution and awaiting a convenient moment to replace it by a government loyal to the Bolshevik regime. In their official statements the Bolsheviks recognized the Rada's authority in Ukraine. Shortly before the departure of the Soviet delegation for Brest-Litovsk, Leon Trotsky expressed the desire that "The Ukrainian toiling masses convince themselves in fact that the All-Russian Soviet government placed no obstacles on the part of Ukraine's self-determination, whatever forms it may take, and that the Russian government recognizes the People's Ukrainian Republic fully and most sincerely."[96]

The uneasy truce between Petrograd and Kyiv was short-lived. Early in December the Rada aroused the ire of the Bolsheviks when, not recognizing their right to represent an all-Russian government, it sent a note to the newly established governments on the territory of the former empire proposing the formation of a central Russian government for the purpose of obtaining a general democratic peace.[97] Tensions between Kyiv and Petrograd mounted in the first half of December when the Rada began disarming Bolshevik-dominated Russian troops in Kyiv and deporting them beyond the frontiers of the UNR; and when, on grounds of neutrality, the Ukrainian government permitted passage through UNR territory to Don Cossacks who were returning from the front to the Don region while denying such permission to Bolshevik troops sent to fight the anti-Soviet forces in the Don.[98] As a result the UNR government received an ultimatum on 17 December signed by Lenin and Trotsky; it accused the Rada of pursuing a deceptive, bourgeois policy, and

---

95. Bunyan and Fisher, 283–4.
96. Pipes, 118.
97. Khrystiuk, 2: 54–5.
98. Ibid., 82.

declared, among other things, that if the Rada failed to assist the Bolsheviks in their fight against the Don Cossacks, "the Soviet of People's Commissars will consider the Rada in a state of open warfare against the Soviet Government in Russia and in the Ukraine."[99] The General Secretariat promptly rejected this ultimatum, stressing the right of the Ukrainian people to self-determination and reminding the Council of People's Commissars that it had no right to intervene in the internal affairs of the Ukrainian republic. Although there were several attempts at reaching a peaceful solution between the two governments, all of them failed.

When it became obvious that the Bolsheviks were determined to set up a Soviet regime in Ukraine by force of arms, the UNR government adopted a firmer attitude toward peace. On 24 December the General Secretariat addressed a note to all belligerent states announcing its decision to send a delegation to Brest-Litovsk. In an attempt to placate the Entente and those circles in Kyiv that were unyielding in their opposition to the idea of a separate peace, it explained that its decision to participate in the negotiations at Brest-Litovsk was reached in the hope that the conference would be a preliminary step toward the conclusion of a general peace.[100] But in view of the military and political realities of the day it had become quite clear that a separate peace was inevitable. In a last attempt to dissuade the Ukrainians from concluding one, Tabouis advised them neither to fight nor to sign a peace treaty, citing as examples Belgium and Serbia, which had allowed the enemy to overrun them but remained loyal to the Entente.[101]

The fledgling UNR government, however, opted for the road of survival. By the end of 1917 it faced both the inevitablity of a Bolshevik invasion and occupation of Ukraine by the Central Powers, for which the rich supplies of grain there were by then a vital necessity. The peace that was concluded between the Central Powers and the UNR on 18 February 1918 prevented, temporarily at least, the first catastrophe and softened somewhat the hardships of the latter.[102] The friendship of the Entente representatives, however, appeared to be irretrievably lost as a result. At the same time a conflict with

---

99. Bunyan and Fisher, 439–40.
100. Khrystiuk, 2: 95–6.
101. Cited in John S. Reshetar, Jr., *The Ukrainian Revolution, 1917–1920: A Study in Nationalism* (Princeton: Princeton University Press, 1952), 105–6.
102. The decision to send a fully authorized delegation to the peace negotiations at Brest-Litovsk was reached by the Rada as late as 28 December, when a Bolshevik invasion of Ukraine was already in progress. The General Secretariat explained that since a federal government for all of Russia was nonexistent, the UNR had no choice but to send its own delegation to negotiate peace. Khrystiuk, 2: 97–8; Elie Borschak, "La paix ukrainienne de Brest-Litovsk," *Le Monde Slave*, 1929, no. 4, 33–62; no. 7, 63–84; no. 8, 199–225; and Anna Procyk, "The Ukrainian Treaty of Brest-Litovsk," M.A. thesis, Columbia University, 1967.

a military force now forming in the Don, close to Ukraine's eastern border, was more than a likely possibility, for, from the perspective of the Russian White generals and Russian political leaders dedicated to the idea of the empire's indivisibility, the conclusion of a separate peace with the Central Powers placed the UNR government in the same category of "traitors" or "German agents" as the Bolsheviks.

The Nationality Question in Russian Liberal Thought

Russian liberalism, like Russian socialism, was rooted in the rationalistic thought of the Enlightenment, which emphasized the general rather than the particular and imparted no special value or utility to the peculiarities of each nation's language and culture. It focused on the rational human being, whose scientific progress and domination of nature would lead to a more perfect society. Basing themselves on the materialistic worldview of the Western-oriented Russian intelligentsia of the preceding generation, the Russian liberals were convinced that a just and more perfect order could be reached most speedily and efficiently under the influence of the most advanced cultures. Thus, according to this line of thought, Russian culture, with its undisputed preeminence within the empire, had the right to leadership and dominance not because the Russians were the ruling nation, but because Russian advanced cultural achievements would benefit all of the empire's inhabitants in the march of history toward progress.

When the fragility of the empire was revealed during the Revolution of 1905, the liberals assigned Russian culture an additional task: to serve as the glue that held the sprawling multinational state together. It came to be viewed as the most reliable unifying force of the heterogeneous, multinational colossus once coercion and oppression were removed by an enlightened, democratic Russia, i.e., a Russia the liberals championed with great determination and zeal. Just as their counterparts in the Austrian Empire half a century earlier, the Russian liberals called for the cultural hegemony of the Russian nation in the name of universal human progress. "The Germans in Austria," wrote the liberal leader Johann Nepomuk Berger in 1861, "should strive not for political hegemony, but for cultural hegemony among the peoples of Austria. [They should] carry culture to the east, transmit the propaganda of German intellection, German science, German humanism."[103] Feelings and sentiments were of no consequence in this purely materialistic

---

103. J. N. Berger, *Zur Lösung der Österreichischen Verfassungsfrage* (Vienna, 1861), 19, cited in Carl E. Schorske, *Fin-de-Siècle Vienna: Politics and Culture* (New York: Vintage Books, 1981), 117.

scheme of thought. In fact, they were viewed as signs of backwardness and thus as serious impediments to progress.

The sensitive issues of the multinational nature and unity of the Russian Empire were discussed most thoroughly and openly in a series of articles in the prestigious journal of Russian liberal thought, *Russkaia mysl'*, on the eve of the First World War.[104] At the beginning of 1911 Petr B. Struve, the editor of the periodical and the future political advisor of the White generals, initiated a discussion of the nationality question by inviting members of the non-Russian intelligentsia to present their views. In the first series of articles, a spokesman for the nationalities, the prominent Jewish intellectual Vladimir I. Zhabotinskii, called attention to the fact that Russians constituted only forty-three percent of the empire's population, and that while it was respectable, this figure by no means justified their claim to hegemony. Although Zhabotinskii expressed a deep esteem and admiration for Russian culture, he pointed out that the natural homeland of this culture was within the boundaries of "Great" (i.e., ethnic) Russia, and that it had exceeded its boundaries as a direct result of the centuries-old oppression and absence of law in Russia. Zhabotinskii ended his article with a note of warning:

> We the aliens [i.e., non-Russians] foresee only one of two possibilities: either there will never be freedom and law in Russia, or everyone of us will voluntarily take advantage of this freedom first of all to develop our unique national personality and to emancipate ourselves from an alien culture. Either Russia will follow the path of decentralization, or it will be impossible for it to have even the most elemental principles of democracy, beginning with universal suffrage. For Russia progress and *Nationalitätenstaat* are synonymous, and any attempt to overlook this truth ... is bound to end in failure.[105]

In his reply to these arguments, Struve presented one of the most unambiguous and candid interpretations of the nationality question in Russia from the liberal point of view. To him Russian hegemony was not only justifiable, but also inevitable in view of what he saw as the undisputed

---

104. Especially interesting are: V. I. Zhabotinskii, "Pis'ma o natsional'nostiakh i oblastiakh: Evreistvo i ego nastroeniia," *Russkaia mysl'*, January 1911, 95–114; Ukrainets [Bohdan Kistiakovs'kyi], "K voprosu o samostoiatel'noi ukrainskoi kul'ture," May 1911, 131–46; P. B. Struve, "Chto takoe Rossiia," January 1911, 175–8; and his "Obshcherusskaia kul'tura i ukrainskii partikularizm: Otvet ukrainstvu," January 1912, 65–86. For further information on Struve, see Richard Pipes, *Struve: Liberal on the Right, 1905–1944* (Cambridge: Harvard University Press, 1980).

105. Zhabotinskii, 114; for an interesting discussion of Zhabotinskii's views on the nationality question, see Olga Andriewsky, "*Medved' iz berlogi:* Vladimir Jabotinsky and the Ukrainian Question, 1904–1914," *Harvard Ukrainian Studies* 14, no. 3/4 (1990), 249–67.

superiority of Russian culture. Except for the Finns and Poles, argued Struve, no other nationality in the empire possessed a national culture in the true sense of the word: "One can partake in local cultural life in Warsaw and Helsingfors without knowledge of the Russian language, but without the mastery of Russian one cannot partake [in the cultural life] of Kyiv, Mahileu, Tbilisi, or Tashkent."[106] Furthermore, none of the nationalities, according to Struve, possessed the potential for further development without the support of Russian culture. By accepting this support and depending upon it, the minority cultures had voluntarily submitted to Russian hegemony: "Among the alien peoples ... Russian culture reigns supreme not only because of the Russians' physical superiority and numerical predominance. This hegemony rightfully belongs to Russia because of its spiritual power and wealth."[107] To corroborate his argument, Struve pointed out that at the University of Kazan lectures were delivered in Russian not only because this was a legal requirement and the police saw to it that it was enforced, but simply because no other language was sufficiently developed to be used at a higher institution of learning. Struve agreed the Baltic nationalities could have followed the path of Finland, but once this path was closed to them by the Russification of the University of Dorpat, they were drawn by the "inexorable forces of history" into the sphere of Russian culture.

By these arguments Struve attempted to prove that Russia was destined to evolve into a unitary nation-state and that the many nationalities comprising the Russian Empire, in view of their cultural inferiority, were bound to assimilate by adopting the Russian language, Russian culture, and, in general, the Russian way of life. Of course, Struve was willing to concede that the inferior local cultures on the periphery of the empire could, theoretically at least, develop and even eventually reach the high level of Russian cultural development, but to him this endeavor of creating a "multitude of cultures" in the empire would consume too many valuable human resources, which could be utilized instead for the enrichment of culture in general.

In an article devoted to the Ukrainian question, Struve focused on endeavors by the Ukrainian intelligentsia to preserve and develop Ukrainian culture. The Ukrainian movement's success, he believed, hinged on whether or not it would be joined by the Ukrainian masses. He was confident that the masses would not join in view of the fact that the socioeconomic forces operating in twentieth-century Russia, such as industrialization, urbanization, universal conscription, mass education, and the mass media, were rapidly drawing the Ukrainian population into the realm of Russian culture. Precisely

---

106. Struve, "Chto takoe Rossiia?" 185.
107. Ibid., 187.

because members of the Ukrainian intelligentsia were aware of this fact, Struve's argument continued, they were desperately trying to preserve local particularism not so much because of their conviction, but for selfish and sentimental reasons. It was primarily the Ukrainian intelligentsia's awareness that Ukrainian culture was destined to become extinct that accounted for the intensity of the Ukrainian cultural revival at the turn of the century, claimed Struve.[108]

In spite of his confidence that socioeconomic forces were operating in favor of assimilation, Struve thought it prudent to issue a note of warning that the unity of the empire could be in serious danger if local cultures were given an opportunity to evolve to a higher stage of development. Therefore he most emphatically insisted that Russian must remain the language of instruction in high schools, universities, and even elementary schools, unless, for pedagogical purposes, local languages were considered indispensable for the education of the young. If, in spite of the elemental processes operating in favor of Russification, local particularism continued to grow, and especially if it began to evince higher cultural or political aspirations, the Russian liberal leader urged that "progressive Russian public opinion must energetically, without any ambiguities, enter into an ideological struggle against [minority] 'nationalism' as [it is] a tendency to weaken and partly even destroy the great acquisition of our history—all-Russian culture."[109]

By imparting such an overriding importance to Russian culture in human progress, considering it to be the determining factor of what constituted Russia, and believing it was the only secure bond holding the empire together—from Petrograd to Tbilisi and from Kyiv to Tashkent—the Russian liberal intelligentsia was bound to adopt a hostile attitude not only to the political but also broader cultural rights of the nationalities.[110] The open "ideological struggle" with minority nationalisms advocated by Struve was, naturally, imprudent during the war and the turbulent days of the revolution. Therefore the resolution of the sensitive nationality issue was systematically evaded by the liberal and socialist Russian intelligentsia in the Provisional Government by continually postponing its discussion in the Constituent Assembly.

That this argument in defense of Russian hegemony coincided with the feelings of the ruling elite was most likely not realized even by the more

---

108. Struve, "Obshcherusskaia kul'tura," 70–2.
109. Ibid., 86.
110. The editor of an Ukrainian émigré weekly in Switzerland wrote in 1916, while polemicizing with Miliukov, that the aspirations of the Ukrainian people would sooner be satisfied by the Russian tsar than by the Russian liberals. See V. Ia. Stepankivs'kyi, *L'Ukraine* (Lausanne), 7 October 1916, quoted in V. Svatkovskii report, Geneva, 22 November 1916, N. N. Giers Archives, file 97, Ukraine, Hoover Institution Archives.

astute members of the Russian intelligentsia, liberal and socialist alike. Because of their materialistic, utilitarian worldview they subconsciously submerged their national emotions in the respectable but not overly sophisticated rationalistic formulas fashionable at the beginning of the century. Not being fully aware of their own feelings, they tended to underestimate the strength of the nationalisms in the periphery and viewed them primarily as direct reactions to the shortsighted, reactionary tsarist policies of repression. They occasionally brought the nationality question to the fore in parliamentary debates not because they believed in its intrinsic value, but because it provided them with a convenient pretext to criticize the hated autocratic regime. When the catastrophes of the war and the revolution made them aware of their submerged feelings, their newly awakened national fervor transformed them into the most ardent defenders of Russia's indivisibility. They saw no need to curb their emotions, because they were convinced that their cause was founded on respectable scientific principles of universal human progress. Thus they became the willing partners of the Russian generals, who believed they were bound by their military oaths to defend Russia's territorial integrity.

Nationalism and Federalism in Ukraine

In contrast to Russian liberalism, the nationalism of the subject nationalities had its roots in the ideology of the Romantic era, which stressed the particular rather than the general and the intuitive and the emotional rather than the rational. The ideas of early Romantic historians such as Johann G. Herder were reinforced in the nineteenth century by the writings of the political theorist and publicist Giuseppe Mazzini. In this scheme of thought, each nation is a unique entity with its very own, peculiar nature, which is expressed primarily through its language and culture. Language is not merely an interchangeable tool for the transmission of ideas, but a medium with its own irreplaceable, intrinsic value. If permitted to develop freely, each national culture enriches the treasury of the human quest for truth through its unique and irreplaceable contributions. Human progress is viewed in cultural and spiritual rather than material or scientific terms, and consequently each nation, irrespective of its size or cultural or material development, is viewed as a carrier of a unique vital force capable of enriching humanity. The extinction of a national language or culture is considered an irreplaceable loss and detriment to all humankind. National self-rule or independence is thus justified as a necessary precondition for free, all-encompassing cultural development and a benefit to humankind in general.

The idea that each nation has the right to unhindered existence and full cultural development remained the cornerstone of the worldview of the leaders of the national movements of the subject nationalities even when the Romantic philosophy was no longer in vogue and the indigenous intelligentsia of the empire's periphery was overwhelmed by positivistic ideas. They took for granted that the concept of equality of all men encompassed the equality of all nations. They tried to rationalize the powerful emotional attachment to their native culture and land as a drive toward the realization of the universal principle of equality. Few were aware that a worldview in which the general rather than the particular had precedence or in which scientific progress and utility, rather than sentiments and feelings, were paramount could not provide valid arguments in favor of unhindered cultural development of the subject nationalities. If languages and cultures had no transcendent value, if they were easily interchangeable and were merely tools for the transmission of information, why should the less developed ones be cultivated? In fact, in light of the prevalent worldview, could not the principle of equality of all men be better defined and interpreted as an equal opportunity for all tsarist subjects to become Russians? In accordance with this line of reasoning, Struve was right. If the uniqueness of culture was of little consequence in the course of human development and material progress and scientific achievements were paramount, all efforts to revive the warped cultures of the oppressed nationalities could, indeed, be considered superfluous or, in the words of Struve, a waste of "valuable human resources" and time. Among the leaders of the nationalities, few were aware that the ideas of the Enlightenment, now reinforced by materialism and social Darwinism, favored the ruling nations and, consequently, the dominant cultures. Their lack of understanding that cultural Darwinism was inherent in all progressive ideologies of the day—including socialism—and their lack of awareness of the powerful role of emotions in historical processes made the Ukrainian socialists in the Rada during the autumn and early winter of 1917 reluctant to opt for independence. Instead they clung tenaciously to the abstract concept of larger state formations and to the principle of federation.

At the turn of the century only the more perceptive members of the non-Russian intelligentsia understood the subtler nature of nationalism. A good example is the prominent sociologist, jurist, and scion of an eminent Ukrainian family from Kyiv, Bohdan Kistiakovs'kyi.[111] In his student years, like many of his contemporaries, Kistiakovs'kyi went through a Marxist phase and attempted to combine Ukrainian cultural nationalism with Marxism. Later he joined Struve in editing a liberal émigré journal that promoted the idea that

---

111. For an excellent summary of his career and worldview, see Andrzej Walicki, *Legal Philosophies of Russian Liberalism* (Oxford: Clarendon Press, 1987), 343–59.

the victory of constitutionalism in the Russian Empire would provide a satisfactory solution to the major problems of the subject nationalities. Personal observations and further study of the nationality question convinced him, however, that this was an illusion. In the above-mentioned debate on the nationality question in *Russkaia mysl'*, Kistiakovs'kyi readily acknowledged the overwhelming power of Russian culture, for which he, like Zhabotinskii, had great admiration. But he refused to deduce from this that an independent, unique Ukrainian culture had no possibility of developing and flourishing. He was baffled and fascinated by the sudden Ukrainian cultural rebirth in the preceding century: "I am completely unable to give a more or less satisfactory explanation of how it was possible for Ukraine in the nineteenth century, in spite of horrible conditions, to produce more than eighty poets, novelists, and playwrights."[112] For him the phenomenon of Ukrainian nationalism, and nationalism in general, defied rational explanations:

> It should be recognized that the Ukrainian nation is endowed with a separate will, or a certain mystical force, that prompts it to assert its independent national individuality. This will expresses itself through different representatives of the Ukrainian nation in a variety of forms, sometimes with a weaker and sometimes with a stronger force. Of course, this is not a solution, only a different formulation of the historico-cultural riddle.
>
> In any case, if the Ukrainian striving for an independent culture is a divine cause, it cannot be defeated by earthly forces. The words of Gamaliel, in the Acts of the Apostles, about newly emergent Christianity may be applied to all cultural movements. Every genuine cultural movement is a manifestation of the divine spirit in humankind; therefore it is sacred, and to do violence to it is a sin.[113]

A perceptive thinker and observer of human nature, Kistiakovs'kyi recognized that Russian liberal and socialist arguments regarding the desirability and inevitability of the dominance of Russian culture could not be defeated on the basis of purely rational explanations. Unless one recognized the transcendent quality of national cultures and the important role of sentiment and feeling in the evolution of the human community, one could not provide convincing arguments in support of the cultural renaissance or political self-determination of the subject nationalities. Russian liberal leaders were aware of this, and this awareness, in light of their deeply rooted rationalism, reinforced their conviction of the righteousness of their stand on the nationality question during the revolution and civil war.

112. Ukrainets, 143.
113. Ibid., 146.

II

"Russia One and Indivisible" and Ukraine

> *The Volunteer Army as a National Factor in the Renaissance of Great Russia, One and Indivisible* (Ekaterinodar, 1919).
> A propaganda pamphlet in English.

While the ideological plans and foundations of the White movement were being developed by the imprisoned generals in Bykhau, the first concrete steps toward the establishment of the VA were taken by Kadet leaders in Moscow together with Gen. Alekseev, the only eminent officer not directly implicated in the ill-fated Kornilov plot:

> In the month of October the Union for the Salvation of the Motherland was organized in Moscow. The founders of this association were principally representatives of the Kadet party. This union authorized me to continue the task of saving the motherland with all means and measures [available]. It was with this purpose that I arrived in the Don, the only safe haven on which were converging [the] refugees, officers, and students of military schools from whom the Volunteer Army was organized by me.[1]

Both Alekseev and the imprisoned generals in Bykhau had considered the Don region as a possible refuge when and if the need arose for one. Especially in Bykhau high hopes were entertained for the Don Cossacks[2] as

---

1. S. A. Piontkovskii, ed., *Grazhdanskaia voina v Rossii 1918–1921 gg.: Khrestomatiia* (Moscow: Izdatel'stvo Kommunisticheskogo universiteta im. Ia. M. Sverdlova, 1925), 496–7.
2. During the March revolution the Don Cossacks established their own provisional autonomous government by electing a council called the Krug. On 2 July 1917 the Krug elected Aleksei Kaledin, a general of the Russian army dismissed in spring of 1917 for his opposition to the military reforms of the revolutionary government, its military head, or ataman. Kaledin was implicated in the Kornilov affair, and the Provisional Government ordered his arrest. In defiance of the Petrograd authorities, the Krug refused to turn over its leader. In spite of these differences

potential allies of the movement they hoped to organize, in spite of the fact that the Cossack leader, Kaledin, very emphatically tried in his correspondence with the Bykhau prisoners to dispel the illusion that the morale of his men remained unaffected by the revolution.[3]

Alekseev was well informed about the true state of affairs in the Don. He considered the Kuban Cossacks[4] to the south of the Don much stronger and healthier as a fighting force; being well attuned to the political trends of the time, however, he mistrusted them because of their separatist tendencies. Separatist currents were especially strong among the Black Sea Cossacks, who were of Ukrainian origin and represented the dominant element in the Kuban Rada. In an interview with Boris Suvorin, which took place shortly after Alekseev's arrival in the Don, the general spoke with great indignation about

---

between the Don Cossacks and the Provisional Government, when the Bolsheviks seized power in Petrograd the All-Cossack Congress condemned the Bolsheviks and pledged its support to the deposed authority. It also extended invitations to all opponents of Bolshevism to join them in the struggle against the usurpers in Petrograd. Thus the Don appeared an ideal base for the White movement. In reality the situation was quite different, because the Don Cossacks, especially those returning from the front, proved highly susceptible to pacifist propaganda and showed no inclination to fight either the Germans or Bolsheviks. They viewed Kaledin's conservative government with suspicion and hostility. For an account of these events in the Don, see V. Dobrynin, *Bor'ba s bol'shevizmom na iuge Rossii: uchastie v bor'be donskago kazachestva* (Prague: Slavianskoe izdatel'stvo, 1921); K. P. Kakliugin, "Voiskovoi ataman A. M. Kaledin i ego vremia," *Donskaia letopis'* 2: 108–70; S. V. Denisov, *Zapiski: Grazhdanskaia voina na iuge Rossii, 1918–1920 gg.* (Istanbul: the author, 1921).

3. Denikin, *Ocherki*, 2: 99–102.

4. The Kuban Cossacks were organized as a military unit in 1850 out of the Black Sea Cossacks and the *lineitsy*. The former were the descendants of Zaporozhian Cossacks, who were resettled in the Kuban by Catherine II after their stronghold on the Dnieper rapids was destroyed in 1775. Most likely for reasons of security, Catherine settled ethnic-Russian Don Cossacks between the settled territory in the Kuban and the mountain tribes of northern Caucasia. These constituted the second group, the *lineitsy*. The Black Sea Cossacks remained conscious of their background, and they and the *lineitsy* did not integrate. At the beginning of the twentieth century contact between Ukraine and the Kuban was established, and soon clandestine Ukrainian organizations appeared in Ekaterinodar. With the outbreak of the revolution in 1917, the Kuban Cossacks established a legislative council, the Rada, and elected Aleksandr Filimonov, a *lineets*, as their ataman. Unlike in the Don, the Kuban ataman had very little authority, and all power rested with the Rada, which was dominated by the Black Sea Cossacks. The Kuban premier, Luka O. Bych, and the speaker of the Rada, Mykola S. Riabovol, were strongly in favor of close cooperation with the Central Rada in Kyiv. It was under their influence that the Kuban Rada proclaimed its independent existence as early as October 1917. For an account of the revolution and the civil war in the Kuban, see D. E. Skobtsov, *Tri goda revoliutsii i grazhdanskoi voiny na Kubani* (Paris: n. p., n. d.); G. K. Pokrovskii, *Denikinshchina: God politiki i ekonomiki na Kubani, 1918–1919 gg.* (Berlin: A. I. Grzhebin, 1923); A. P. Filimonov, "Kubantsy, 1917–1918," in *Beloe delo: Letopis' beloi bor'by*, vol. 2, ed. A. A. von Lampe (Berlin: Russkoe natsional'noe knigoizdatel'stvo "Mednyi vsadnik," 1927), 62–107; M. P. Vatatsi, "The White Movement, 1917–1920: Memoirs," Hoover Institution Archives.

the separatist inclinations of Luka Bych, the Kuban premier, which he viewed as an outgrowth of the personal ambitions of the socialist politician.[5] The Don Cossacks, while very sensitive about the question of their privileges and regional autonomy, defended most resolutely the territorial unity of the Russian state.[6] When the Ukrainian Central Rada issued its First Universal proclaiming Ukraine's autonomy, an All-Russian Cossack Congress led by the Don Cossacks passed a resolution stating that the Cossacks stood for the indivisibility of Russia; despite the protests of the Kuban delegates, the congress pledged its unswerving support for the Provisional Government and its orders against the universal.[7] Thus, in selecting the Don region as a base of operations for the future VA, Alekseev was not guided by purely military considerations. Nor did he envisage only military objectives for the movement he was organizing.

Alekseev's ideas and plans were set forth in a letter he wrote shortly after his arrival in the region's capital, Novocherkassk, to the General Headquarters in Mahileu. In it he explained that he wanted to take advantage of the Don as a temporary haven for his work because the region was rich in resources and peaceful enough that it could serve as a base for economic recovery when "after the conclusion of peace Russia would be in a position to tear itself away from German capital and industry and from the Teutonic pressure for world conquest."[8] A firm economic base and order, in turn, would create favorable conditions for the establishment of strong authority first on the local and later on the all-Russian level. The principal task of the new army Alekseev hoped to organize from among officers, cadets, and volunteers would be to protect this political center. The former supreme commander harbored no illusions that his call for the salvation of Russia would elicit a mass response. He was quite cognizant of the fact that the movement he was organizing would have to depend almost exclusively on Russian officers and Russian intelligentsia. Commenting wryly that the Russian "valiant army" would most likely respond to Lenin's order for an armistice with a spontaneous dispersion in the direction of their homes, the old general nonetheless asserted confidently that this would not "change the general scheme for the salvation of Russia." For this undertaking to succeed, Alekseev foresaw two principal tasks: (1) political—a press, agitational propaganda, intelligence, and "special work in connection with the [Central] Rada; and (2) mili-

---

5. Boris Suvorin, *Za rodinoi: Geroicheskaia epokha Dobrovol'cheskoi armii, 1917–1918 gg.* (Paris: O. D. i ko., 1922), 17.
6. Khrystiuk, 1: 82.
7. Ibid.
8. Alekseev's letter to Lieut. Gen. M. K. Diderikhs, Novocherkassk, 8 [21] November 1917, published in *Beloe delo* 1 (1926): 77–82.

tary—formation of new military units and the strengthening of the existing Cossack forces. After compiling a detailed list of all the military units and materiel he felt could be utilized for the movement, Alekseev ended his letter by calling attention to two issues. Both dealt with developments in Ukraine.

Alekseev saw the Central Rada as "an intelligent, serious opponent" that was skillfully led and subsidized from outside. Therefore the general advised that a way be found to discredit the Ukrainian political leaders and to expose the Rada as a treacherous and alien body. Because Russian counterintelligence had been dismantled in Kyiv, Alekseev urged that a new apparatus be established in the Ukrainian capital for the sole aim of monitoring the Rada's activities. Steps in this direction had to be undertaken immediately because even though according to the latest reports, "the Rada did not as yet have strong roots, with every month its position was being strengthened and was increasing the number of its supporters." Alekseev considered an open struggle with the Ukrainians untimely because of the lack of resources, but finding ways to discredit the Ukrainian leaders he considered both useful and possible.[9] The second urgent matter he warted to bring to the attention of General Headquarters was the question of the Black Sea Fleet, which had to be prevented, the general urged, from joining the Rada's side.[10]

Alekseev's preoccupation with developments in Ukraine is of interest because his letter was written before the formal proclamation of Ukraine's independence and before a separate peace with the Central Powers was considered by the Rada. Moreover, Ukraine was not alone in exhibiting a national revival.[11] Certainly Ukraine's proximity to the Don made Alekseev especially alert to developments in Kyiv. But more importantly, it was at this time that the anti-Bolshevik Russian regiments being expelled by the Rada from Kyiv began arriving in Novocherkassk together with Kyiv's prominent Russian political leaders. Judging from the content of the letter, it is more than likely that Alekseev wrote it under the guidance of the Kyiv Russians.[12] The influence of the latter remained strong, especially in the VA's intelligence department, and might explain the preoccupation—one may even call it obsession—of the White movement in the south with the Ukrainian question.

---

9. Ibid., 81–2.

10. The Ukrainianization of the fleet paralleled that of the army and also gained momentum in late 1917. Alekseev's fears were not unfounded; the Admiral of the fleet did indeed subsequently pledge his allegiance to the General Ukrainian Naval Council in Kyiv. Doroshenko, 2: 255–6.

11. Within months of the Bolshevik coup, eight nationalities of the former tsarist empire proclaimed their independence: Finland and Lithuania on 6 and 11 December 1917 respectively; Latvia on 12 January, and Ukraine on 22 January 1918; Estonia on 24 February; and Georgia, Armenia, and Azerbaijan in May. Pipes, 287.

12. In the introduction of his letter Alekseev admits that his plans were developed in collaboration with both local and newly arrived political leaders.

The Political Objectives of the Volunteer Army

One month after the establishment of the Volunteer organization in the Don, Alekseev was joined by the former prisoners from Bykhau.[13] Their lengthy political discussions during their three-month incarceration culminated in the endorsement of a political program authored by Gen. Denikin. It expressed firm commitment to the idea of a Constituent Assembly, to continuing the war in close cooperation with the Entente, and to the protection of Russia's economic and political interests. The issue of the future state structure and the nationality question were to be resolved by the Constituent Assembly.[14] In short, the program adhered rather closely to the principles professed by the Provisional Government. This is not surprising, since many of the generals implicated in the Kornilov affair were moderates. This was particularly true of Denikin.

When the generals began arriving in Novocherkassk, they found there a contingent of about 600 officers, and a dozen prominent political leaders from Moscow and Petrograd. Some of the latter had been delegated to Novocherkassk by newly formed political circles in Russia "to aid General Alekseev in his noble national undertaking with their knowledge, experience, and connections;"[15] others had gone there on their own as soon as they learned of Alekseev's plans. By the end of December the more prominent Kadets, including the leader Miliukov, and several Russian Socialist Revolutionaries, among them the former terrorist Boris V. Savinkov and his colleague K. Wendziagolski, were ready to offer their services to the White cause.[16]

The presence of these civilians in the Don capital proved useful when the question of the VA's leadership arose with the arrival of Kornilov. Because Alekseev had founded the organization and had close ties with influential civilians, many were of the opinion that leadership of the VA should be

---

13. After a formal order for their release was issued by the Military Headquarters in Mahileu, the generals left for the Don by different routes. Denikin, Markov, and Romanovskii arrived early in December. The last to arrive was Kornilov, who reached Novocherkassk on 19 December. Loukomsky, *Memoirs,* 127–130; Denikin, *Ocherki,* 2: 140–55.
14. Ibid. See also A. I. Denikin, "Navet na beloe dvizhenie," Hoover Institution Archives. The original of this unpublished article is in the A. I. and K. V. Denikin Papers.
15. The Kadets Mikhail M. Fedorov and A. S. Beletskii were sent to Alekseev from a clandestine group in Moscow called "Deviatka" formed from various nonsocialist groups shortly after the Bolshevik coup. Denikin, *Ocherki,* 2: 187–8.
16. The more prominent Kadet members in Novocherkassk were the former socialist Petr B. Struve; the jurist Konstantin N. Sokolov; the former Provisional Government members Vasilii A. Stepanov and Andrei I. Shingarev; and Fedorov and Prince Grigorii N. Trubetskoi. K. N. Sokolov, *Pravlenie generala Denikina* (Sofia: Rossiisko-bolgarskoe knigoizdatel'stvo, 1921), 3; K. Vendziagol'skii, "Savinkov," *Novyi zhurnal,* no. 70 (1962), 155; Denikin, *Ocherki,* 2: 187–8.

entrusted to him. But, it was Kornilov who, since September 1917, had been associated with Russia's victory in the war, and it was obvious that he would attract the largest following. Matters were complicated by the fact that there was a deep-seated hostility between the two generals. It was thanks mainly to the mediation of the Kadet leaders that an arrangement was worked out whereby Kornilov was entrusted with the organization and command of the army while Alekseev undertook the direction of financial and foreign affairs. With Kornilov's assumption of command early in January 1918, the Alekseev organization became officially known as the VA.[17] Shortly afterwards Alekseev organized an advisory body—the Political Council—composed of Kadets and Socialist Revolutionaries to assist him in the formulation of financial and foreign policies. The council undoubtedly was meant to be the nucleus of the Russian authority designated as the center of the White movement in Alekseev's letter to Mahileu. With the arrival of Kornilov, who mistrusted the Kadets and Miliukov in particular, this plan had to be shelved.[18] In fact, Kornilov demanded in writing that the council remain only an advisory body and that no question be resolved without the approval of the General Staff.[19]

Early in January 1918 Miliukov prepared an official manifesto of the VA outlining the objectives of the White cause. In it the Russian historian compared the White movement to the great Russian national upheaval of the seventeenth century and called upon the people to defend their sacred land as resolutely and bravely as their forefathers had three hundred years earlier. The formation of a strong military force counterposed to the spreading anarchy and to the "German-Bolshevik" invasion was declared to be the movement's principal task. The manifesto promised that

> The new army will stand guard over civil liberties until the day when the master of the Russian land, the Russian people, can express its will through the election of a Constituent Assembly. Before the will of the people all classes, parties, and groups of the population must bow. It alone will be

---

17. Denikin, *Ocherki*, 2: 188–9. In the spring of 1918, when Kornilov issued the first conscription order, the army ceased to be purely volunteer. After the Kuban and, later, Don Cossacks were subordinated to Denikin in 1919, the official name of the army became the Armed Forces of South Russia (AFSR), although popularly the White forces fighting in the south were called the VA.

18. It is not that Kornilov saw no need for men well trained in the art of politics. He himself had his own circle of political advisors, but he intensely disliked Alekseev's political entourage because of what he considered the Kadets' duplicity in the September 1917 mutiny. The Kadets, while involved in the events that led to the confrontation between Kornilov and Kerensky, managed to come out unscathed.

19. Denikin, *Ocherki*, 2: 193–4.

served by the establishment of this army, and all who are participating in the army's creation will incontrovertibly subordinate themselves to the legal authority established by it through a Constituent Assembly.[20]

Behind the solemn language and patriotic rhetoric, the manifesto embodied some of the basic principles the White leadership would adhere to throughout the civil war: firm commitment to defend Russia as a great power, aspiration to be the guardian of national rather than particular class interests, and relegating the resolution of all important issues, including the nationality question, to a future Constituent Assembly. The manifesto did not call for the restoration of the monarchy or the old political order not because the "counterrevolutionary" leaders considered such slogans inauspicious, but because both Alekseev and Kornilov supported unequivocally the slogans proclaimed by the March Revolution. In fact, with the exception of the Bolsheviks, few contemporaries referred to the VA leaders as counterrevolutionaries. Wendziagolski aptly observed that Alekseev was hardly in a position to proclaim the slogan of "Down with the Revolutionaries and Democrats," as he "on the fateful day for the monarchy, with all his authority as chief of staff ... supported not his monarch and supreme commander but the revolution."[21] Kornilov too, in Wendziagolski's opinion, had no reason to sympathize with the counterrevolutionaries, since the popular military leader "not only on account of his worldview and education but also because of his alien origin[22] had neither racial nor class ties with the reactionaries."[23] Incidentally, as commander of the Petrograd Military District, Kornilov carried out the arrest of the imperial family after the fall of the monarchy. Alekseev and Kornilov's successor, Gen. Denikin, was reproached for harboring "a deep prejudice against the aristocracy,"[24] and a conservative British officer was shocked to find the White movement's leader "morbidly sensitive against aristocrats, courtiers and officers of the ex-imperial guard."[25]

The absence in the manifesto of an unequivocal affirmation of the unity and indivisibility of Russia, a tenet that figured prominently in all subsequent official White proclamations, is striking and can be explained only by the growing difficulties the VA leaders were experiencing in early January 1918. The Bolsheviks proved highly successful in inciting the peasants and some of

---

20. Panina Papers, box 8, file 1.
21. Vendziagol'skii, 174–5.
22. Kornilov was of Buriat-Mongol origin.
23. Vendziagol'skii, 174–5.
24. P. N. Vrangel, *Vospominaniia* (Frankfurt: Posev, 1969), pt. 1, 110.
25. H. N. H. Williamson, *Farewell to the Don* (New York: John Day, 1971), 207.

the younger Cossacks against the Don government of Ataman Kaledin, and by January 1918 a rival Soviet government had been established in the region.[26] It became quite clear to the VA leaders that if their movement had any chance of developing into a fighting force, they would have to move south to the Kuban. In its formative period the small VA could not afford to alienate the independent-minded Kuban Cossacks if it wished to use the Kuban as a base of operations.

Another reason for the omission of the indivisibility principle may have been a somewhat different view on the nationality question that Kornilov appeared to profess in January 1918. Although according to the agreement between the VA leaders, he was entrusted exclusively with the military leadership of the army, he did not consider political questions to be outside his purview. With the cooperation of his personal political advisors, a certain Dobrinskii in particular, Kornilov prepared a draft of his own political program. In substance this document conformed rather closely to the principles of the White movement's leaders and was based, as Kornilov himself pointed out, on the Bykhau program. It called for continuing the war to a victorious end, preserving civil liberties attained by the March Revolution, and postponing the resolution of the agrarian question until the convocation of the Constituent Assembly. On one point, however, Kornilov's views departed considerably from the ideals espoused by the White leaders—on the all-important question of Russia's territorial integrity. Not only did Kornilov show readiness to grant broad autonomy to the borderland states even before the convocation of the Constituent Assembly, but he was also willing to recognize the separate political status of Poland,[27] Ukraine, and Finland: "Poland, Ukraine, and Finland, having formed themselves into separate national state entities," reads article fourteen of the program, "should be supported by the Russian government in their strivings toward state regeneration in order that in this manner the eternal and indestructible union of the brotherly peoples might grow even stronger."[28]

Kornilov's program did not remain a closely guarded secret for long. When rumors regarding its existence reached Alekseev, the old and generally self-composed soldier became so incensed that he angrily demanded to see it immediately. Miliukov, after studying the document, indignantly branded

---

26. Dobrynin, 47.
27. The VA's foreign policy was identical to that of the Provisional Government. Thus Poland's right to independence within its ethnographic borders was fully recognized. For a thorough discussion of the White movement's attitude toward Poland, see Adolf Juzwenko, *Polska a "Biała Rosja:" Od listopada 1918 do kwietnia 1920 r.* (Wrocław, Warsaw, Cracow, and Gdańsk: Zakład Narodowy im. Ossolińskich, Wydawnictwo Polskiej Akademii Nauk, 1973).
28. The program was published in *Arkhiv russkoi revoliutsii* 8 (1923): 285–6; and *Beloe delo* 2: 173–82.

Kornilov an "adventurist" and a "political dilettante," and warned Alekseev that if the program was publicized, broad support for the VA would immediately disintegrate.[29]

Kornilov's program would have constituted a landmark in the evolution of the nationality policy of the White movement and undoubtedly caused a bitter conflict, perhaps even a schism, within the VA, if the events that followed—the costly Kuban campaign and Kornilov's sudden death[30]—had not consigned the document to oblivion.

In the middle of January, when the future of the VA appeared to be especially bleak, Alekseev authorized Wendziagolski, the only non-Russian member of the Political Council, to organize a separate department for the nationalities.[31] Furthermore, by the end of the month, in spite of his dislike and suspicions of the Central Rada, Alekseev appointed Ivan P. Demidov as a special representative to the UNR government in Kyiv.[32] It is not clear what prompted Alekseev to do this, but it is doubtful that he had changed his attitude toward the Rada, of which he had spoken with such opprobrium only two months earlier. Most likely Demidov's appointment was the result of pressure exerted by the Entente representatives, whose governments had appointed commissioners to the UNR government in the hope of averting the conclusion of a peace between the Rada and the Central Powers.[33] Because Entente support was essential for the VA's survival, the old general may have given in to the pressure. Whatever the motive behind Demidov's mission, relations between the VA and the UNR government never materialized because the White movement's envoy reached Kyiv only after it was already in Bolshevik hands.[34] Soon after the Rada's departure from Kyiv, the VA, too, was forced to leave Novocherkassk for the Kuban, where the Bolshevik takeover appeared less imminent. With the withdrawal of the VA from the Don, Alekseev's Political Council dispersed: some members went to Kyiv as soon as the city was cleared of the Bolsheviks, while others emigrated abroad. In the early spring of 1918 the White leaders were preoccupied exclusively with military matters because the VA was fighting for its very survival.

29. P. N. Miliukov Archive, box 8161, file 13, Bakhmeteff Archive.
30. See infra, 58.
31. Vendziagol'skii, 175.
32. Ibid., 178.
33. See supra, 22–3.
34. Vendziagol'skii, 178.

Developments in Kyiv and the Volunteer Army

A. A. Gol'denveizer, a prominent Jewish political leader and a keen observer of developments in Ukraine during the revolution, remarked that life in Kyiv was always "marked by national animosities."[35] The Kyivans' exclusiveness and intolerance were to a large extent the result of Russification policies that had been implemented assiduously by local Russians and Russified bureaucrats. As early as the 1860s, before full-scale Russification became policy, the first editor of *Kievlianin*, Vitalii Ia. Shul'gin,[36] selected the following motto for his paper: "The Southwestern *krai* is Russian, Russian, Russian." "This slogan," observed Gol'denveizer, "would have been ludicrous and absurd in a purely Russian land such as Moscow: it had a definite meaning and political significance in Kyiv, precisely because the Southwestern *krai* was not purely Russian. The aim of V. Ia. Shul'gin and his successors was to make it such."[37]

In Kyiv, Russian-Ukrainian animosities intensified especially with the emergence of the Central Rada as a political factor in Ukraine. Between March and November 1917 several Russian organizations were established in Kyiv to struggle against the Rada's efforts to introduce the Ukrainian language in schools and state institutions. Among the more prominent were the Gogol Union of Little Russians (Soiuz malorosov imeni Gogolia), the South Russians (Iugorossy), the Russian National Union (Russkii natsional'nyi soiuz), and the Non-party Bloc of Russian Voters, which vowed to struggle for the preservation of Russia's cultural and state unity.[38] After the July agreement between the Rada and the Provisional Government, attacks on the Rada in Kyiv's Russian press subsided somewhat; most Russians, as Gol'denveizer points out, considered the agreement an "unavoidable evil."[39]

The uneasy truce between the Ukrainians and the more moderate Russians in Kyiv came to an abrupt end in November when, in the conflict between the Bolsheviks and the pro-Provisional Government forces in the city, the Rada intervened on behalf of the Bolsheviks and ordered the withdrawal of all reinforcements that the military staff in Kyiv had brought in to help suppress

---

35. A. A. Gol'denveizer, "Iz kievskikh vospominanii," in *Revoliutsiia na Ukraine po memuaram belykh*, ed. S. A. Alekseev (Moscow and Leningrad: Gosudarstvennoe izdatel'stvo, 1930), 18.
36. The father of Vasilii V. Shul'gin, the future editor of the same paper and a prominent White politician.
37. Gol'denveizer, 18–19.
38. Memorandums of the Kiev National Center, V.A. Maklakov Archive of the Russian Embassy in Paris, 1918–23, series B, box 20, Ukraine, Hoover Institution Archives.
39. Gol'denveizer, 13. In *Kievlianin*, V. V. Shul'gin protested strongly against the concessions made to the Rada.

the Bolshevik uprising.[40] The forces fighting on the side of the Provisional Government capitulated after a brief struggle, but the local Bolsheviks were too weak to assume power, and thus, according to an agreement concluded by the representatives of the Kyiv military staff, representatives of the Bolsheviks, and emissaries of the General Secretariat, authority in Kyiv passed to the Rada. The agreement stipulated that all military units fighting on behalf of the Provisional Government must be evacuated from the city.[41] On 14 November these units began leaving for Novocherkassk, but only an insignificant number of soldiers joined the VA.[42]

Even before the fighting in Kyiv ended, the Rada proceeded to enlarge the scope of its authority by adding several new secretaries to the General Secretariat[43] and extending its jurisdiction over several new gubernias. On 16 November 1917 the Ukrainian government formally announced that it was assuming all authority in Ukraine, but at the same time it flatly denied that it was striving for full independence of the country. Three days later the formation of the UNR was officially proclaimed in the Third Universal, which nonetheless emphasized again that Ukraine did not consider its ties with Russia severed: "Without separating from the Russian Republic and destroying its unity, we shall firmly establish ourselves on our own land in order that, with our strength, we may help the rest of Russia ... to become a federation of free and equal peoples."[44]

The Rada's insistence on the maintenance of its ties with a future federated Russia should not be viewed merely as a maneuver to placate the influential Russian element in the cities[45] or a measure designed to elicit the support of the Jewish minority, whose leaders favored reconstruction of the Russian Empire on federal principles. In the autumn and winter of 1917 the

---

40. For details of the struggle of the forces loyal to the Provisional Government with both the local Bolsheviks and units of the Rada, see Doroshenko, 1: 161–72; Khrystiuk, 2: 41–9; and V. Manilov, ed., *1917 god na Kievshchine: Khronika sobytii* (Kyiv: Gosudarstvennoe izdatel'stvo Ukrainy, 1928), 324–5.
41. Ibid.
42. The Kyiv military staff was able to gather a considerable number of men for the struggle against the Bolsheviks. There were approximately 10,000 soldiers in Kyiv loyal to the Provisional Government. At the crucial moment, however, many of them either joined the Rada or proclaimed their neutrality. Doroshenko, 1: 165, 171.
43. Among the new secretaries was Dmitrii Odinets, who was put in charge of Russian affairs. Ibid., 172–4.
44. Ibid., 179–81.
45. In the Kyiv municipal council the Ukrainians controlled only twenty percent of the seats. A similar situation existed in other larger cities of Ukraine such as Odessa, Zhytomyr, and Kharkiv. Panas Fedenko, *Ukraïns'kyi hromads'kyi rukh* (Poděbrady: n. p., 1934), 75; Manilov, 415; Doroshenko, 1: 143.

General Secretariat was dominated by the Ukrainian Social Democrats and Ukrainian Socialist Revolutionaries, some of whom may have been convinced, as was pointed out in the UPSR organ *Borot'ba*, that "federation is a higher type of cohabitation by peoples than the existence of separate states."[46]

The activities of the General Secretariat shortly after the Bolshevik coup in Petrograd indicate that such a conviction dominated. Immediately after the fall of the Provisional Government, the General Secretariat established ties with the Cossack governments in the Don and Kuban as well as with General Headquarters in Mahileu,[47] and urged that serious efforts be made to form a central authority.[48] The commander in chief of the Russian armies, Gen. Nikolai N. Dukhonin, replied that he supported the General Secretariat's proposal but that the position of General Headquarters was too weak for such an undertaking, and he proposed that a central government be formed in Kyiv instead.[49] The General Secretariat, however, considered it inconvenient that two governments, one Ukrainian and one all-Russian, would be located in the same city, and therefore it rejected the proposal.

When these negotiations were discussed at a meeting of the Rada on 3 December, the policies of the General Secretariat received general approval. Consequently delegations were sent to the Cossack governments, and on 8 December a special appeal was issued to the Cossack Southeastern Union[50] and the governments of Caucasia, Siberia, Moldavia, Crimea, and Bashkiria urging that they immediately begin negotiations with the General Secretariat "on the question of forming a socialist government for all of Russia."[51] The first response to this appeal came from the Don Krug, and subsequently friendly relations were established with Kaledin's government: the UNR government assured safe passage to the Don Cossacks returning from the

---

46. Quoted from an article published on the occasion of the proclamation of the Third Universal by Doroshenko, 1: 186.
47. At this time the leader of the Russian Socialist Revolutionaries, Viktor Chernov, together with other Russian political leaders, was negotiating at General Headquarters the formation of a socialist coalition government under the protection of the generals. Oliver Radkey, *The Sickle under the Hammer* (New York: Columbia University Press, 1963), 76–91.
48. This implies that the General Secretariat did not recognize the Bolshevik government as a central authority.
49. It was Gen. Lukomskii who, in a letter from Bykhau, first suggested to Dukhonin that the military headquarters be moved to Kyiv, where the safety of the officers could be assured with the aid of the somewhat more reliable troops of the Southwestern Front. Lukomskii, *Vospominaniia*, 1: 266.
50. Early in October the Don, Kuban, Terek, Astrakhan, Kalmyk, Ural, and Dagestan Cossacks held a conference in Vladikavkaz at which they resolved to form a Southeastern Union. The Cossacks guaranteed each other complete independence with respect to their internal affairs and pledged themselves to a united struggle against the Bolsheviks. Denikin, *Ocherki*, 2: 182.
51. Doroshenko, 1: 205.

Russian-German front to Novocherkassk, while Kaledin agreed to transfer Ukrainian units from the Don to Kyiv.[52]

Cooperation with Kaledin's government in the Don could not help but lead to a direct confrontation between the Rada and the Bolshevik government. Indeed, in the ultimatum that the Rada received from Petrograd, the demand that the Rada immediately stop cooperating with the "counter-revolutionary Kadet-Kaledin uprising" figured most prominently.[53] Considering the Bolshevik demand an interference in Ukraine's internal affairs, the Rada refused to comply, and the transfer of the Don Cossacks to Novocherkassk continued.[54] Simultaneously with the General Secretariat's rejection of the Bolshevik ultimatum, the UNR government issued its second appeal to all newly formed republics and autonomous regions to cooperate in the formation of a central all-Russian government.[55] The war with the Bolsheviks, which began in the second part of December, was an important factor in the Rada's decision to conclude a separate peace with the Central Powers. It was only at this time that the Entente states, which had been showing considerable interest in developments in Ukraine since the spring of 1917, began taking serious steps in the direction of establishing official diplomatic relations with the UNR government. At the end of December 1917 Gen. Tabouis was informed by the French ambassador in Romania, de Beaupoil de Saint-Aulaire, that the Entente governments were examining the possible conditions for an official recognition of the UNR government, and early in January 1918 he appointed Tabouis as the commissioner of the French Republic in Ukraine.[56] Similarly, the British government designated the former British consul at Riga, John Picton Bagge, as its representative to the UNR. In an official statement, Bagge declared that his government "would support to the utmost of its ability the Ukrainian government, [by] maintaining order and combating the Central Powers, who are the enemies of democracy and humanity."[57] The French government also tried to induce the United States to recognize the Rada as the government of Ukraine. On 9 January the French ambassador in Washington sent an official note to the State Department stating that his government was maintaining de facto relations with the Rada and that "the reports it has received about the Austro-German activities at Kiev led it to the conclusion

---

52. Ibid.
53. Bunyan and Fisher, 439–40.
54. Doroshenko, 1: 216–17.
55. Ibid.
56. Arnold D. Margolin, *From a Political Diary* (New York: Columbia University Press, 1946), 182; Doroshenko, 1: 236–7.
57. V. Vynnychenko, *Vidrodzhenia natsiï (Istoriia ukraïns'koï revoliutsiï [marets' 1917 r.–hruden' 1919 r.])*, vol. 2 (Vienna: Dzvin, 1920), 241–3.

that it could not defer any longer taking a more clearly defined attitude toward the Ukraine ... [and that it was therefore necessary to instruct Gen. Tabouis] to notify the Ukrainian Government that the French Government is glad actually to recognize it as an independent government ... [and that the French Ambassador was interested whether the government of the United States] would be inclined to take a similar step."[58] The United States government's reply was negative.

It is important to note that the prospect that the UNR would join the Allied war effort raised high hopes in some Entente capitals and even won sympathy for the Ukrainian government among some Russian diplomats abroad. Vasilii A. Maklakov, the Provisional Government's ambassador in Paris who continued to represent Russia's interests there after the Bolshevik coup, recalled these hopes in a letter to his Kadet colleagues at VA Headquarters:

> You cannot imagine what impression this has created here, and how favorably disposed toward Ukraine the reports in the press [in Paris] have become.... Essentially it was from this moment that Ukraine became the object of [Entente] interest. The questions that were asked were: what is Ukraine, what is its national composition, what is the basis for the differences in psychology [between the Ukrainians and the Russians]? These were questions that were examined from every aspect in specialized and general literature. It was hoped that if Northern [ethnic] Russia had died, it would be possible to save Southern Russia [Ukraine]. And I shall not conceal the fact that even we, Russians here, began to cling, as a drowning man to a straw, to this possibility, thinking perhaps it is true, perhaps because the land is more agricultural, Bolshevism will disappear there and Ukraine will be able to maintain armies on the German Front.[59]

While Maklakov's spirits were buoyed at the prospect of Rada-Entente cooperation, the local White circles in Kyiv became seriously alarmed that the close ties the General Secretariat established with the Entente representatives in Kyiv might eventually lead to official recognition of the UNR by France and Britain. While they could not openly work against the Ukrainian government, these circles did try to hinder relations between the UNR foreign ministry and the Entente by gaining influence in the French and British missions in the Ukrainian capital and winning over at least some of their

---

58. United States, Department of State. *Papers Relating to the Foreign Relations of the United States, 1918,* vol. 2, *Russia* (Washington, D.C.: U.S. Government Printing Office, 1931), 655.
59. V. A. Maklakov to Ekaterinodar, 12 May 1919, P. N. Wrangel Military Archives, file 135, Hoover Institution Archives.

members to the Russian point of view on the Ukrainian question. They were especially successful in this endeavor with Emile Henno of the French mission in Kyiv. Henno became one of V. V. Shul'gin's closest collaborators, and in the months immediately following the conclusion of World War I he worked tirelessly to prevent rapprochement between the Entente and Ukraine.[60]

Russian Interpretations of the Ukrainian Question

The Kyiv Russians and Russified Ukrainians based their interpretation of the Ukrainian question on three principles: (1) "Great Russia", "Little Russia,"[61] and Belarus are three branches of one Russian people; (2) the Russian literary language and Russian culture are the common achievements of the three branches of the Russian people; and (3) "Little Russia" is an inseparable part of a unitary Russia. In their contacts with Entente representatives, the Kyiv Russians stressed the fact that the preponderant majority of Little Russians was loyal to the idea of the unitary Russian state and to the Entente; and that Little Russia, which has been incorrectly called Ukraine, is a region most distinctly Russian in character with a population most distinctly Russian among the three branches of the Russian people. Furthermore, they tried to persuade the Entente representatives that Ukrainians were not a nation but a political party nurtured by Austria-Hungary and Germany and that the idea of Ukrainian statehood had emerged from an insignificant, treasonous part of the local population involved in the Austro-German plan to dismember Russia.[62]

Interpretation of the Ukrainian question by Russian leaders from Moscow and Petrograd was essentially the same, although they attempted to be somewhat more scholarly and sophisticated. They, too, stressed the common origin of the three branches of the Russian people, but took into consideration the fact that the western (Belarusian) and southwestern (Ukrainian) branches lived from the mid-thirteenth to the mid-seventeenth centuries under the influence of Western culture, while for two hundred years the northeastern branch was under the Mongol yoke. Although they recognized that Little Russia enjoyed a period of independence in the seventeenth century, they emphasized that in 1654 it voluntarily "united" with Muscovy. The subsequent

---

60. Shul'gin's letter to Sergei D. Sazonov, 8 March 1919, Wrangel Military Archives, file 132.
61. The Kyiv Russians and VA leaders habitually used the term "Little Russia" when referring to Ukraine.
62. Report of the Committee for the Convocation of a National Russian Congress of South Russia, Wrangel Military Archives, file 129.

260 years of Great and Little Russian political, social, religious, and economic coexistence, the argument continued, had brought about the rapprochement (*sblizhenie*) of the two fraternal peoples. Furthermore, forty years of compulsory military service and industrial and agricultural development were leading to their complete merger (*sliianie*). While they pointed out that the Ukrainian movement should not be considered purely a product of Austro-German intrigue—the bureaucratic mistakes of the tsarist regime contributed as well—they believed the tsarist restrictions imposed on the Ukrainian cultural and political activities were justifiabled from the point of view of Russia's state interest and security.[63]

On the basis of such arguments the Russian leaders of Kyiv, Moscow, and Petrograd denied the existence of a separate Ukrainian nation. In practice this meant that they flatly rejected Ukraine's right to autonomy within the Russian state. (It has been previously noted that not only the Ukrainians were denied this right.) Both before and after the revolution most Russian politicians resolutely opposed the idea of a Russian federation based on the national principle.[64]

The conclusion of a separate peace between the UNR and the Central Powers on 9 February 1918 seemingly confirmed the allegations of the Russians both in Kyiv and abroad that the Ukrainians were closely tied with Germany and Austria-Hungary, even though the Rada stubbornly pursued an independent course in open defiance of the wishes of the German Mlilitary Command in Ukraine. When, on 29 April, the Rada issued a radical land reform, the Germans replaced the intractable Ukrainian socialist government with a conservative regime that they hoped would cooperate more willingly in securing Germany's main objective in Ukraine, the procurement of food supplies from the countryside. This change was facilitated by the fact that the agrarian reforms sponsored by the socialist Rada angered not only the German High Command and the large landowners in Ukraine, but also provoked opposition among the well-to-do peasants. On 7 April 1918, 1,500 wealthy peasants gathered in Lubny to protest the reforms, charging that they were ruinous to the country. A conservative Ukrainian Democratic Agrarian party, consisting of landed nobles and wealthy peasants, had been in existence since May 1917. It was not, however, the leaders of this party who engineered the overthrow of the Rada, but rather a Ukrainian People's Hromada, formed on the initiative of Gen. P. Skoropads'kyi and Mykola Sakhno-Ustymovych, which had approached the German military authorities with a proposal that the Rada be deposed and replaced by a conservative Ukrainian government. The

---

63. A good summary of this point of view is contained in an article that appeared in an Italian newspaper on 2 April 1918; copy in the Maklakov Archive, series B, box 20, Ukraine.
64. See supra, 16.

Germans were more than willing to accept this plan in view of the Rada's intransigence.[65]

The conservative coup was planned well in advance. On the same day that the German-backed government of Hetman Skoropads'kyi[66] assumed power, it decreed a set of Laws for the Provisional State Structure of Ukraine that in essence restored the tsarist legal order in the country.[67] These laws, which were to serve as the provisional constitution of the state until the convocation of a Ukrainian diet, were signed by the hetman and the premier, Sakhno-Ustymovych. The latter exerted strong efforts to form a cabinet from members of Ukrainian nonsocialist parties, but the more prominent Ukrainian political leaders refused to cooperate.[68] Sakhno-Ustymovych resigned, and consequently many government posts were filled by former tsarist officials and bureaucrats.[69] This resulted in a highly anomalous situation: the so-called Ukrainian State, which under the hetman's rule became more and more Ukrainian,[70] was administered by Russians or Russified Ukrainians, most of

---

65. For these developments see Serhii Shemet, "Do istoriï Ukraïns'koï demokratychno-khliborobs'koï partiï," *Khliborobs'ka Ukraïna* (Vienna) 1: 67–79; Oleh S. Fedyshyn, *Germany's Drive to the East and the Ukrainian Revolution, 1917–1918* (New Brunswick: Rutgers University Press, 1971), 133–57; Report from Odessa, 5 February 1919, Wrangel Military Archives, file 132; and Doroshenko, 2: 28–9.

66. Hetman Pavlo P. Skoropads'kyi was a descendant of the brother of the eighteenth-century Cossack hetman Ivan Skoropads'kyi. In the summer of 1917, as a general of the Russian army, he undertook the task of Ukrainianizing the corps he commanded. After the fall of the Provisional Government he supported the Rada and became the commander of a new, volunteer military unit, the Free Cossacks. Because of differences with the socialist leaders of the Rada, he resigned from his post. Doroshenko, 2: 22–41 and passim.

67. Gol'denveizer notes that when he first saw the laws in the press, he immediately sensed something familiar. After comparing the new provisional constitution with the laws of 1906, he noticed that, with few exceptions, the former repeated the latter. Gol'denveizer, 37.

68. Only one member of the Ukrainian Socialist Federalist party (the Ukrainian equivalent in political outlook to the Kadet party) accepted a post in the hetman's government—the future historian Dmytro Doroshenko, who was named foreign minister.

69. The first cabinet of the hetman's government, headed by Fedir A. Lyzohub, a former chairman of the Poltava Zemstvo Board, did not consist of reactionaries, although the policies it introduced were unmistakably conservative. Several ministers were members of the Kyiv branch of the Kadet party. The latter's acceptance of posts in the government and the subsequent approval by the regional congress of the Kadet party of cooperation with the hetman led to a schism in the People's Freedom party. The central party organs and a minority of the Kyiv branch strongly censured their colleagues' activities. A considerable number of Kadets in Ukraine were of Ukrainian or Jewish origin. Protocols and resolutions of the Kadet party on this question are located in the Miliukov Personal Archives, box 1.6.6.1., file 29.

70. The government's accomplishments in education and culture were truly impressive. A new Ukrainian state university was opened in Kamianets-Podilskyi, and several chairs of Ukrainian history, law, language, and literature were established in existing institutions of higher learning. A Ukrainian Academy of Sciences, National Gallery, National Museum, and State Archives were

whom, while highly qualified, were indifferent to the idea of Ukrainian statehood. The supply of experienced Russian administrators in Kyiv increased every day, since under the hetman Ukraine became a refuge for diverse Russian political and civic leaders from Petrograd and Moscow.

Russian Anti-Bolshevik Organizations in Kyiv

Almost simultaneously with the formation of the VA, through the efforts of the former tsarist minister of agriculture Aleksandr V. Krivoshein a secret organization of various non-socialist political and civic leaders was formed in Moscow to organize a struggle against the Bolsheviks. Early in 1918 a second group—the Left Center—came into being; it consisted of Kadets, right Socialist Revolutionaries, and Popular Socialists and announced a political program under the slogan of the "Constitutional Assembly." Initially these Russian political groups were pro-Entente and supported the VA. The German military success in the spring of 1918 led to dissension within the Left Center, however, and it split into a Right Center, which consisted of monarchists who were inclined to cooperate with the Germans if they helped them to overthrow the Bolsheviks, and a National Center consisting primarily of Kadets who stood for maintaining loyalty to the Entente and unequivocally endorsed the VA's political program.[71] In the summer of 1918 the National Center invited Alekseev to become its honorary chairman, and in a letter addressed to the White center it explained that

> the Russian state authority, in order to be a national state authority, should be formed without the participation of enemies who only recently defeated Russia. ... We consider that Russia's interests do not coincide with those of Germany. And no matter how hopeless and difficult the Bolshevik yoke may be, to look for salvation in Germany is senseless and futile. With the aim of working toward the liberation from the [Bolshevik] yoke, we should work in the hope of the rebirth of the national spirit of the people and should maintain our relations with the Allies, knowing that their interests coincide with ours.[72]

The National Center's association with the VA remained close throughout Alekseev and Denikin's leadership of the White movement. Especially loyal

---

also founded. More than fifty Ukrainian high schools were organized, and several university scholarships were established. Doroshenko, 2: 336–71.
71. Wrangel Military Archives, file 129; Miliukov, *Russia Today and Tomorrow,* 130–2; Denikin, *Ocherki,* 3: 78.
72. Wrangel Military Archives, file 129.

to the White cause was the Kyiv branch of the center, which consisted of those Kadets who refused to cooperate with the Skoropads'kyi government and of some members of the Non-party Bloc of Russian Voters, including V. V. Shul'gin. The branch set before itself the task to struggle against Ukrainian independence, to support the VA, and to enlighten the Entente on the true state of affairs in Ukraine.[73] The center was especially active in trying to hinder the Ukrainianization policies pursued by the Skoropads'kyi regime and in organizing opposition to the hetman's endeavors to convene a Ukrainian State Diet.

In addition to the political organizations that originated in Moscow, several new political and civic associations sprang up in Kyiv. The most important was the Council of Members of the Legislative Houses (of the four Russian State Dumas and the State Council) led by a former tsarist minister of agriculture, Count Aleksei Bobrinskii, and consisting primarily of pro-German monarchists. Members of the Zemstvo and City boards also organized themselves into a separate association. The Representatives of Industry, Commerce, and Finance, better known under the acronym Protofis, established their organization during the first days of the Skoropad'skyi regime and proved to be especially active in the economic life of the new state. The first and especially the last of these organizations actively supported the conservative Ukrainian government. A prominent member of Protofis, Sergei M. Gutnik, was the minister of trade in that government.[74]

It is not difficult to understand the willingness of the large landowners, Protofis members, and some ultraconservative monarchists to cooperate with the Skoropads'kyi regime. Although that regime stood for Ukraine's independence, at the same time it was restoring the principles upon which the old order was based—a step no other larger political center on the territory of the former empire was willing to undertake. To the men gathered in these organizations, personal interests mattered more than national peculiarities. Even if some of them were irritated by the rapid pace of Ukrainianization, they were willing to tolerate it as long as a secure base for economic reconstruction was being built at the same time; they probably considered Ukrainianization a temporary phenomenon that would be considerably modified once order was restored in Russia. Their principal enemies were the Bolsheviks, and if the spread of Bolshevism could be arrested with the aid of Germany or through the efforts of an independent Ukrainian state, they were willing to take advantage of such aid even at the expense of the territorial unity of Russia.

---

73. Resolutions of the National Center, Kyiv, 30 October 1918, Wrangel Military Archives, file 129.
74. M. S. Margulies, *God interventsii,* vol. 1 (Berlin: Z. I. Grzhebin, 1923), 13–15; Gol'denveizer, 39; Denikin, *Ocherki,* 4: 184–6.

None of these explanations and rationalizations seemed justifiable to the leaders of the VA and its adherents in Kyiv. The White generals had nothing but contempt for Protofis members' "internationalism" and Germanophilism, which they saw as treason.[75] To the VA leaders—both military and political—Skoropads'kyi and his entourage were all traitors because they cooperated with the Germans and because they actively supported Ukraine's independence. When rumors of alleged negotiations between the VA and the hetman's government spread in Kyiv, the local members of the National Center immediately sent a letter of alarm to VA Headquarters, in which they stated that

> There can be no justification for any kind of negotiations with the traitor Skoropads'kyi and with the Ukraine he is heading; the rumors and reports of alleged negotiations between the Volunteer Army and "Skoropadia" have produced a depressing atmosphere among the members of the National Center, because if the Volunteer Army recognizes Skoropads'kyi and Ukraine, this will lead to their universal and final recognition.... The National Center in Kyiv has resolved to concentrate its efforts exclusively on the struggle against Ukrainian independence.[76]

The Kyiv members of the National Center need not have worried, because by this time leadership of the VA was securely in the hands of Denikin, whose ideology and political orientation coincided even more closely with that of the National Center than Alekseev's.[77] A short pamphlet devoted especially to the VA's relations with Ukraine tersely explained why official contacts with Skoropad'skyi's government had been flatly rejected by VA Headquarters:

> The Volunteer Army has set before itself the task of restoring a unitary and indivisible Russia within its former boundaries (with the exception of ethnographic Poland) through Russia's liberation from the Bolsheviks and through voluntary unification of all its disjoined regions into one entity. Therefore all efforts by some people and parties to create division among the Russian people or to sever this or that district is regarded as treason. Because of this basic principle, the Volunteer Army did not recognize as the legal authority in Little Russia the government of Hetman Skoropads'kyi, who took

---

75. Denikin, *Ocherki*, 4: 183.
76. Ibid., 187.
77. When Alekseev died in early October 1918 after a prolonged illness, Denikin assumed the title of supreme commander of the VA and became the undisputed leader of the White movement in the south.

advantage of a foreign power hostile to Russia for the purpose of creating an "Independent Ukrainian State."[78]

By the time Denikin assumed both military and political control of the VA, the formative stage of the White movement had ended, and its political objectives and the means for achieving them had been defined. Its principal aim was the restoration of the territorial unity and indivisibility of the empire within the prewar frontiers—a task that called for the repulsion of the Austro-German armies from Russia and the destruction of both the Bolsheviks and the new independent governments in the borderlands. The White generals harbored no illusions that this formidable undertaking could be accomplished through the efforts of the small corps of volunteers who had answered their call. Therefore their immediate aim was neither to fight the Bolsheviks nor to organize an anti-German front, but to form a military and political center professing unswerving loyalty to the Entente, a center that, by not recognizing the Treaty of Brest-Litovsk, would, in principle at least, keep Russia in the war. They were confident that the defeat of the Central Powers would lead to the fall of the borderland governments and would make the defeat of Bolshevism an easy task, especially since it was taken for granted that France and Britain would hasten to aid the White cause.

---

78. *Kratkaia zapiska istorii vzaimootnoshenii Dobrovol'cheskoi Armii s Ukrainoi* (Rostov: Delo, 1919), 3.

III

An Indivisible or a Democratic Russia: The Root of the White Dilemma

At the time of the Skoropads'kyi coup in Kyiv, the VA was recovering from one of its most difficult and costly campaigns. The march from Novocherkassk to the Kuban in February 1918 proved to be most inauspicious. The Kuban Cossacks received the White generals with mistrust and even open hostility. Even before the arrival of Alekseev and Kornilov in the Kuban, the Cossacks were repeatedly warned by Bych, the energetic Kuban premier, that an alliance with the VA could only lead to their subjugation to a military dictatorship and that "to aid the Volunteer Army means to prepare a new absorption of the Kuban by Russia."[1] Only after the Bolsheviks scored several important victories in the Kuban and occupied its capital, Ekaterinodar, were the Cossacks willing to cooperate with the Volunteers. In an agreement drawn up between the White generals and the Kuban military and political leaders at the end of March 1918, the Cossacks agreed to subordinate their forces to the VA Command, but only if the latter guaranteed in writing that it would not interfere in Kuban civil affairs and would fully recognize the authority of the Kuban Rada and its government.[2]

Kornilov, the principal negotiator of the Kuban-Volunteer agreement, was determined to help the Cossacks clear their territory of Bolsheviks. In fact he singlehandedly insisted on taking Ekaterinodar by storm at a time when the rest of the VA General Staff was of the opinion that continuing the attack on the Kuban capital would be suicidal. What upset the White commanders, particularly Denikin, Romanovskii, and Markov, was the fact that Kornilov insisted on the attack not because he was convinced that the operation could

---

1. Denikin, *Ocherki*, 2: 254. For the developments in the Kuban, see V. G. Naumenko, *Iz nedavnago proshlago Kubani*, vol. 2 (Belgrade: n. p., 193?), 5–6; and "N. S. Riabovol," *Vol'noe kazachestvo*, August 1936, 11–13.
2. "N. S. Riabovol," 12–13; Denikin, *Ocherki*, 2: 279.

succeed, but because he saw it as the only way to end his life with honor. "Lavr Georgievich, why are you so inflexible on this matter?" Denikin asked Kornilov on the eve of the planned attack. "There is no way out, Anton Ivanovich," replied Kornilov. "If we do not take Ekaterinodar, there is nothing left for me but to put a bullet through my head."[3]

The attack on Ekaterinodar did not take place on 13 April as scheduled, but not because Kornilov was persuaded to give his troops a respite. In the early morning hours of the attack he was killed by a shell that exploded in his office at VA Headquarters.[4] Denikin, whom the ailing Alekseev appointed commander in chief, immediately rescinded Kornilov's plan and ordered an immediate retreat to the Don. The end of the Kuban campaign marks the beginning of Denikin's leadership of the White movement.

A White General in a Liberal Saddle

Although Denikin lacked Kornilov's charisma and Alekseev's endearing personal qualities, he possessed a strong will and a great independence of mind. It was his worldview that most strongly affected the political program of the White cause. Four basic principles guided Denikin's outlook: (1) Russia's indivisibility; (2) loyalty to the Entente; (3) implacable hostility to Germany and its alleged agents—the Bolsheviks and the leaders of the pro-independence movements in the borderlands; and (4) postponement of all decisions regarding the political, economic, and social structure of the state until the convocation of a Constituent Assembly.

The first principle was of foremost importance. "The preservation of Russian statehood was the symbol of faith to General Alekseev, to me, and to the entire Volunteer Army," writes Denikin. "It was an orthodox symbol not permitting any doubts, vacillations, or compromises."[5] As the commander in chief of the VA, Denikin considered it his duty and moral obligation to do everything in his power to restore the might, glory, and greatness of Russia. This seemed to him possible only if the territorial integrity of the empire, forged "in the course of three centuries by the heroic feats of its gatherers, by the blood of its soldiers, by the toil of its people," was preserved.[6] Denikin firmly believed that to achieve this objective, the White cause must become an all-embracing movement of all nationally conscious citizens of Russia. The

---

3. Denikin, *Ocherki*, 2: 295.
4. B. Kazanovich, "Ataka Ekaterinodara i smert' Kornilova," Bakhmeteff Archive; Denikin, *Ocherki*, 2: 304.
5. Denikin, *Ocherki*, 3: 39.
6. Ibid., 6.

latter, in Denikin's opinion, could only come from the educated classes of Russian society, "because the people in the general meaning of the word, or the 'toiling masses,' according to another terminology, at this period of the revolution were totally indifferent to the purely spiritual aspect of the question."[7] To attract the support of every nationally conscious Russian irrespective of political persuasion, Denikin tried to keep the image of the VA "above politics" and its leadership independent of political parties and organizations. "A 'Unitary, Great, and Undivided Russia' could be understood by everyone clearly, but matters become complicated when one goes further"[8] was Denikin's firm reply to everyone who reproached him for refusing to commit to a more precisely defined political program. In the spring and summer of 1918 the new VA leader faced strong pressure to proclaim the restoration of the monarchy as one of the principal aims of the White cause. At this time it was estimated that eighty to ninety percent of the army was monarchist. Shul'gin, Gen. Lukomskii, and even Miliukov tried to persuade Denikin that the idea of the monarchy was indispensable for the success of the movement.[9] Denikin remained adamant in his refusal to emblazon the monarchist slogan on the banner of the VA. "What right does a small circle of people have to decide the fate of the country without the knowledge of the Russian people?" wrote the general indignantly. "As far as I am concerned, I will not fight for the form of government. I am leading a struggle for Russia only."[10]

Denikin's confidence that the White movement would eventually evolve into an all-embracing national struggle for the restoration of the great Russian state was reinforced by the general and unequivocal condemnation by Russian public opinion of the peace treaty of Brest-Litovsk concluded between the Bolsheviks and the Central Powers in March 1918,[11] "by which Russia politically withdrew to the beginning of the seventeenth century."[12] The entire Russian press, with the exception of the official Soviet media, reverberated with condemnations and protests against the treaty. "No matter how diverse were the external forms of this protest," Denikin discerned in them an "expression of national sentiment."[13] Through the treaty, Denikin believed, the treachery of Bolshevism was fully revealed. He condemned the

7. Ibid., 10.
8. Ibid., 130–1.
9. Ibid.; Miliukov, "Dnevnik," 4 July 1918, 73.
10. Denikin, *Ocherki*, 3: 132.
11. For a thorough treatment of this treaty, see J. W. Wheeler-Bennett, *The Forgotten Peace: Brest Litovsk, March 1918* (London: Macmillan, 1938).
12. Denikin, *Ocherki*, 3: 7.
13. Ibid., 10.

Bolsheviks not because of their social and economic goals, but because he considered their government and leadership to be basically non-Russian.

> The basic vicious ailment of the Soviet government was the fact that *this government was not national*.... Never before in its history, ever since the Tatar yoke, have the representatives of Russia—who at the time of its dismal fall were Messrs Ioffe, Bronshtein [Trotsky], and Briliant [Sokolnikov] respectively—subjected themselves to greater humiliation than at the conference of Brest-Litovsk.[14]

But in the opinion of the White leader, the "aliens" in the Bolshevik government were not the only ones guilty of Russia's "dismemberment." Equally responsible for Russia's misfortune were the leaders of the borderland nationalities. Whether these men were socialists, liberals, or monarchists, Denikin was determined to struggle against them with equal vehemence because their endeavors presented a serious threat to the unity of Russia.

Many factors shaped Denikin's outlook, but his passionate devotion to the state must have been instilled in him in his youth and during his early career. From his brief and incomplete memoirs it is clear that he highly idealized his father, who, though born a Russian serf, retired from the army with the rank of captain.[15] The elder Denikin died early, and therefore the youth of Anton Ivanovich was "difficult and cheerless." He knew that in order to escape the poverty and obscure surroundings of his youth, he had to follow his father's example. One factor in Denikin's background could have presented a hindrance to his military career. Unlike his father, he was not a "pure Russian." His father married an impecunious Polish noblewoman in the town of Wrocławek in Warsaw gubernia, where Anton Ivanovich was born and spent his childhood. In his monumental *Ocherki russkoi smuty,* Denikin is silent on his half-Polish origin, but he describes in great detail the injustices and discrimination officers of Polish origin experienced in the Russian army:

> Of all the nationalities of the Russian state in the officers corps, the government practiced discrimination against the Poles only. This traditional distrust assumed unjust and offensive forms. According to a secret edict, a series of restrictions were imposed on the Polish officers.... For individuals who wished to pursue a military career and wanted to clear a path for themselves through a [military] academy, there was only one solution: to compromise one's own conscience and accept Orthodoxy. Among the commanders I knew, for example, only one Pole, Gen. Gurchin, although there were at least a dozen Germans.[16]

14. Ibid., 6.
15. A. I. Denikin, *Put' russkogo ofitsera* (New York: Izdatel'stvo im. Chekhova, 1953).
16. Denikin, *Ocherki,* 1, pt. 2, 128.

There is no question that Denikin considered himself Russian. Even though he spent his formative years in a Polish town and conversed with his mother and relatives in Polish only, he appears to have identified totally with his father. In spite of this fact, a feeling of insecurity must have plagued Denikin during his career. The fact that his "reliability" might be questioned when the time of his promotion came up must have instilled in Denikin a passion to prove that he was a Russian, to bend over backwards to attest to his loyalty, devotion, and dedication to Russia. What was a habit in his early career could have evolved into an obssession later in his life. A movement founded on the principle of Russia's unity and indivisibility could not have found a more dedicated leader than Denikin.

One of Denikin's first important military decisions as commander in chief of the VA involved the launching of the second Kuban campaign at the end of June 1918. When Denikin's troops reached the southern borders of the Don early in May, the situation in Novocherkassk was quite different from the one the generals had left there only two months earlier. The appearance of the German armies along the western borders of Cossack territory, the arrival of a small but well-disciplined unit under the command of Col. Mikhail G. Drozdovskii from the Romanian front, and the blunders committed by the local Soviet leaders in the Don tipped the scale in favor of the anti-Bolshevik forces in the region. By May the capital of the Don was again in Cossack hands, this time with a government even more conservative than Kaledin's.[17] On 16 May the Don Krug elected a former tsarist officer, Petr N. Krasnov, as its ataman. Under Krasnov the government followed not only a conservative, openly restorationist policy, but also proved willing to secure order and peace in the Don with the aid of German bayonets.[18] Only two days after his election, Krasnov revealed his pro-German sympathies by writing a letter to the German emperor in which he asked for the recognition of the Don as an independent state until the convocation of the Russian Constituent Assembly.[19] Shortly afterward the ataman delegated Gens. A. V. Cheriachukin and Mikhail A. Svechin to establish friendly relations with Skoropads'kyi and to seek German aid. Among other things, the delegation was instructed to obtain

17. Kaledin committed suicide shortly after he was informed by Alekseev that the VA was leaving the Don. Ia. M. Lisovoi, ed., *Belyi arkhiv: Sbornik materialov po istorii i literature voiny, bol'shevizma, belago dvizheniia i t.p.,* vol. 1 (Paris: n. p., 1926), 99–100.

18. All laws established by the Provisional Government were abolished, and the principle of private property was reestablished. The ataman was invested with dictatorial powers until the convocation of the next Krug. G. P. Ivanov, "Osvobozhdenie Novocherkasska i Krug Spaseniia Dona," *Donskaia letopis'* 3: 59–60, 323–6.

19. For the text of the letter, see Denikin, *Ocherki,* 3: 66–7. Krasnov wrote a second letter to the emperor in July 1918; a copy is located in the A. V. Cheriachukin Papers, file 1, Hoover Institution Archives.

arms and ammunition for the Don, to gain Ukrainian and German cooperation in transporting the Cossacks and officers to the Don, to secure the Ukrainian government's acceptance of the Don's claims to the Tahanrih district,[20] to restore rail and other communications between Ukraine and the Don, and to establish trade relations with Ukraine.[21]

While Denikin strongly censured Krasnov's dealings with the Germans, he readily accepted arms and ammunition from Novocherkassk because they were indispensable for his rapidly growing army.[22] At a conference between the Don ataman and the VA leaders at the end of May 1918, Krasnov promised substantial material aid to Denikin and, among other things, gave his approval for the opening of several enlistment bureaus in Rostov and Novocherkassk. Krasnov's generosity to the Volunteers, even though it might have brought about serious differences between the Don and the German Military Command, was motivated by his desire to win over Denikin for a joint campaign against the Bolshevik stronghold at Tsaritsyn, which represented a serious menace to the security and stability of the Don. Denikin, an able if not brilliant commander by most accounts, must have been well aware of the strategic importance of the city as a railroad junction with many ammunition factories and military supplies that could serve as a connecting link between the VA and the incipient White movement in Siberia.[23] Yet he categorically rejected Krasnov's plan. The Don ataman pleaded with Denikin, arguing persuasively that in addition to the strategic considerations for taking Tsaritsyn, it would also provide the VA with a purely Russian base and the VA would then not have to depend on the support of the Kuban Cossacks. No argument, however, proved sufficiently convincing for the strong-willed general. It seems that, already at the time of the conference with Krasnov, Denikin must have been thinking of a second Kuban campaign. What prompted him to give this matter serious consideration was the possibility of a secret agreement between the exiled Kuban government, then only tenuously

20. According to the treaty of Brest-Litovsk, the Tahanrih district was to be ceded to the UNR. *Texts of the Ukraine "Peace"* (Washington: Department of State, 1918).
21. The Cheriachukin-Svechin mission proved very successful. During the summer of 1918 alone the Don received from Kyiv 11,651 rifles, 46 cannons, 88 machine guns, 109,104 rounds of artillery shells, and 11,594,721 rounds of rifle ammunition. P. N. Krasnov, "Vsevelikoe Voisko Donskoe," *Arkhiv russkoi revoliutsii* (Berlin) 5 (1922): 207–10; K. P. Kakliugin, "Donskoi ataman P. N. Krasnov i ego vremia," *Donskaia letopis'* 3: 68–163.
22. At the end of the first Kuban campaign, the VA had barely three thousand men; by June it had almost ten thousand. E. V. Pavlov, ed. *Markovtsy v boiakhi pokhodakh za Rossiiu v osvoboditel'noi voine, 1917–1921* (Paris: n. p., 1922), 246–7.
23. The revolt of the Czech Legion in Cheliabinsk broke out on 14 May 1918 and the Socialist Revolutionary members of the disbanded Constituent Assembly were organizing a government in Samara. David Footman, *Civil War in Russia* (London: Faber and Faber, 1961), 98–9.

allied with the VA, and Skoropads'kyi's government.[24]

From the start the agreement between the Kuban Cossacks and the VA was on shaky foundations. In spite of their military subordination, the Cossacks retained much of their separate identity, and the Kuban government formulated its policies independently of the VA. On the eve of Denikin's conference with Krasnov, in open defiance of the stand adopted by the VA with respect to the Germans and the Ukrainian government, a Kuban delegation headed by the speaker of the Kuban Rada, Mykola Riabovol, whose pro-Ukrainian sympathies were well-known, left for Kyiv to request aid from Skoropads'kyi.

In addition to Riabovol, the delegation included two members of the Rada with unmistakably pro-Ukrainian sympathies, Kuz'ma Ia. Bezkrovnyi and Hryhorii V. Omel'chenko; two Russians, the Kuban minister of agriculture D. E. Skobtsov and a Kadet member of the Rada, P. M. Kaplin; and the chairman of the Committee of the Caucasian Mountain Peoples, Sultan Shakhin-Girei, who had just concluded an alliance with the Kuban government. The delegation arrived in Kyiv on 28 May 1918. A week later it was very warmly welcomed by the hetman and the members of his government. Skoropads'kyi greeted the delegates with a highly patriotic speech: "I am very happy that through you, the Kuban Cossacks, I have an opportunity to greet the descendants of the glorious Zaporozhian Host, who in their incessant struggle for the freedom of Ukraine were forced to leave the [region of the] Dnieper Rapids for the mountains of the Caucasus, where they, in spite of many hindrances, remained faithful to their Motherland—Ukraine. In view of this, I hope that the celebrated Kuban Cossacks will march hand in hand with the youthful Ukrainian State in order to attain those objectives that guided the actions of our forefathers." In response, a member of the Kuban delegation declared that the Kuban would always live in complete union with "Mother Ukraine."[25]

According to Dmytro Doroshenko, Skoropads'kyi's foreign minister, the government in Kyiv considered the Kuban as a historical part of Ukraine that sooner or later would be united with the Ukrainian republic. As soon as the Kuban emissaries arrived in Kyiv, Doroshenko initiated secret negotiations with the Ukrainian members of the delegation to that end. The negotiations proceeded smoothly but did not remain secret for long. Soon Krasnov's ambassador to Kyiv, Gen. Cheriachukin, learned about them and became considerably alarmed, because unification would include territories claimed

---

24. The Kuban government retreated with the Cossacks and the VA from Ekaterinodar, and they established joint headquarters in the southern Don region.

25. Doroshenko, 2: 196.

by the Don.[26] Rumors of the negotiations also reached the Kuban government, which instructed its delegation to terminate the secret talks at once and instead concentrate on the question of military aid.

Denikin must have foreseen the danger of a union between Ukraine and the Kuban. The union would have strengthened the Ukrainian republic considerably, providing it with a sizable military force while at the same time depriving the White cause of half of its army.[27] Furthermore, it would have provided Germany with an opportunity to penetrate even farther east and to take control of the entire northeastern Black Sea coast. The danger must have appeared imminent when it was learned that several Kuban Cossack settlements near Azov had risen up against their local soviets and had turned to Germany for aid. The Germans not only enabled these settlements to exist independently of the Soviet regime, but also began stockpiling with great haste considerable military supplies in the strategically important littoral region.[28] In addition, the VA's agent in Kyiv, Col. O. Riasnianskii, learned of the arrival there of two regiments, one Austrian and one German, with no clear destination. Riasnianskii suspected they were destined for the Kuban.[29] The expansion of German influence in the southwestern corner of the former Russian Empire and the simultaneous strengthening of a newly formed border republic might have appeared more dangerous to Denikin than the Bolshevik stronghold at Tsaritsyn, and they must have played a role in his decision to reject Krasnov's proposal for a joint anti-Bolshevik campaign against Tsaritsyn. This was a decision for which he was harshly criticized by his contemporaries and subsequently condemned.[30]

26. Ibid., 195. The Don emissary in Kyiv, Gen. M. A. Svechin, was astonished to see in Skoropads'kyi's office a map of Ukraine that included not only the Tahanrih and Rostov districts and the Donets Basin—regions claimed by the Don—but also the entire Kuban. N. A. Svechin, "Dopolnenie k vospominaniiam," pt. 2, 1–20, Bakhmeteff Archive.

27. The Germans systematically hindered the development of the Ukrainian army. Several regiments were ordered to disband. The occupying forces were careful to see to it that no local power grew strong enough to present a menace to them. Doroshenko, 2: 392. At this time the VA consisted of 9,000 men, half of whom were Kuban Cossacks. Denikin, "Navet na beloe dvizhenie," 39–40.

28. Sokolov, *Pravlenie generala Denikina*, 18–23. Sokolov, a member of the Kadet party and the Political Council, had most likely been sent to the Azov region for intelligence purposes.

29. Miliukov, "Dnevnik," 22 June 1918, 29.

30. Russian émigré historians have argued that the capture of Tsaritsyn would have resulted in a decisive victory for the White movement in the civil war. The Soviet government would then have been cut off from Transcaucasia and the Caucasus, thereby enabling the White armies to clear Transcaucasia of the Bolsheviks with ease. Denikin is blamed for the failure of Krasnov's plan. A. A. Zaitsov, *1918 god: Ocherki po istorii russkoi grazhdanskoi voiny* (Paris: n. p., 1934), 198; N. N. Golovin, *Rossiskaia kontr-revoliutsiia v 1917–1918 gg.* (Paris: Biblioteka "Illiustrirovannoi Rossii," 1939), vol. 5, bk. 10, 30–7, and bk. 11, 7–21. Denikin replied to his critics most fully in "Navet na beloe dvizhenie."

What has been considered Denikin's greatest military blunder could be viewed as a success if examined from the point of view of Russia's territorial unity. As events were to prove, the Ukrainian government was indeed determined to annex the Kuban and was working tirelessly in that direction. Soon after Denikin's forces appeared on the northern fringes of the Kuban, the Ukrainian War Ministry transferred a division commanded by Gen. O. Natiiv from Kharkiv gubernia to the Azov region.[31] According to the principal architect of the Ukrainian annexation of the Kuban, Doroshenko, these plans fell apart because of sabotage in the Ukrainian War Ministry. Although Doroshenko avoids mentioning anyone by name, he avers that a high official in the Ukrainian government who was in close touch with the VA saw to it that the order for the disembarkation of Ukrainian troops on the Black Sea coast was delayed long enough for Denikin to occupy the principal cities in the Kuban. Once Ekaterinodar was in Denikin's hands, the Germans gave orders to halt the Kuban campaign because they did not wish to see a clash between the VA and the Ukrainian army.[32]

The second Kuban campaign underscored once again that for the White movement Russia's chief enemy was Germany and Russia's principal danger lay in what was viewed as the successful execution of Germany's plan—Russia's dismemberment either through conquest or through the support of centrifugal forces within the empire. The strengthening of a separatist government that Ukraine's unification with the Kuban would have effected, even if it was resolutely anti-Bolshevik, represented a serious peril to the state's territorial unity. Therefore no matter how promising the capture of Tsaritsyn might have been for the anti-Bolshevik struggle, Denikin went ahead with his plans for the second Kuban campaign. The VA's strong-willed commander was to repeat similar moves or "blunders" a number of times. Only a few months after their occupation of the Kuban, Denikin was preparing his troops for a march on socialist but resolutely anti-Bolshevik Georgia.[33] A year later he ordered his troops to march westward on Kyiv,

31. Doroshenko, 2: 197. The Germans agreed, after some hesitation, to replace Natiiv's regiment on the Ukrainian-Soviet border with their own troops. They also promised to help the Ukrainians with the disembarkation of troops on the Azov coast. Sokolov's observations indicate that in the early summer of 1918, preparations for a Kuban campaign were well under way. The two German divisions whose arrival Riasnianskii reported in June were most likely replacements for the Ukrainian troops on the Ukrainian-Soviet border.
32. Ibid.
33. When Denikin was preparing for his campaign against Georgia, he casually remarked to Premier Bych: "It is sufficient for me to send one or two divisions and there will be nothing left of the Georgians." To this the Kuban premier replied caustically: "Of course, if it is your objective to conquer Georgia—incidentally, there are no Bolsheviks there." Quoted in Margulies, 1: 348.

even though he was urged to concentrate his troops in the northeast against the Bolsheviks. From the point of view of a successful anti-Bolshevik struggle, these strategic decisions were irreparable blunders. From the point of view of the struggle for "Russia One and Indivisible," however, Denikin's plan was both logical and advantageous to the White cause.

A Black Knight in the White Army

The VA most resolutely refused to establish official relations with the conservative Ukrainian government of Hetman Skoropads'kyi. But it did follow very diligently developments in Ukraine; it was in an excellent position to do so because one of its best organized intelligence agencies was located in Kyiv. The agency, operating under the cryptic name Azbuka, was established sometime in March 1918 by Vasilii Shul'gin,[34] most likely in compliance with the plan outlined by Alekseev in one of his first letters from Novocherkassk.[35] When the VA established its headquarters in Ekaterinodar, Shul'gin transferred Azbuka's main office to the Kuban capital. His agency, financed in part by the General Staff, remained closely tied with the VA.[36]

Shul'gin's association with the White leaders predated the revolution. He was an active member of the Progressive Bloc, a member of the Duma Committee, one of the two civilians who helped Alekseev to persuade the tsar to abdicate, and an intermediary between the secret officers' organizations and the civilians in the events that led to the Kornilov mutiny in September 1917. Shul'gin's ties with the VA remained close, and his influence on White policy makers remained considerable, especially during the first year of Denikin's leadership, in spite of the fact that unlike the supreme commander of the White movement, he was a staunch conservative and monarchist.[37] What he had in common with Denikin and the influential Kadets in the Political Council was his fanatical devotion to a united Russia and an implacable hostility toward Germany. It was because of the Germanophile tendency of the monarchist bloc and the readiness of his conservative colleagues to compromise on the Ukrainian question that he broke his ties with the right-

---

34. Letter from V. V. Shul'gin to the Military Governor of Odessa, January 1919, Wrangel Military Archives, file 132.
35. See supra, 37–9.
36. Denikin, *Ocherki*, 3: 86.
37. Shul'gin's influence in Ekaterinodar was so strong that some members of the White movement referred to him as the chief of the VA's political department. Letter from Shul'gin to an unknown addressee in Omsk, 15 February 1919, Wrangel Military Archives, file 132.

wing parties and joined the National Center in Kyiv.³⁸ It was his profound conviction that any form of cooperation with Germany would inevitably lead to the disintegration of Russia and that a monarchy restored with German aid would therefore be irretrievably compromised.³⁹ Although Shul'gin reproached Alekseev and Denikin for eschewing the monarchist principle, he nonetheless unhesitatingly offered his services to the VA because it resolutely stood for an indivisible Russia.

Shul'gin's almost religious devotion to the concept of Russia's unity predetermined his attitude toward the nationalities. In prerevolutionary times he had earned a reputation as a rabid anti-Semite and an impetuous Ukrainophobe.⁴⁰ With respect to the future structure of the empire, Shul'gin envisaged Russia divided into autonomous regions with boundaries determined not on the nationality principle but "on economic, geographic, and other factors that would assure the attainment of the higher objectives for everyone."⁴¹ As for the Ukrainian question, he urged a division of Ukraine's territory into three autonomous regions: New Russia, with Odessa as its center; Little Russia, with Kyiv as its center; and a Kharkiv region, with Kharkiv as its center. The official language was to be Russian, government officials were to use Russian only, and Russian was to be the language of instruction in all educational institutions.⁴²

Shul'gin presented his views on the Ukrainian question in great detail in a declaration in which he and a fellow member of the Kyiv National Center, Anatolii I. Savenko, declined to accept Ukrainian citizenship. In this official letter addressed to Skoropads'kyi's government, Shul'gin categorically refused to recognize any historical, ethnic, socioeconomic, or political basis for the existence of a separate Ukrainian state.⁴³ In his talks with Entente representatives Shul'gin argued that the Ukrainian idea had no roots whatsoever among the people of the south; he explained away the resounding successes of Ukrainian political organizations during the elections to the Constituent Assembly in November 1917—the Ukrainian parties received seventy-five percent of the entire vote in Ukraine—as being the result of the ignorance of

---

38. Denikin, *Ocherki,* 4: 186.
39. Denikin, *Ocherki,* 3: 85; Miliukov, "Dnevnik," 5.
40. After the civil war, as an émigré, Shul'gin continued to polemicize both with the Ukrainians and the Jews. He ridiculed the leaders of the Ukrainian revolution and published books and articles grossly anti-Semitic in character. See his *Ukrainstvuiushchie i my* (Belgrade: N. Z. Rybinskii, 1939) and *Chto nam v nikh ne nravitsia* (Paris: Russia Minor, 1929).
41. Letter from Shul'gin to an unknown addressee in Omsk.
42. Ibid.
43. "Is it Possible to Recognize the Ukrainian State?" (Motives for rejecting Ukrainian citizenship by V. V. Shul'gin and A. I. Savenko), Maklakov Archive, series B, box 20, Ukraine.

the masses and the cunning tactics of the Ukrainian political leaders.[44]

It is difficult to ascertain whether Shul'gin truly believed in the ideas he propounded so zealously. Reports issued by his own agency, not to mention the observations of others, contradicted at times his favorite contention that the Ukrainians were not a nationality but a political party subsidized by Austria-Hungary and Germany with the aim of dismembering Russia.[45] Shul'gin's sincerity and honesty is not of great consequence here, however. What is important is that his views were supported by the VA's political leaders. With the establishment of a more-or-less permanent and secure base for the VA in the Kuban, the leaders of the White movement could again devote more time to political questions, and it was Shul'gin who was authorized to prepare a plan for the establishment of a new political consultative body for the VA. His draft on the Special Council, as the new advisory body was to be called, was approved by Alekseev on 31 August 1918, only two weeks after the Volunteers entered Ekaterinodar.[46] The draft, which had to be kept secret from the Kuban Rada in order not to exacerbate relations with the Cossacks, envisaged broad tasks for the council: it was responsible for working out plans for regional administration and local self-government and for preparing provisional legal projects of state organization "aimed at the restoration of Russia as a great power within its former borders." Moreover, it was the council's task to establish contact with Russian governments, political parties, and prominent individuals who defended the idea of Russia's unity, in order to prepare them for the moment when the organization of the new Russian state would be possible.[47] Alekseev was designated the chairman of the council, and Gens. Denikin, Abram M. Dragomirov, and Lukomskii, deputy chairmen.

While the various departments of the Special Council were being organized, two Kadet jurists, Konstantin N. Sokolov and Vasilii A. Stepanov, were authorized to prepare the White movement's constitution; while doing so, they were to make a special effort to reconcile the VA's authority with the

---

44. On the results of the elections, see Oliver H. Radkey, *The Election to the Russian Constituent Assembly of 1917* (Cambridge: Harvard University Press, 1950), esp. 18 and 30.

45. Reports of the Don envoy to Ukraine, Gen. Cheriachukin, on the situation in Ukraine differed considerably from those supplied by Azbuka. Cheriachukin Papers, file 4.

46. The Political Council established at Novocherkassk dispersed when the VA set out on its first Kuban campaign. Alekseev subsequently established a political bureau, but it played no significant role in the VA. When Shul'gin arrived in Ekaterinodar in the middle of August, he was appalled by the casualness with which political matters were dealt with by Alekseev's youthful and inexperienced assistants. Letter from V. V. Shul'gin to an unknown addressee, 9 February 1919, Azbuka report, Wrangel Military Archives, file 132.

47. Sokolov, 30–1; Denikin, *Ocherki*, 3: 264.

rights of the Kuban Rada.[48] According to this constitution, which was ready for approval by the end of September, the Special Council was defined as a consultative assembly of the commander in chief, who had the authority to appoint and dismiss the chairman of the council and the heads of departments.[49] The constitution introduced only minor changes in the structure of the council. Interestingly, neither Shul'gin nor the Kadet legal experts deemed it necessary to include a department of nationalities within the council. What the constitution did define in great detail, however, was the question of the Kuban's self-government. Matters such as local police, maintenance of prisons, sanitation, medicine, local trade, industry, agriculture, and education—provided that instructions were given in the Russian language—were left within the purview of the Kuban district government headed by the ataman, while foreign relations, military command, justice, the post, and foreign trade were reserved for the center. The Kuban Rada never acquiesced to the limitations imposed on its government by the constitution. Even though no other region under VA control was granted as much self-government as the Kuban, already during the drafting of the constitution the Kuban political leaders showed great dissatisfaction with the proposed autonomy framework and defended steadfastly the right of their government to conduct its own commercial and foreign relations and the right of an independent Cossack army.[50] The question of Kuban autonomy and the authority of the VA Command was never resolved peacefully. In the autumn of 1919, after the VA had developed into a secure military force and did not have to depend on the support of the Kuban Cossacks, the command "resolved" the Kuban question by dispersing the Rada and eliminating the leaders of the Cossack government through execution or assassination.[51]

In contrast to Skoropads'kyi and Krasnov's political programs, the VA constitution recognized as valid all legislation enacted by the Provisional Government and assured all citizens equality before the law irrespective of nationality, social status, or religion. The Kadet authors of the constitution were somewhat apprehensive that such liberal principles would not be acceptable to the more conservative military leaders such as Dragomirov and Lukomskii.[52] Their fears proved groundless. In spite of the continuing influx of conservative officers into the VA and the increasingly important role that

---

48. Sokolov, 34.
49. The full text of the constitution is in Denikin, *Ocherki*, 2: 267–9; excerpts of it translated into English are in James Bunyan, ed., *Intervention, Civil War and Communism in Russia, April–December 1918: Documents and Materials* (Baltimore: Johns Hopkins Press, 1936), 48–9.
50. Denikin, *Ocherki*, 2: 267–9.
51. Pokrovskii, 240–7; Denikin Papers, box 24, file "Police and Counterintelligence."
52. Sokolov, 37.

the two conservative generals began playing in the political affairs of the White movement—after Alekseev's death in October 1918 Dragomirov became chairman of the Special Council[53]—Denikin's outlook coincided so closely with that of the Kadets that he unhesitatingly approved the constitution on 4 October 1918.[54]

As in the political program of the generals imprisoned in Bykhau and in the VA manifesto, the constitution endorsed unequivocally the achievements of the March Revolution. That the White leaders continued to subscribe to a rather liberal program in spite of the prevalence of conservative views among the officers was partly the result of Denikin's ability to assert and maintain his political authority and partly the result of the White movement's dependence on Entente support (it was believed that France and Britain would aid anti-Bolshevik Russia only if it pursued liberal objectives). It was also, to a great degree, the result of the readiness of prominent Kadets to aid the White army.

The number of distinguished Russian liberals at VA Headquarters increased substantially when the congress of the People's Freedom party convened in Ekaterinodar at the end of October 1918. The resolutions adopted at this congress coincided so closely with the declared objectives of the VA that Denikin jestingly chided his Kadet colleagues for plagiarizing his program.[55] Of the Kadet leaders who remained closely associated with the VA during Denikin's leadership, the most important was Nikolai I. Astrov, the left-wing member of the party's Central Committee who was known during the revolution as a "progressive" and "conciliationist" for his advocacy of cooperation with the moderate socialist parties.[56] During the civil war Astrov was simultaneously a member of the National Center and the socialist-dominated Union of Regeneration. In Denikin's Special Council Astrov was a minister without portfolio, but he performed the duties of a minister of the interior. His influence in the political apparatus of the VA was so strong that the right-wing parties ridiculed Denikin for being Astrov's "plaything."[57] A close associate of Astrov was Sofia V. Panina, a prominent Kadet intellectual and social activist best known as the founder of the Peoples' House, a shelter for the underprivileged in St. Petersburg, who was the deputy minister of education and minister of welfare in the Provisional Government.[58] The aforementioned jurists Stepanov and Sokolov were also devoted followers of

---

53. Ibid., 43.
54. Denikin, *Ocherki,* 3: 271.
55. N. I. Astrov, "Vospominaniia," Panina Papers, box 5, 501.
56. Rosenberg, 202–4, 212, 217–18.
57. Margulies, 1: 170.
58. Rosenberg, 278–9.

Denikin. The former was a specialist on labor legislation who had been closely tied with Miliukov in prerevolutionary days, and the latter became head of the important propaganda department of the Special Council. Of these men and women, only Sokolov had a reputation as a "conservative" Kadet, primarily because of the anti-Semitic tendencies of the Department of Public Information he headed.

Although both the right and left wings of the Kadet party were represented in the VA's political apparatus, it was the influence of the left wing that proved to be stronger, partly because the better known right-wing members became disqualified from participating in the Special Council because of their pro-German orientation in the spring of 1918,[59] and partly because of Denikin's close ideological and personal ties with the left-wing members. Panina, Astrov, and Stepanov were not only Denikin's closest political collaborators; they also formed a part of the small social circle of the VA commander and his wife in Ekaterinodar.[60] Thus, even though Denikin took great pains to emphasize that he was able to keep the VA "above politics," in actuality the White movement under his leadership consistently pursued the Kadet political goals. As the conservative Vasilii I. Gurko wrote in his reminiscences, "The Command of the [Volunteer] Army declared itself apolitical, but in fact it was, with respect to politics, under Kadet hypnosis."[61] Denikin complained bitterly that the field commanders habitually referred to the Special Council as "Kadet."[62]

---

59. Among them were Baron Boris Nol'de, Prince Trubetskoi, Sergei A. Kotliarevskii, and Miliukov. P. N. Miliukov Personal Archive, box 1.6.6.1., file 25; S. P. Mel'gunov, *Grazhdanskaia voina v osveshchenii P. N. Miliukova* (Paris: "Rapid-Imprimerie," 1929), 33–4. Ironically Miliukov, who was one of the staunchest advocates of a pro-Entente orientation as foreign minister of the Provisional Government, attempted to draw the VA into an alliance with Germany in the spring of 1918. In spite of the VA Command's categorical rejection of any dealings with the Germans, he established contact with the German High Command in Kyiv. In his meeting with a representative of the German military, Maj. Haase, on 21 June 1918, Miliukov presented the conditions that would allow the Germans and VA to come to terms. The greatest stumbling block proved to be the Treaty of Brest-Litovsk: on the question of Russia's territorial unity and integrity Miliukov refused to compromise and insisted that only Poland had the right to separate from Russia. With the exception of providing some special status for Ukraine, he refused to accept the principle of federation, firmly declaring that he believed in the "unity of citizenship, unity of territory, and sovereignty of the central organs." Because the Germans refused even to consider the revision of the Brest-Litovsk treaty, negotiations were broken off after two more meetings. Miliukov Personal Archive, box 1.6.6.1., file 1; Miliukov, "Dnevnik," 10–40.
60. Dimitry V. Lehovich, *White Against Red: The Life of General Anton Denikin* (New York: W. W. Norton, 1974), 298.
61. V. I. Gurko, "Iz Petrograda cherez Moskvu, Parizh i London v Odessu, 1917–1918 gg.," *Arkhiv russkoi revoliutsii* 15 (1924): 38.
62. Denikin, *Ocherki*, 4: 207–8.

Interestingly, the concept of being "above parties" (*nadpartiinost'*) and "above classes" *(nadklassnost')* was a distinct characteristic of the Kadet political program. "The Kadet party—the People's Freedom party," announced a Kadet pamphlet during the revolution, "is distinguished from all other parties in that it struggles for all citizens, and not for a particular social class.[63]" *"Nadpartiinost'"* and *"nadklassnost'"* were not merely propaganda slogans. The Kadets, though predominantly professionals and intellectuals, did not, in fact, represent or defend the interests of a particular class. Their nonpartisanship was an extension of their deep sense of nationalism and patriotism. Above all else, they defended the interests of Russia as a great power and sought to raise it to the level of the leading progressive European nations. Nonpartisanship and nationalism were the two elements that brought together two otherwise diverse groups during the war and the revolution: the apolitical officers of the Russian army, represented by Alekseev, Kornilov, and Denikin, and the highly politicized intelligentsia of Constitutional Democracy; neither group was from or represented a particular class. Their partnership heightened and reinforced nationalism and nonpartisanship to such an extent that the former at times assumed a grotesque, fanatical form, and the latter resulted in the neglect of pressing social and economic problems.

"Bolsheviks of the Right" in the Civil War

Denikin's success in clearing the Kuban and its neighboring districts of the Bolsheviks and in establishing a political apparatus in Ekaterinodar coincided with a series of Entente victories in the West and the collapse of the Central Powers in October 1918. The allied triumph boded well for the future of the VA. For the governments and parties that cooperated with the Central Powers in struggling against Bolshevism, however, this sudden change in the international arena necessitated an immediate shift both with respect to internal policies and foreign orientation. Both the Don and Ukrainian governments hastened to strengthen their position internally and to seek aid from outside.[64] The expected German withdrawal made the Don and Ukraine vulnerable to Bolshevik invasion from the north. Both governments hoped, therefore, that the Entente states would not refuse them aid for the maintenance of peace and order.

---

63. N. O. Losskii, *Chego khochet Partiia narodnoi svobody (Konstitutsionno-demokraticheskaia)* (Petrograd: n.p., 1917), 6.
64. Doroshenko, 2: 392–3; A. D. Chernogorchevich's report to Adm. Neniukov, Odessa, December 1918, Wrangel Military Archives, file 143.

The first step of the Skoropads'kyi government, after dispatching envoys to the Western capitals, was to elicit the cooperation of the various Ukrainian socialist parties working together in the Ukrainian National Union.[65] Before a working agreement with these parties could be established and a new government acceptable to them could be formed, however, the Kadet ministers in the hetman's government demonstratively resigned, explaining that

> At present, Ukraine is faced with two possibilities: either it will build and strengthen the state by taking advantage of the decline and disorder in Russia, or it will help Russia to rise again in an alliance with other states built on the ruins of Russia. If Ukraine remains indifferent to the struggle with the Bolsheviks, it will never be forgiven by its neighbors. If, on the other hand, it will help Russia to defeat the Bolsheviks, it will be sure of free development in alliance with Russia.[66]

The Kadet ministers' position on Ukraine's relations with Russia received full approval at a Protofis meeting on 22 October. The resolution adopted there stated that "close cooperation between the two parts of the former empire is indispensable for their economic development."[67] The change in the international situation induced some members of the Union of Agrarians, the staunchest supporters of Skoropads'kyi's government, to declare that they, too, considered Ukraine's independence an expedient to building a federation with Russia. The Agrarians demanded equal rights for the Russian language in Ukraine.[68]

To cement the relationship between Ukraine and the Don into a firm alliance, a meeting was arranged between the hetman and Ataman Krasnov on 2 November at the Skorokhodove railway station east of Poltava. After discussing economic and military matters, the two leaders decided, on the hetman's initiative, that a conference should be convened in Kyiv to which representatives of the Don, the Kuban, the VA, and, if possible, Georgia, Poland, Belarus, Finland, and Siberia should be invited to discuss the future structure of Russia, the status of regions and states that severed their ties with the center, the precise boundaries between the former and the latter, and the

---

65. On these developments see Doroshenko, 2: 377–402; Khrystiuk, 2: 120–2.
66. Maklakov Archive, series B, box 20, Ukraine; Doroshenko, 2: 394.
67. Doroshenko, 2: 396.
68. Azbuka report, October 1918, Wrangel Military Archives, file 141; Doroshenko, 2: 396, 404–5. On the question of Ukraine's future status, a split occurred in the Union of Agrarians. The smaller landowners declared themselves for independence, while the larger proprietors, represented by Count Geiden, Dussan, and Nenarokhomov, insisted that Ukraine should become part of a federated Russia.

possibility of a concerted struggle against the Bolsheviks.[69] The meeting proceeded amicably, although Skoropads'kyi and his advisors were somewhat taken aback when Krasnov announced that he viewed the Don-Ukrainian alliance only as the beginning of "that great task the hetman was destined to accomplish," namely, the reunification of the former Russian Empire.[70] From the start of the revolution the Don Cossacks were staunch defenders of Russia's territorial integrity. This was why Denikin considered it possible to maintain relations with the Don ataman in spite of Krasnov's open Germanophilism.

The pressure in favor of Ukraine's federation with Russia increased after the return of Skoropads'kyi's emissaries from the Western capitals. The Entente states categorically insisted that Ukraine must establish federal ties with Russia to receive their support.[71] Under such pressure, partly to please the Entente and partly to retain the sympathy of his former Russophile supporters, on 14 November the hetman dismissed the Ukrainian cabinet formed only a month earlier and issued an edict in which he announced Ukraine's intention to join a future federated Russia:

> We are faced with a new political task. For a long time the Allies have been friends of the former great and united Russian state. Now, after the great turmoil in Russia, the conditions of its future existence have definitely changed. The former vigor and strength of the All-Russian state must be restored on the basis of the federal principle. In this federation Ukraine deserves a

---

69. Report on the situation in Ukraine, September 1918 to February 1919, Cheriachukin Papers, file 4. Krasnov immediately informed VA Headquarters of the planned conference. Denikin, *Ocherki*, 4: 192.

70. Doroshenko, 2: 412.

71. Shortly after the collapse of the Central Powers, the Ukrainian ambassador to Bulgaria, Oleksander Shul'hyn, established contact with the American ambassador there. The latter informed Shul'hyn that the Entente states were resolutely opposed to the existence of an independent Ukraine, but favored its unification with a federal Russia. Shul'hyn continued negotiating with members of the Entente Military Command, but they also insisted that Ukraine must federate with Russia. Skoropads'kyi sent the former Russian Ambassador to Peking, Ivan Korostovets', to the United States to request aid. En route to Washington, Korostovets' stopped in the temporary Romanian capital, Jassy, which at that time was the headquarters of Entente diplomats and members of the Entente Military Command. On 7 November 1918 Korostovets' met privately with the French envoy, de Beaupoil de Saint-Aulaire, and the British representative, Sir George Barclay. To Korostovets''s request that Entente troops be dispatched to Ukraine to replace German forces and thus prevent a possible Bolshevik invasion of the country—Korostovets' pointed out that the Germans hindered the development of the Ukrainian army—the two Entente representatives made no definite commitment, but expressed hope that the Ukrainians would defend their territory and would struggle together with loyal Russian armies for the reestablishment of order, and that the Germanophile ministers in the hetman's government would be replaced by individuals enjoying the confidence of the Entente. Doroshenko, 2: 209–10.

leading role, because it was from Ukraine that law and order emanated throughout the country, and it was within its borders that for the first time the citizens of former Russia, humiliated and oppressed, found refuge.[72]

Simultaneously the hetman announced the formation of a new, predominantly Russian cabinet headed by Sergei N. Gerbel', a powerful landowner who had served as governor of Kharkiv gubernia under the tsarist regime. Georgii Afanas'ev replaced Doroshenko as the foreign minister.[73]

With the publication of the proclamation and the formation of the Gerbel' government, it appeared to many, especially to Entente diplomats, that all obstacles to a close union between the hetman and the VA had been eliminated. The prospect of this alliance appeared even more probable in view of the fact that Skoropads'kyi's government had not exhibited hostility toward the VA and had not hindered the activities of an unofficial VA recruitment bureau in Kyiv headed by Gen. Lomnovskii.[74] Official relations between Kyiv and Ekaterinodar did not exist, however, and when Denikin wrote a letter to Skoropads'kyi in July concerning the arrest of a VA officer in Kyiv, he was careful not to address him as head of a state.[75] Skoropads'kyi, naturally, was offended and did not reply.

The hetman's first official note to Ekaterinodar was sent only after the federation proclamation. It concerned an order, issued allegedly by Denikin and published in several Kyiv newspapers, declaring all officers of the former Russian Empire subordinated to the supreme commander of the VA.[76] In a note Afanas'ev, the new foreign minister, expressed confidence that the papers had not transmitted Denikin's orders correctly "because subordination of officers serving in Ukraine to you [Denikin] would lead to confusion and the loosening of discipline in the Ukrainian Army. This is especially dangerous at a moment when the Ukrainian forces, in agreement with the Don and parallel to the VA, are being prepared for the struggle against the Bolsheviks

---

72. Khrystiuk, 3: 120–1.
73. Doroshenko, 2: 451.
74. In the summer of 1918, two VA officers, Cols. Riasnianskii and Lopukhovskii, were arrested in Kyiv. The latter was soon released because he was engaged in recruiting officers for the VA only. In Riasnianskii's possession a letter from Alekseev to Shul'gin was found; therefore he was imprisoned on charges of espionage. Miliukov, "Dnevnik," 23 June 1918, 31.
75. Denikin, *Ocherki*, 4: 206.
76. In addition to the officers recruited by Lomnovskii for the VA in Kyiv, there were several other military formations there not tied directly to Skoropads'kyi's government. They were recruited with German aid by members of the monarchist bloc to fight the Bolsheviks. Some of these regiments declared their allegiance to Denikin after the publication of the order in the Kyiv press. Azbuka Report, 12 January 1918, Wrangel Military Archives, file 131.

and for the restoration of Russia's unity."⁷⁷ Afanas'ev requested Denikin to take appropriate measures to correct the situation.

The publication of the order in Kyiv's newspapers required extreme caution on the part of Denikin, pointed out a pamphlet specifically devoted to relations between the VA and Ukraine.⁷⁸ So that, on the one hand, the VA would not be interfering directly in the internal affairs of Skoropads'kyi's government—the direct result of which would have been "confusion in the defense activities of the Southwestern *krai*," and, on the other, would not be "dampening the patriotic fervor of the Russian Volunteers in Little Russia," Denikin prepared a carefully worded reply to Afanas'ev on 17 November:

> The order appearing in the Kyiv newspapers was not given to General Lomnovskii. The representative of the Volunteer Army in Kyiv was only authorized to unite the leadership of all Russian Volunteer regiments in Ukraine, at was at the same time obliged to coordinate his activities in every way with the interests of the region, exerting all efforts toward the struggle with the Bolsheviks but, at the same time, not interfering in the internal affairs of the region. Once Ukraine has entered onto the path of Russian statehood, it will be necessary to come to an agreement on the question of a united front, a united command for the struggle with the Bolsheviks, and a single Russian representation at the international [peace] congress. The Volunteer Army proposes three principles as the condition of the agreement: (1) a united Russia; (2) struggle with the Bolsheviks; (3) loyalty to the agreements with the Allies and full rejection of the German orientation."⁷⁹

This unexpected proposal could have led to the establishment of relations between the White movement and Skoropads'kyi. It was disregarded by the hetman's government, however, partly in view of the difficult situation in which it found itself at the end of November—on the same day the edict on federation was issued, a Ukrainian nationalist uprising against the hetman broke out in Ukraine⁸⁰—but mainly because the conditions presented by Ekaterinodar were not acceptable to Skoropads'kyi. The edict on federation made it quite clear that the Ukrainian government was not at all prepared to subordinate itself to the VA or to any Russian authority. What the hetman's government was proposing was the establishment of a federal Russian state through the concerted efforts of all governments that had emerged on the ruins of the former empire, on the basis of full equality and parity.

77. *Kratkaia zapiska*, 6–7.
78. Ibid., 7–8.
79. Ibid.
80. Doroshenko, 2: 416–24.

Instead of responding to the VA's conditions, Skoropads'kyi's government wired a circular note on 22 November in which, in compliance with the decision accepted at the meeting with Krasnov, it invited the representatives of the Don, the Kuban, Georgia, and the VA to a conference in Kyiv.[81] The chairman of the VA's Special Council, Gen. Dragomirov, responded positively to this invitation but again raised conditions not acceptable to Skoropads'kyi. The VA authorities insisted that the conference be held either in Ekaterinodar or in the Crimea and that the Georgian government, in view of its separatist position "hostile to the VA and Russia," be excluded.[82] Before the VA's reply was received in Kyiv, Skoropads'kyi notified all the above-named governments that the conference was to take place on 5 December in Kyiv. It never convened, however, because by that date the Ukrainian capital was surrounded by the insurgent troops of the socialist UNR Directory.[83] A week later the hetman abdicated and fled from Kyiv.[84]

With Skoropads'kyi's abdication, the tenuous ties that had begun to emerge between the conservative government in Kyiv and the VA were terminated. It is doubtful that they could have solidified into an alliance even if the hetman had been able to survive the nationalist uprising. Denikin never trusted Skoropads'kyi, who, it was brought to the VA's attention, only a week before the edict on federation advised his Council of Ministers: "in all relations, with both our close neighbors and all other states of the world, we stand and shall stand on the principle of an independent and sovereign Ukrainian state."[85] Even for the insignificant exchange of messages between Kyiv and Ekaterinodar, the VA apologetically explained to the Entente that "having set before itself the task of gathering together the Russian land, the Volunteer Army Command had reason to believe that the hetman's government, in view of its internal difficulties, had remembered at last its filial obligations to a common motherland and would conduct in the future policies of complete unification."[86] The hetman's idea of a loose federation implied in the edict of 14 November by no means conformed to the VA's understanding of the future Russian state. Skoropads'kyi continued to pursue an independent course. For this he and the Russian monarchist bloc in Kyiv—

81. *Kratkaia zapiska,* 11–12; Denikin, *Ocherki,* 4: 192–3.
82. Ibid.
83. The insurgent forces of the Ukrainian National Union formed, on 14 November 1918, a five-member Directory of the UNR consisting of Volodymyr Vynnychenko, Symon Petliura, Fedir Shvets, Andrii Makarenko, and Opanas Andriievs'kyi. Doroshenko, 2: 418–19.
84. Sviatoslav Dolenha, *Skoropadshchyna* (Warsaw: M. Kunyts'kyi, 1934), 140; Doroshenko, 2: 424.
85. Denikin, *Ocherki,* 4: 192.
86. *Kratkaia zapiska,* 11.

which, according to Denikin, encouraged the Ukrainian government to assume a haughty attitude toward the VA—were mercilessly denounced by the military and political leaders in Ekaterinodar.[87]

Skoropads'kyi's edict on federation was followed by additional concessions to the Russians in Kyiv. On 18 November, in view of the fact that most of his Ukrainian units had deserted him and joined the forces of the Directory,[88] Skoropads'kyi appointed a conservative Russian general, Count Fedor Keller, as the supreme commander of all military forces in Ukraine.[89] This won him the support of Russian conservatives in Kyiv, who were grouped together in a newly formed organization called the Council of Russia's State Unity.[90] The hetman's concessions to the pro-Russian sentiment in Kyiv did not soften the attitude of the National Center, which continued to oppose him as resolutely after the edict on federation as it did before. Shortly after the publication of the edict, at a joint meeting of the All-Russian National Center, the Kyiv branch of that organization, and the VA representatives passed a resolution declaring that "all relations with the 'traitor Skoropads'kyi' are inadmissible and immoral."[91] Subsequently the National Center advised Denikin that "the hetman's unilateral declaration concerning the federative structure of future Russia cannot predetermine the expression of the will of the All-Russian National Assembly."[92] The moderates of the National Center opposed Skoropads'kyi's government primarily because of its pro-Ukrainian orientation and its conservative political character. In Kyiv the National Center strove energetically to prevent any association between the VA and the existing government in Ukraine from developing. "In Kyiv the hetman is so unpopular that any identification of the Volunteer Army with his name would be detrimental to the prestige of the Volunteer Army in leftist circles," noted a report from Kyiv to Denikin.[93] Any connection between the hetman and the VA, emphasized that report, would have been most inoppor-

---

87. Ibid., 8.
88. Doroshenko, 2: 421.
89. Ibid., 419.
90. A trend toward uniting the conservative circles in Kyiv appeared already in August. The leading figures were the former tsarist minister of agriculture Krivoshein, Count Vladimir Bobrinskii, and Ihor O. Kistiakovs'kyi. While the outcome of the war was still in doubt, it was assumed that anti-German and anti-Ukrainian elements would not join the organization. In addition to the members of the State Duma and State Council, the new organization was joined by the All-Russian Church Council, the Governing Senate, and Protofis. "Brief History of the Activities of the Council of State Unity," Wrangel Military Archives, file 129; *Kievskaia mysl'*, 26 November 1918.
91. Denikin, *Ocherki*, 4: 196.
92. Volkov's report on the situation in Kyiv, Azbuka report, 18 November 1918, Wrangel Military Archives, file 151.
93. Ibid.

tune, because rumors had already spread in Kyiv that "both the pro-Russian coup executed by the hetman and the formation of the conservative government were directed by General Denikin," and therefore the local population was beginning to associate the VA with the forces of restoration and conservatism.[94]

The success of the insurgent forces of the UNR Directory and the possibility that Kyiv would fall into the hands of the socialist Ukrainian parties before Entente aid was available softened somewhat the intransigent attitude of some of the members of the National Center toward Skoropads'kyi. "Under existing circumstances," wrote an agent of the center, "it was most convenient to retain the government that exists until the arrival of Allied and Russian reinforcements, which alone would be able to restore order here in the struggle against anarchy and forces hostile to Russia."[95] The question of not associating Denikin's name with the hetman's reactionary government, and at the same time providing necessary aid to the existing authority until a more opportune time, was solved in an ingenious way: Lomnovskii subordinated his units to Keller without providing them with the VA banner.[96] Keller, with whom VA representatives managed to maintain cordial relations, retained his post for a brief time only. Although he had promised, before assuming the post of supreme commander, not to interfere in affairs of state, it was difficult to stay away from politics, especially since he had been the candidate for the Russian throne supported by the monarchist bloc in Kyiv.[97] When Keller began overstepping the limits of his authority, and especially when he began ignoring the hetman and the government and evinced obvious dictatorial pretensions,[98] Skoropads'kyi dismissed him and appointed in his stead Prince Pavel Dolgorukov, a Russian general who proved to be more amenable to Skoropads'kyi's directives.[99]

Keller's dismissal and the success of the Directory's forces in the vicinity of Kyiv prompted some leaders of the diverse Russian political circles in the city to work toward unifying their activities. A series of meetings at which representatives of the monarchist bloc, the Council of State Unity, the National Center, and the socialist Union of Regeneration gathered to discuss a common course of action were arranged, but had no practical result. On the

---

94. Ibid.
95. Ibid.
96. Denikin, *Ocherki,* 4: 197–9.
97. Brief history of the activities of the Council of State Unity, Wrangel Military Archives, file 129.
98. A group of officers close to Keller were preparing a conspiracy to overthrow the hetman and transfer all authority to Keller. E. N. Trubetskoi, "Iz putevykh zametok bezhentsa," *Arkhiv russkoi revoliutsii* 18: 147.
99. Doroshenko, 2: 420.

question as to who should be the supreme commander of all armies in Russia, the monarchist bloc and the Council of State Unity voted for the commander in chief of Ukraine, while the National Center and the Union of Regeneration voted for Denikin.[100]

With the appointment of Dolgorukov, relations between VA representatives and the Supreme Command in Kyiv rapidly deteriorated. Dolgorukov completely disregarded Lomnovskii's presence, countermanded his orders to the VA units, and finally, when rumors reached him of treasonous activities in some VA regiments, ordered Lomnovskii's arrest.[101] Although Lomnovskii was soon released and promised to cooperate in the defense of Kyiv, Dolgorukov was never forgiven by the VA for the harsh treatment of its representative. Ironically, the National Center welcomed the Lomnovskii-Dolgorukov quarrel because, as one Azbuka report put it, the incident "disassociated the Volunteer Army from the monarchist bloc and the hetman's government."[102]

Lomnovskii's orders to his troops, after his humiliating arrest, to defend Skoropads'kyi against the forces of the Directory utterly confused the VA officers in the city; few understood his explanation that "the situation had changed, that the Directory was a prelude to Bolshevism,"[103] and only an insignificant number followed his orders. Kyiv was defended by a small number of VA officers and students.[104]

Various explanations have been advanced for the poor showing of the VA in the struggle against the Directory. One Azbuka agent noted that officers refused to follow Lomnovskii's orders because of their hatred of the hetman; they did not wish to die defending Skoropads'kyi, whom they considered a traitor to Russia.[105] Another agent observed that in view of the political chaos in Kyiv and Lomnovskii's weak and irresolute character, Russian officers were beginning to lose faith in the White cause; some even considered the possibility of joining the Red Army, where the position of the officers was beginning to improve. "And what is more," rationalized the disgruntled officers, "your own people will not consider you an enemy [after joining the Red Army]."[106]

Pondering this question, Denikin subsequently observed that in view of the situation in Kyiv, the VA officers had no choice but to avoid the conflict. From the Russian national point of view, both the leftist leaders of the

---

100. Denikin, *Ocherki*, 4: 198.
101. Azbuka report, 12 January 1919, Wrangel Military Archives, file 131.
102. Ibid.
103. Denikin, *Ocherki*, 4: 199.
104. Azbuka report, 12 January 1919.
105. Azbuka report, 17 December 1918, Wrangel Military Archives, file 131.
106. Azbuka report, 12 January 1919.

Directory and the conservative Skoropads'kyi milieu were contemptible because they stood for Ukrainian statehood and pursued aims detrimental to Russia. The officers must have been asking themselves, speculated Denikin, "Should one defend the authority of the hetman and the Ukrainian State?... Should one defend the hetman against [the socialist Symon] Petliura?"[107] From the political point of view, too, the officers had little choice. They must have argued, explained Denikin, "On that side: 'all power to the soviets,' on this side: 'all power to Protofis.' Which is better?"[108] The only choice was to stay away.

Protofis was one of the staunchest supporters of Skoropads'kyi's government before the collapse of Germany. Denikin equated in this instance the "internationalism" of the Bolsheviks with the "internationalism" of the industrial, commercial, and financial circles in Kyiv. Both groups, though on the opposite side of the political spectrum, had many non-Russians in their midst. Azbuka agents in Kyiv referred to Protofis and the monarchist bloc as "Bolsheviks of the right." By this they meant that both groups were ready to come to terms with the enemy for personal or party gain at the expense of Russia.[109]

The fall of Skoropads'kyi was inevitable after 14 November. The edict on federation, on the one hand, deprived him of Ukrainian support—the Ukrainian regiments, one by one, began deserting him after the proclamation—and, on the other, it did not gain him sufficient support from Russians who, after the Entente victory, were certain that France and Great Britain would restore Russia's unity. The few Russian monarchists who supported the hetman to the end had at their disposal only an insignificant number of reliable troops who were far from sufficient to resist the rapidly growing army of the Directory. The Entente troops on whose support the hetman counted—and it seems that it was primarily desire to win the the aid of France and Britain that prompted Skoropads'kyi to issue the edict on federation—were too far away to provide any meaningful assistance. It is true that the French consul Emile Henno, who had just arrived in Odessa, implicitly recognized Skoropads'kyi's government in his declaration of 22 November and thus strengthened somewhat the prestige of the hetman's authority in Kyiv, but in practice this recognition did little to stem the tide of opposition to Skoropads'kyi.[110]

107. Denikin, *Ocherki,* 4: 199.
108. Ibid., 200.
109. Denikin, *Ocherki,* 4: 183; Azbuka reports, Wrangel Military Archives, file 131.
110. Excerpts from *Kievskaia mysl'*, 23 November 1918, in the Maklakov Archive, series B, box 20, Ukraine.

Skoropads'kyi's rule in Ukraine illustrated graphically the basic difference in the attitude on the nationality question between the right (monarchist) and liberal (VA and National Center) Russians. Both groups indubitably defended the idea of Russia as a great power. The right, however, was willing to see Russia restored with the aid of Germany and the newly formed nation-states, even if this meant territorial concessions to the former and broad political autonomy for the latter. The conservative circles were confident that the monarchy would provide the necessary unifying element for a multinational Russia. Some, no doubt, hoped that once an absolute monarchy was reestablished, the political rights granted to the peripheral states could be easily abrogated if they proved to be disadvantageous to the center.

The liberals, on the other hand, were resolutely opposed to any concessions to the nationalities and regional governments, even in the darkest hour of the VA, primarily because such concessions would create a historical precedent and strenghten the international position of the border states. The leaders of the VA and the National Center insisted from the very beginning—just as the Provisional Government did in 1917—that only an All-Russian Constituent or People's Assembly would have the right to decide such weighty political issues as the future structure of the state. What was required was a military victory for the White armies, the restoration of the lost territories, and the regeneration of the former might of the vast empire. Only then would Russia be in a position to discuss the status of its constituent parts. Therefore the liberals resolutely opposed the idea of "federation from below," the restoration of the Russian Empire through the concerted effort of all its parts, because in this manner the latter would be in a position to wrest not only exorbitant cultural concessions, but—with the help of the Entente— also political concessions from a weak and prostrated Russia.

Under the shock of Russia's collapse as a great power, the Kadets became obsessed with the defense of Russia's state interests, particularly with the restoration of the empire within its prewar borders. Reconstruction of Russia as a great power was inconceivable without the restoration of Russian cultural supremacy throughout the former multinational state. The Russian liberals pursued this objective without any inhibitions or second thoughts as to the appropriateness of this endeavor from the liberal point of view, for they believed, or persuaded themselves to believe, that Russian cultural hegemony in a liberal state would promote enlightenment and progress for all.

IV

The Questions of Russia's Indivisibility and Ukraine at the Paris Peace Conference

During the first year of its existence, the White movement received only a negligible amount of aid from the Entente. Nonetheless, the military and political leaders of the movement's principal center, the VA, assumed that France and Great Britain would readily support the White cause after the Central Powers had been defeated. To Denikin and his associates the signing of the armistice on 8 November 1918 did not signify the end of the World War. Rather, they believed it was only a matter of time before the armies of the Entente appeared on the shores of the Black Sea. Their hopes were bolstered by the sympathetic attitude the Entente's military and diplomatic representatives showed at VA Headquarters in Ekaterinodar. Upon his arrival there, Gen. Frederick C. Poole, the head of the British military mission, assured Denikin that the Entente's "aims were identical to yours—the establishment of a united Russia."[1] Similarly, Lieut. Erlich, the French diplomatic representative, expressed confidence that "the glorious tricolor flag of a great, united, and undivided Russia" would soon replace the red banner atop the Kremlin.[2]

Denikin had no reason to doubt these sentiments, since dispatches from his own emissaries in the West were most encouraging. In mid-November Gen. Dmitrii G. Shcherbachev, the former Russian commander on the Romanian front, reported that the results he had achieved in his conference with Gen. Henri Berthelot, the commander of the French forces in Romania, far exceeded the VA's expectations.[3]

---

1. Denikin, *Ocherki*, 4: 37.
2. Ibid.
3. E. G. Val', *K istorii belago dvizheniia: Deiatel'nost' general-adiutanta Shcherbacheva* (Tallinn: the author, 1935), 34–7.

Shcherbachev was not the only one representing VA interests in Romania. He had the support of Stanislav A. Poklevskii-Kozel, the former Russian ambassador in Bucharest, of Col. N. S. Il'in, the former president of the Russian Red Cross, and of his own former aides. All of them were residing in Jassy, the temporary Romanian capital. But the VA cause was championed most ardently and energetically by Emile Henno,[4] a French military agent from Gen. Tabouis's mission to Ukraine. Both in Jassy, where he assumed the title of French consul to Kyiv, and previously, during his stay in Kishinev, Henno maintained close contact with Shul'gin, the head of the White intelligence agency Azbuka, and with other White political leaders.[5] It was on Henno's initiative that the first conference between Entente emissaries and White representatives was convened.

When it was clear that the Central Powers were losing the war, Henno suggested to de Beaupoil de Saint-Aulaire, the French ambassador in Jassy, that a Russian advisory council be formed to supervise the anticipated intervention of Entente forces in the peripheries of the former empire. He also suggested that Shul'gin was best qualified to prepare the groundwork for the formation of such a council. The French ambassador expressed some interest in the proposal, but felt that other Russian political leaders should also be consulted. At Henno's request, however, he agreed not to contact them until Shul'gin had arrived or responded to specific questions about the intervention.[6]

Henno described his conversation with the French ambassador in a letter to Shul'gin and invited him to come to Jassy. He assured Shul'gin that the Entente governments would provide Russia with substantial economic and military aid, noting that "the restoration of Great Russia is indispensable for the political balance of power, because this alone can guarantee peace in the near future." The Entente's program, he commented, could be summed up as follows: "reestablishment of a united and undivided Russia, coupled with support for the restoration of the monarchy, which the majority of the Russian population desires." Henno further stated that as "a convinced and sincere adherent of the reestablishment of the Great Russian Empire," he had firmly supported this idea both in Paris and in his dealings with the French

---

4. Henno's position and mission in Ukraine still remain a mystery. Although he had a letter of appointment as vice-consul in Kyiv, French Foreign Minister Stephen Pichon denied Henno's appointment on two occasions in the Chamber of Deputies. Henno was never listed in the diplomatic-consular register of France. He was most likely a military agent of the French, and this may explain his close contacts with Shul'gin and the latter's intelligence agency Azbuka. *Annales de la Chambre des Députés: Débats parlementaires* (Paris, 1919), pt. 1, 1250, 1305–6 (debates of 24 and 26 March 1919.)

5. Shul'gin's letter to Sergei D. Sazonov, 18 March 1919, Wrangel Military Archives, file 132.

6. Henno's letter to Shul'gin, 19 October 1918, Wrangel Military Archives, file 129.

ambassador in Jassy.[7] As evidence of his efforts, Henno enclosed copies of two telegrams he had sent early in October 1918 informing the French government of the situation in Ukraine. In these communiqués he had conveyed Shul'gin's interpretation of the Ukrainian question, noting that since "the Ukrainian national idea does not in fact exist, any program aimed at restoring the Russian Empire will be welcomed by the mass of the intelligentsia." Henno concluded his letter by stating that despite the important functions Shul'gin was performing at VA headquarters in Ekaterinodar, he hoped the latter would soon come to Jassy to begin preparations for the first meeting between Entente representatives and loyal Russians. Such a meeting, he emphasized, "will be the first step towards the rebirth of Russia and will return Ukraine to its motherland."[8]

Henno never questioned Shul'gin's views on the political climate in Russia or on developments in Ukraine. He assumed that as the head of Azbuka, Shul'gin was well-informed and therefore excellently suited for the prospective role in Jassy. Entente representatives, however, took a more guarded view of Shul'gin's interpretation of events in Ukraine.[9] Consequently, when the Russian contingent in Jassy appeared interested in meeting to establish a liaison between the Entente and the White movement, Saint-Aulaire approved the arrangements for such a meeting despite having promised Henno that he would take no action until Shul'gin's arrival. The Russian representatives in Romania considered the meeting particularly timely in view of the arrival in Jassy of a delegation headed by Volodyslav Dashkevych-Horbats'kyi that was sent by Skoropads'kyi's government to negotiate for aid.[10]

On 30 October 1918 a Russian Provisional Committee was formed under the chairmanship of Poklevskii-Kozel. Shortly thereafter invitations to Jassy were dispatched to VA headquarters and to representatives in Kyiv of all Russian political parties and newly formed groups that endorsed the platform of "Russian statehood."[11] The latter included the Council of State Unity, composed predominantly of moderate conservatives; the National Center, which united prominent members of the Kadet (People's Freedom) party and ultra-reactionary members of the Union of the Russian People in Kyiv; and the Union of Regeneration, which represented the socialist organizations. Each

---

7. Ibid.
8. Copies of Henno's telegrams to Paris, 9 and 16 October 1918, Wrangel Military Archives, file 129.
9. Miliukov, "Dnevnik," 29 October 1918, 214.
10. D. Doroshenko, 2: 154.
11. P. N. Miliukov, "Iasskoe soveshchanie," *Kievskaia mysl'*, 25 November 1918, Giers Archives, file 97, Ukraine.

group elected four or five delegates—among them such distinguished political figures as the former tsarist minister Krivoshein, the Kadet leaders Miliukov and Fedorov, and the Popular Socialist A. A. Titov.[12]

The invitation to Jassy did not come as a surprise to Miliukov and his colleagues, who had just returned from a regional Kadet party conference in Ekaterinodar. Shul'gin, though not a member of the party, had been invited to participate in the conference. At one of the meetings he not only apprised the Kadets of Henno's letter, but also read a memorandum he had prepared for the VA command setting forth his views on the intervention.[13]

The memorandum began with a statement of the basic task of the White movement, which was tersely formulated as "the restoration of an independent and united Russia." Those who subscribed to this view were termed "allies"; those who opposed it—the Bolsheviks and the nationalities—were considered enemies. In great detail, the memorandum proceeded to outline the White movement's program for Ukraine. The first task was the overthrow Skoropads'kyi's government. It was to be replaced by a provisional military regime that would rule Ukraine with the aid of Entente forces until a permanent government was established. Russian was to be reinstituted as the state language, although there were to be no legal sanctions against the use of the "Little Russian dialect" in state and zemstvo institutions. All higher and secondary education was to be conducted in Russian, but private schools were free to use any language. The memorandum also dealt with the question of Russia's representation at the future peace conference. It stated categorically that only those governments that had demonstrated their devotion to a united Russia could speak for the country; moreover, it insisted that these governments reach an agreement on the question of Russia's delegation to the peace negotiations. Although the Entente's moral and military support was taken for granted, it was regarded primarily as an inspiration for the White armies "to clear the Russian land of the Bolsheviks and of other states that did not acknowledge the unity of Russia."[14]

The Kadet leaders were rather disconcerted by Shul'gin's sharp division of all governments within the former empire into "hostile" and "allied" states and its reduction of the task of the White movement and the Entente intervention to occupying Ukraine and eliminating all remnants of Ukrainian nationalism. In the ensuing discussion Miliukov argued persuasively that not only was the Ukrainian issue only one facet of the nationality question of Russia's borderlands, but the implementation of Shul'gin's policy in Ukraine would make the nationalities hostile to the VA. Furthermore, he pointed out

12. Miliukov, "Dnevnik," 9 November 1918, 239–48.
13. Ibid., 218–21.
14. Shul'gin's memorandum to the Special Council, Wrangel Military Archives, file 151.

that the annexation of Galicia would become a complicated issue were the Ukrainian language to be supplanted by the term "Little Russian dialect."[15]

Although Shul'gin's memorandum was severely criticized by the assembled delegates, Miliukov's plea for moderation toward the nationalities went unheeded when the Kadet leaders prepared an appeal to the Entente concerning Russia's foreign policy and the intervention. Their appeal did not call the states that had separated from Russia "hostile forces," but it denied the nationalities any meaningful role on the international scene.[16]

Before Shul'gin left for Jassy, Sergei D. Sazonov, the chairman of the VA's diplomatic section and a former tsarist foreign minister, asked him to transmit a letter to Poklevskii-Kozel concerning the situation in Ukraine, based exclusively on intelligence reports from the Kyiv branch of the National Center. The object of concern was the planned uprising by the Ukrainian National Union against Skoropads'kyi. Sazonov considered such an uprising extremely dangerous, because the conspirators wanted the conflict with the hetman to appear as both a struggle against Germanophile tendencies in Ukraine and an attempt to establish a democratic government that was favorably disposed toward the Entente. In addition, the Ukrainian National Union was widening its base by eliciting support from Jewish socialists, who had agreed to cooperate because, Sazonov explained, they were similarly opposed to the slogan of a "united Russia." According to information from Kyiv sources that Sazonov thought completely reliable, the Ukrainian National Union had the secret support of the Germans, who regarded a successful coup as another opportunity to continue the dismemberment of Russia. The Kyiv local groups "that accept the platform of Russia's unification," Sazonov's letter continued, "are impatiently awaiting the arrival of the Volunteer Army or the Allies, firmly convinced that such aid will lead to a victory of all healthy elements within Little Russia and will rapidly liquidate the intentions of the Ukrainian National Union, which are so detrimental to both the interests of the Allies and Russia."[17] Sazonov authorized Poklevskii-Kozel to make the contents of the letter known to the Entente ambassadors in Jassy and to request that they transmit the information to their governments as soon as possible. Sazonov did not request an immediate dispatch of Entente troops to Ukraine or temporary moral support for Skoropads'kyi. Military aid was geographically impossible, and moral support for the hetman was never advocated by the White leaders, even as a last resort. Indeed, the White representatives always emphasized that they had systematically spurned all

15. Miliukov, "Dnevnik," 13 October 1918, 220.
16. Denikin, *Ocherki*, 4: 236–7.
17. Letter to the Russian ambassador in Romania, Stanislav A. Poklevskii-Kozel, from the Diplomatic Department of the VA, Wrangel Military Archives, file 143.

overtures by the Ukrainian government to establish relations with Ekaterinodar because they considered the hetman's policy a betrayal of Russia.[18]

Shul'gin and the Russian political leaders in Kyiv left for Jassy before Skoropads'kyi issued his edict of 14 November announcing the Ukrainian government's intention to federate with Russia. But even had they been aware of the hetman's new policy, their attitude toward his government would not have changed, for the VA military leaders, as well as their political advisors, were resolutely opposed to both the federative principle and the idea of the reconstruction of Russia from below—the two principles on which Skoropads'kyi's edict was based. Even the Russian conservatives in the State Council of Russia, inclined as they were to support the hetman and the Ukrainian government while the outcome of the war was uncertain, reverted to the idea of Russian territorial unity once it became obvious that the Entente was winning the war. The opposition of Russian political leaders to any compromises with the nationalities—particularly with the Ukrainians—manifested itself with unmistakable clarity during the conference at Jassy.

Divided at Home, United Abroad

The Ukrainian question became the object of a heated debate already at the first meeting in Jassy, on 16 November. There, to the dismay of the Russian delegation, Henno announced his intention of leaving immediately for Kyiv.[19] In the interval between this meeting and Henno's letter to Shul'gin exactly a month earlier, various Ukrainian delegations had visited Jassy. In the course of negotiations with them, the highly impressionable French vice-consul became persuaded that it was advantageous for the Entente to recognize the existing Ukrainian government in Kyiv. Henno's explanation that "the hetman had recently changed his political orientation and had expressed willingness to place himself at the disposal of the Allies" by no means calmed the Russian delegates. Miliukov very tersely explained why it did not:

> The French consul's presence in Kyiv has both a positive and negative aspect. His participation in local affairs could contribute to the smooth process of Russia's unification considered desirable both from the Allied and Russian point of view ... but at the same time it [Henno's presence in

---

18. VA appeal to the Allies, Wrangel Military Archives, file 143.
19. A summary of each meeting at Jassy is in the Wrangel Military Archives, file 143, under the heading "Zhurnaly Iasskago soveshchaniia." Altogether there were sixteen meetings. A detailed report on the conference prepared by Astrov for Denikin is in the Denikin Papers, box 24.

Kyiv] could be a sign of approval for the hetman's position, which is unacceptable to us.[20]

Henno did not give in easily. He continued to argue that Skoropads'kyi's government was in an extremely precarious position, even according to its own representatives, who were exerting strenuous efforts toward the establishment of an Entente representation in Kyiv in order to strengthen Skoropads'kyi's position. Henno noted that the socialists of the Ukrainian National Union were also seeking Allied support, and that under the circumstances his presence in Kyiv would be to the advantage of both the Allies and Russia. What Henno failed to understand was that for the Russian representatives, especially the Kadets who were most closely linked to the VA, even temporary recognition of Ukrainian separatism, which his presence in Kyiv would imply, could impair support for the idea of Russia's territorial unity. It was precisely Miliukov and Fedorov who opposed Henno's trip to Kyiv most vehemently, and it was at their insistence that the French consul resolved to postpone his departure.

Developments in Ukraine were also the subject of discussion during the second meeting of 16 November, at which Col. Novikov reported on the distribution of military forces in the vicinity of Kyiv. Because the situation appeared extremely dangerous to the pro-Russian political groups in Ukraine, the meeting unanimously decided to appeal to the Entente governments to announce their official position on the question of Russia's unity. Miliukov and Titov were entrusted to draft the appeal as well as general instructions for Henno's impending trip to Kyiv. Two principles, which Miliukov announced would guide both documents, were unanimously approved: (1) the Entente should not do anything that would provide grounds for the recognition of an independent and separate Ukrainian state; and (2) the Entente should avoid doing anything that would give the Ukrainian government hope for the future resolution of relations with Russia.[21]

The first conference between the Russian delegation and the Entente ministers in Jassy took place on 17 November in the British embassy. The Russian's were warmly greeted by Ambassador Barclay with reassuring words that "the Allies will do all that is in their power to help Russia in its struggle against the Bolsheviks, to reestablish its unity, its political and economic existence."[22]

---

20. "Zhurnal" no. 1, 16 November 1918, Wrangel Military Archives, file 143.
21. "Zhurnal" no. 2, Evening Session, 17 November 1918, Wrangel Military Archives, file 143.
22. Minutes of the conference between the Russian Delegates in Jassy and the Allied representatives, 17 November 1918, at 3 P.M. in the British embassy, Wrangel Military Archives, file 143.

On behalf of the Russians, Miliukov thanked the Entente ministers for initiating direct relations with the "state-conscious elements of Russia" and read a statement of principles unanimously endorsed by the Russians at a previous meeting. The statement was based entirely on the VA's foreign-policy program: (1) denunciation of the Treaty of Brest-Litovsk and the recognition of a unitary Russia within its August 1914 borders, with the exception of Poland; (2) non-recognition of the new states established with the aid of Germany, whose aim was to divide Russia; (3) a single Russian diplomatic representation now and at the future peace conference; (4) a single Russian command for purging the Bolsheviks from Russia; and (5) recognition of the great merits of the VA in the drive for the reconstruction of Russia. Miliukov proceeded to review in detail the situation in Ukraine, and ended his speech with a patriotic appeal: "The delegation expects that the first armed forces of the Allies will arrive with this firm decision: not to recognize the different state formations the Germans have created with the intention of dismembering Russia, and to return to Russia the flag of St. Andrew, the symbol of its unity."[23] Only a month earlier Miliukov had criticized Shul'gin for imparting too much importance to the Ukrainian question, yet at this first meeting with Entente diplomats he was so carried away with the situation in Ukraine that his colleague Fedorov had to state that the principles Miliukov had outlined represented only a part of the general intervention plan.

The Ukrainian question assumed even greater importance when new Russian delegates who had arrived from Kyiv brought news of Skoropads'kyi's edict on federation with Russia, of the Ukrainian National Union's uprising, and of the formation of the UNR Directory. The hetman's edict was ignored, but the delegation immediately undertook steps designed to prevent the Directory's victory in Ukraine. First, two officers were dispatched to appeal to French Headquarters in Istanbul for immediate intervention.[24] Second, the delegates proceeded to prepare a new appeal to the Entente governments. In it the Directory was linked with Bolshevik and anarchist bands, and its victory, it was pointed out, would only facilitate a Bolshevik invasion from the north. To forestall this possibility, speedy execution of the following measures was urged: (1) an immediate dispatch of Entente troops to Odessa, even in small numbers, which would then proceed to Kyiv; (2) a declaration announcing unequivocally that the Entente supported the "forces of order" in Russia; and (3) a warning to the Germans that they would be held responsible if they aided the Ukrainian insurgents either by selling arms to them or by impeding the Russian officers from using the arms of the Kyiv

---

23. Untitled document in the Giers Archives, file 97, Ukraine.
24. "Zhurnal" no. 7, afternoon session, 18 November 1918, Wrangel Military Archives, file 143.

arsenal.[25] The third step the delegation took was to expedite Henno's departure and to prepare for him the declaration he was to issue in the name of the Entente upon his arrival in Kyiv. This carefully worded document was directed against the Directory without expressing any support, even by implication, for Skoropads'kyi's government. In fact, according to the instructions Henno received, his activities in Kyiv were to be guided exclusively by the "principle of the unity and indivisibility of Russia."[26]

Even after news of Skoropads'kyi's edict reached Jassy, the Russians refused to have any official dealings with the Ukrainian delegation conferring simultaneously but separately with the Entente diplomats. Only on one occasion did Miliukov agree to meet with Dashkevych-Horbats'kyi to discuss the hetman's edict. Miliukov expressed annoyance that Skoropads'kyi had the audacity "to dictate to all Russia the form of state structure it should assume." Furthermore, he openly admitted that the proclamation on federation with Russia "creates a situation that is even more dangerous than before, because in the eyes of the Allies—thanks to Ukrainian propaganda abroad—it [federation] could appear acceptable." He expressed surprise that the hetman did not mention the VA in his edict and thus ignored the fact that the Entente governments were ready to recognize Ekaterinodar as the center from which an All-Russian government would emerge, and to which all other state formations on Russian soil would have to be subordinated. Expressing the views of his party and the VA, Miliukov stressed the need for a unified command and a single Russian representation at the future peace conference.[27]

Miliukov assumed the same self-assured posture when, on the same day, he discussed Bessarabia with the Romanian prime minister, Ion Bratianu. To Bratianu's argument that Bessarabia rightfully belonged to Romania because it was unjustly taken by Tsar Aleksander I, the Russian historian angrily snapped back that if one would consider such reasoning valid for Georgia, the Baltic lands, and other borderlands, the disintegration of Russia would never stop. "Our first task," explained Miliukov, "is to oppose disintegration in principle and to put an end to it."[28]

The Russian delegation's stance was self-confident only on the surface. In its midst a nervous and agitated atmosphere prevailed. Even though the Russians never doubted that substantial Entente aid would be forthcoming, they were not certain whether the White centers would be the only recipients.

---

25. "The Second Appeal of the Russian Delegation in Jassy to the Allies," Giers Archives, file 97, Ukraine; untitled document in Wrangel Military Archives, file 143.
26. Margulies, *God interventsii*, 1: 38–9.
27. Miliukov, "Dnevnik," 18 November 1918, 299–300.
28. Ibid., 295–9.

The Entente ministers, while reassuring the Russians that they would do everything in their power to restore Russia's unity, were, at the same time, negotiating with Skoropads'kyi's representatives. According to Henno, contacts had also been established between the Entente diplomats and the Ukrainian National Union. What was most distressing was that the Entente ministers, on whose initiative the conference had convened, appeared most inattentive to the Russian delegation's meetings. One of the late arrivals in Jassy, Vasilii I. Gurko, was shocked to see that at the first meeting he attended, there were no other Allied representatives besides Henno.[29]

Once the second appeal was dispatched to the Western capitals and Henno had departed for Kyiv, the delegation set aside the Ukrainian problem. During its last days in Jassy it discussed more general questions. But unlike the stand it took on the question of Russia's unity, it failed to reach unanimity even on such important issues as the nature of authority during the struggle for the reconstruction of the empire. Finally, at the suggestion of the British ambassador, it decided to omit controversial issues from its final communiqué to the Entente governments.[30] This document again emphasized the principle of the empire's territorial integrity, stressed the inadmissibility of non-Russian delegations in international relations, and urged the subordination of all anti-Bolshevik forces to the commander in chief of the VA.[31]

Although the Russian delegation had been negotiating for aid exclusively on behalf of the VA, Ekaterinodar was not officially represented at Jassy. Shul'gin, the one delegate who, according to Henno's plans, was to play the leading role at the conference, fell ill en route and never attended the meetings.[32] Shul'gin's task, however, was very ably assumed by Miliukov, who, even though he disagreed in theory with the political outlook of the White intelligence agent, saw to it in practice that every resolution adopted at the conference would conform to the ideology espoused by the VA. This was true in particular on the question of political concessions to the nationalities. In his efforts, the Kadet leader did not encounter any serious opposition. The representatives of the socialist and moderate, conservative parties at Jassy, together with the Kadets, recognized the merits of the VA,

---

29. V. I. Gurko, "Iz Petrograda cherez Moskvu, Parizh i London v Odessu," *Arkhiv russkoi revoliutsii*, 15 (1924): 49; the attitude of the Allied ministers toward the Russian delegates is well documented in Robert H. McNeal, "The Conference of Jassy: An Early Fiasco of the Anti-Bolshevik Movement," in *Essays in Russian and Soviet History*, ed. J. S. Curtiss (New York: Columbia University Press, 1963), 221–36.

30. Miliukov, "Iasskoe soveshchanie."

31. The Third Appeal of the Russian Delegation to the Allies, Giers Archives, file 97, Ukraine.

32. Denikin, *Ocherki*, 5: 7. The only information available on Shul'gin is that he arrived on 18 November and brought new information from Ekaterinodar. "Zhurnal" no. 5, Morning Session, 18 November 1918, Wrangel Military Archives, file 143.

and although their political views differed widely, they were willing to recognize Ekaterinodar as the center from which Russia's regeneration should begin. It was the belief in Russia's unity and indivisibility that bonded the representatives of the diverse parties at Jassy, beginning with the constitutional monarchists and ending with the Popular Socialists. Miliukov described the proceedings of the conference in the most glowing terms, and he praised all the participants for their patriotism and for hiding their party differences from the Entente representatives in the name of an indivisible Russia.[33]

In spite of initial disappointments, by the time the conference was drawing to an end the Russian delegation recovered its former enthusiasm and optimism. In fact, on its last day in Jassy, 23 November, it decided not to disband but to continue its work in Odessa, where Entente troops were expected to arrive shortly. Furthermore, it decided to send a four-man delegation to Paris to press for what were considered to be Entente obligations to Russia.[34] In spite of the Jassy Conference's optimism and great expectations as to its future role, the communiqué it issued on 23 November was its last act of any significance on behalf of the White cause.

The Nationality Question in International Politics

The White leaders' jubilant anticipation of large-scale and speedy Entente intervention was short-lived. Gen. Shcherbachev was the first to learn that the plans of Entente aid presented to him by Berthelot were rejected in Paris.[35] To the Jassy Conference participants, the first severe blow occurred upon the arrival of the four-man delegation in Istanbul en route to Paris. Because of Miliukov's secret negotiations with the Germans in the spring of that year,[36] the delegation not only was refused an audience with Franchet d'Esperey at French Military Headquarters, but was denied permission to proceed further. Only after the mediation of the British embassy was the group able to travel to Paris. It arrived in the French capital only to suffer further humiliation. The French socialist press raised a stormy protest against Miliukov's presence. Consequently, on the express orders of Georges Clemenceau, Miliukov was expelled from France.[37]

This humiliating treatment of the delegation did not mean that the Entente representatives in Paris had no interest in Russia. On the contrary, they were

---

33. Miliukov, "Iasskoe sovieshchanie."
34. "Zhurnal" nos. 14 and 15, 23 November 1918, Wrangel Military Archives, file 143.
35. Val', *K istorii belago dvizheniia,* 42–3.
36. See supra, 71, n. 59.
37. Miliukov, "Dnevnik," 467–95; Margulies, 1: 85; Gurko, 53–5.

very much concerned with developments in Eastern Europe and, in general, were favorably disposed to the reestablishment of Russia's territorial unity, though not necessarily the reestablishment of a highly centralized tsarist state.[38] The Jassy delegation, in spite of its pretensions, was not an officially appointed representation of any of the White centers in Russia. Thus this unpleasant incident had no lasting effect on relations between the Entente diplomats and White representatives.

Efforts to form an official Russian representation at the Paris Peace Conference were undertaken early in Ekaterinodar. It was for this purpose that the aforementioned Council on Foreign Affairs chaired by Sazonov was established at the end of October 1918. In addition to the former tsarist foreign ministers, the council was to consist of five prominent political leaders, predominantly Kadets, and one representative each of the Don and Kuban Cossacks. Both Cossack groups demanded parity on the council, and when their request was flatly rejected, they refused to participate. In the end Sazonov alone was selected to represent VA interests at the peace negotiations. He was to be guided by the general principle of Russia's territorial integrity outlined in the foreign-relations program.[39]

Sazonov departed for Paris at the end of December 1918. He embarked on his new assignment with great enthusiasm, convinced that his principal task, to gain support for Russia's unification at the conference table, would be greatly facilitated by what he perceived as an unmistakable trend toward consolidation at home. The Transcaucasian nationalities, he announced in an interview on the eve of his departure, had almost completely lost interest in separatism because their political leaders and the people at large had already freed themselves "from the folly of nationalism and were trying to correct their mistakes."[40] The only exception was Georgia, but Sazonov dismissed it as of no consequence because he "could not conceive a Georgian republic standing alone surrounded by nationalities and provisional state formations gravitating toward a unitary, indivisible Russia."[41] As for Ukraine, Sazonov accepted unreservedly Shul'gin's views and position on this question: there were no ethnic or historical foundations for separatism in Ukraine, and if a separatist trend did exist, he was convinced that it was solely the product of German efforts to dismember Russia.

---

38. For an excellent presentation of Entente attitudes toward Russia on the eve of the Paris Peace Conference, see John M. Thompson, *Russia, Bolshevism, and the Versailles Peace* (Princeton: Princeton University Press, 1966), 62–81.

39. Denikin, *Ocherki*, 4: 237.

40. News reports from *Kievskaia mysl'*, 16 November 1918, in the Maklakov Personal Archive, series B, box 20, Ukraine.

41. Ibid.

Upon his arrival in Paris, Sazonov astounded Western diplomats and correspondents by speaking of Russia "as though it were unchanged, still an Ally and powerful member of the Entente."[42] Thus, from the start, Sazonov was received in Paris as an archconservative unable to comprehend the spirit of the new era.[43] His rigid position on the question of Russia's territorial unity was considered an outgrowth of his association with the tsarist regime, although the newly appointed VA diplomat was merely expressing views fully endorsed by the liberal and socialist Russians of the National Center and Union of Regeneration. Sazonov's conservatism stigmatized the movement he was representing; this stigma was difficult to erase because in the course of the conference the VA did not soften its attitude toward the borderland states. In Paris an inflexible attitude toward the nationalities was interpreted as reaction pure and simple.

The VA's foreign minister was spared the embarrassment of being evicted from Paris, but he was treated in a most humiliating manner by Clemenceau, who not only refused to see him but even warned the peace conference against giving Sazonov an opportunity to present his views at the negotiating table "lest it be alleged that the Conference is conspiring with tsarism."[44]

Fortunately for the VA, Sazonov was not the only one representing the White cause in Paris. Since the early autumn of 1918, the Provisional Government's ambassador to Paris, Vasilii A. Maklakov, had been working strenuously to assure a place for Russia at the conference table. Maklakov was acutely aware of Russia's precarious international position in 1918, that for the Entente Russia ceased to be an equal partner in the Alliance with the Peace of Brest-Litovsk, the White movement notwithstanding. Russia's place at the conference table, something that was taken for granted in Ekaterinodar, was still very much in doubt, at least until the Entente granted formal recognition to one of the Russian anti-Bolshevik centers operating on the territory of the disintegrated empire.

Partly because of the lack of information about developments in Russia after the Bolshevik seizure of power and partly because the Entente governments were considering recognizing the Russian socialist Directory in Ufa just before it was overthrown by a more conservative group supporting Kolchak in Omsk,[45] Maklakov believed the Siberian center had the best

---

42. Quoted in Thompson, 71.
43. Maklakov's letter to Maksim M. Vinaver, Paris, 7 March 1919, Wrangel Military Archives, file 151.
44. *Papers Relating to the Foreign Relations of the United States: The Paris Peace Conference, 1919*, vol. 4 (Washington: Government Printing Office, 1943), 53–4.
45. On the coup and subsequent developments, see Stephen Michael Berk, "The Coup d'Etat of Admiral Kolchak: The Counterrevolution in Siberia and East Russia, 1917–1918." (Ph.D. diss., Columbia University, 1971); Golovin, op. cit., vol. 4, bk. 9, 30–40, 74–83; Miliukov, *Russia*

chances of being recognized by France. Therefore he viewed it as the rallying point for all the other anti-Bolshevik centers. With this idea in mind, Maklakov wired a lengthy telegram to the minister of foreign affairs in Omsk at the end of October 1918, urging him to take steps immediately to come to an agreement with Ukraine, the Crimea, the Don, and the Caucasian republics. If some form of an agreement could be reached, advised Maklakov, Entente recognition of Omsk as an all-Russian government would be more readily granted, because the Entente states "would like to avoid the possibility that a government recognized by them as all-Russian would be rejected at the congress [the peace conference] by large territories [of the former empire]." It would be easy at the conference table to disregard the Bolsheviks and smaller borderlands, explained the Russian diplomat, but not such large entities as Ukraine, which constituted the richest and the most heavily populated parts of former Russia. Maklakov evinced special interest in the developments in Kyiv, especially in the fate of the Skoropads'kyi regime once the Germans withdrew beyond the borders of Ukraine. "Now it is impossible to predict what government will succeed [the hetman], but no matter what government it will be," advised the Russian Ambassador, "it is necessary to have it on our side." Moreover, Maklakov suggested that aid be extended to the Ukrainian government against the Bolsheviks, but warned prudently that this aid be offered not in the form of assistance from a supreme ruler "claiming authority there, but from a Russian patriot defending Ukraine against the Bolsheviks."[46]

Just as the political leaders of the White centers, isolated as they were from developments in the West, could not comprehend the extent of Russia's weakness in the international arena, so from abroad Maklakov failed to grasp the nature of the forces struggling for power in the former empire. Like the Entente statesmen and diplomats, he viewed the White movement primarily as anti-Bolshevik and was confounded by its unwillingness to reach a compromise with the borderland states also threatened by Bolshevism. Interestingly, Maklakov did not mention Denikin and the VA, either because he thought that some form of an agreement already existed between the two White anti-Bolshevik centers, or simply because of the lack of information in Paris on developments in the southwestern part of Russia in autumn of 1918.

Unification of the Russian anti-Bolshevik centers proved to be difficult, let alone an agreement with the nationalities. It took more than six months of strenuous effort on the part of the indefatigable Russian diplomat before Denikin in Ekaterinodar and Nikolai V. Chaikovskii, on behalf of the

---

Today and Tomorrow, 152–5; Footman, op. cit., 118–33.
46. Telegram from Maklakov to Golovachev, 31 October 1918, Maklakov Archive, box 18, Russia-Ukraine.

Arkhangelsk government,[47] formally recognized Kolchak as the supreme White leader.[48]

Maklakov proved to be much more successful in uniting the Russian representatives abroad. It was on his initiative that the Russian Political Conference of ambassadors of the defunct Provisional Government and of important political leaders came into being in January 1919.[49] The former head of the Provisional Government, Prince L'vov, became the conference's chairman, while such eminent but diverse political leaders as the former tsarist foreign minister Aleksandr P. Izvol'skii, the liberal-turned-conservative Struve, the former terrorist Savinkov, and the Popular Socialist Chaikovskii were its members. Sazonov too, after some hesitation, decided to join the conference, but not before receiving Denikin's approval; in his person, both the Ekaterinodar and the Omsk governments were represented (in the beginning of January 1919 Kolchak authorized Sazonov to represent his government as well.)[50] The conference, or more precisely its inner body, the Russian Political Council consisting of L'vov, Maklakov, Sazonov, and Chaikovskii, became the official voice of the White movement in Paris.

The organization of the Russian Political Conference was no mean achievement on Maklakov's part, considering that some of his colleagues had serious misgivings about this body and argued that a weak and unofficial Russian representation at the peace negotiations would be worse than nothing because it could be compelled to make concessions to the nationalities.[51] The conference proved to work rather well, in spite of the diversity of political convictions among its members. The Political Council always displayed unanimity in its official pronouncements[52] even though it was torn by serious friction, especially between Sazonov and the three other members.[53]

A serious shortcoming of the Political Conference, from the point of view of the Entente diplomats and political leaders, was its entirely Russian composition. Maklakov was acutely aware of this deficiency; in spite of strong opposition from his colleagues, he worked hard to attract the cooperation of the diplomats of the new borderland governments. Cognizant

---

47. On the Archangelsk government, see S. P. Mel'gunov, *N. V. Chaikovskii v gody grazhdanskoi voiny: Materialy dlia istorii russkoi obshchestvennosti, 1917–1925 gg.* (Paris: Librairie "La Source," 1929).

48. Telegram from Sazonov to Denikin, 22 June 1919, Maklakov Archive, box 23, Union of Russian Governments.

49. On the formation of the conference, see Maklakov's letter to Fisher, 31 March 1934, V. A. Maklakov Personal Archive, Hoover Institution, box 2; Mel'gunov, *Chaikovskii,* 96–100.

50. Denikin, *Ocherki,* 4: 237–8.

51. Miliukov, "Dnevnik," 468–71.

52. Maklakov's letter to Fisher, 5–6.

53. Maklakov's letter to Vinaver.

of his lack of knowledge when it came to the nationality question, Maklakov asked Boris A. Bakhmeteff, the Russian ambassador in Washington, to send him literature on this vital issue, especially on those nationalities that would have to be taken into account at the peace conference.[54] It was primarily through the Russian ambassadors in the Western capitals that the Russian Political Council was kept abreast of the numerous diplomatic activities abroad of the other nationalities.

As early as January 1919, largely through Maklakov's efforts, the Political Conference forwarded a declaration to the French foreign minister, Pichon, in which it assured the French government that the future Russian state would be constructed on democratic principles. The declaration devoted particular attention to the nationality question:

> the new Russia will be obliged to begin a new policy toward the various nationalities. The reactionary [tsarist] regime, in view of its very nature, could not recognize the special rights of the nationalities. The political status of the nationalities in the framework of the state will depend on the degree of their cultural and historical traditions. The elaboration of an agreement between the rights and interests of the nationalities and the vital interests of the state will be the principal task that will have to be resolved not only with the reestablishment of a Russian state on new principles, but also in harmony with the reorganization of international relations.
>
> After the revolution of 1917, the new Russia declared the independence of Poland, eliminated all infringements of the Finnish constitution, began reexamining the ties between Russia and Finland, and raised the question of the autonomy of the Baltic and other nationalities. This work, which was interrupted by the Bolshevik uprising, should be completed. The new Russia will strive to eliminate at the very core the artificial reasons for unhealthy separatism, which is nurtured by the memories of old wrongs, by the lack of confidence in the old regime, and by the exasperation with Bolshevik despotism. The unity of a state should not be continuously and constantly bolstered by fear; rather, this unity should become organic, for it corresponds equally to both state and national interests. Political experience provides sufficient examples of how to realize this unity either through federation or autonomy so that this problem, no matter how complicated it may be, might be solved.[55]

Only a few weeks later, on 9 March 1919, a separate declaration dealing exclusively with the nationality question was forwarded to the president of the

---

54. Telegram from Maklakov to Bekhmeteff, 29 November 1918, Maklakov Archive, box 18, Russia-Ukraine.
55. Declaration of the Russian Political Conference in Paris presented to Minister of Foreign Affairs Pichon, Wrangel Military Archives, file 135.

Paris Peace Conference. It was signed by the four members of the Political Council and presented on behalf of the Arkhangelsk, Ekaterinodar, and Omsk governments. This lengthy document, in addition to reiterating the general sentiments expressed in the memorandum to the French foreign minister, made some provisional but very specific commitments to the nationalities of the former empire:

> The [Allied] Governments recognize that (a) all questions connected with the territories of the Russian State in its boundaries of 1914, with the exception of ethnographic Poland, (b) and also question on future organization of nationalities living within these boundaries, cannot be solved without the consent of the Russian people. Thus no final decision can be reached before the Russian people are able to express freely their will and to take part in the regulations of these questions.
>
> Desiring, on the other hand, to foster the aspirations of nationalities in the organization of their national life and in defending it from anarchic dissolution, the Governments have decided to postpone the question of their final organization, but to recognize temporarily the regime which has been established there in accordance with their present needs and, primarily, with the military, financial, and economic necessities of the interested populations.
>
> In view of this, the Governments are inclined to consider the authorities established by these nationalities as governments *de facto*—inasmuch as these authorities are inspired by democratic principles, enjoy the confidence of the population, and are prepared to help their people in regard to their political and economic organization.[56]

While the first part of the declaration conformed fully with the basic principles on the nationality question espoused by the Provisional Government and the White movement, the second went beyond what Denikin and Kolchak were willing to endorse. Recognition of the existing governments of the new states, even though conditional and temporary only, was a revolutionary step for the political groups connected with the Provisional Government and, subsequently, the White movement. Until this time only the two extremes of the Russian political spectrum, the Bolsheviks and the monarchists, showed readiness to make such far-reaching concessions to the new nation-states.

The Political Council submitted the declaration on its own initiative without consulting the governments it was formally representing. That this step did not result in an immediate protest by Denikin's Special Council was

---

56. Declaration addressed to the president of the Peace Conference by the Russian Political Conference in Paris, 9 March 1919, Delegation Propaganda (Authenticated): Russia (Anti-Bolshevik) Documents presented to the Peace Conference—Memoranda, Hoover Institution; Arnold Margolin, *From a Political Diary: Russia, The Ukraine, and America, 1905–1945* (New York: Columbia University Press, 1946), 191–2.

partly due to the poor communications between Paris and Ekaterinodar, and partly a result of the undefined relationship between the White authorities and the Political Council in Paris. While Denikin tacitly approved of the Political Council representing Russia's interests at the peace conference and did not object to Sazonov's participation in that body, he never authorized it to speak on behalf of the VA. In turn, the members of the Political Council did not consider themselves subordinate to the governments they professed to represent, and at times they acted independently of them. That a complete rupture of relations between Paris and Ekaterinodar did not result was mainly because of the VA's helplessness in foreign affairs, but also because the Political Council was never recognized by the Entente governments as the official delegation representing Russia at the peace talks.[57] Its declarations, while tending to improve the White image abroad, were not politically binding and were therefore of little practical consequence.

The conciliatory attitude the Political Council adopted toward Russia's former national minorities was largely the result of Maklakov's determined effort to reach some form of understanding with the numerous delegations of the borderland governments in Paris. Maklakov was not only a realist far removed from the atmosphere of rabid nationalism engendered in the White centers by the disintegration of the empire and the war; as the most important Russian diplomat in the West, he had the most thorough understanding of Entente sentiments and intentions toward Russia. He was fully aware that the Entente governments were willing to aid the White movement not out of a sense of obligation to restore the power and political influence of a faithful but unfortunate ally, but mainly because of their own interest in the destruction of Bolshevism and the restoration of peace in Eastern Europe. And the destruction of Bolshevism appeared possible from Paris only through a concerted effort by all anti-Soviet forces operating on the territory of the former empire: the White armies, the Entente expeditionary units, and the military formations of the governments of the nationalities. Furthermore, to Maklakov an agreement with the borderland governments appeared indispensable not only for an effective struggle against Bolshevism but also for creating a favorable impression in the Western capitals. There the inflexible White position on Russia's indivisibility was associated with extreme conservatism and reaction, and, as Sazonov's reception in Paris vividly demonstrated, Western statesmen were particularly keen not to arouse negative public opinion in their countries by appearing to associate with what were believed to be dark forces of tsarist reaction in Russia.

---

57. Although a tenuous relationship between Paris and Ekaterinodar continued to exist throughout the duration of the peace conference, it was wrought with tension. Denikin wrote about the Political Council with bitterness and indignation. See his *Ocherki,* 4: 238, 241.

Being deeply convinced that for the White movement to have any success in the struggle against Bolshevism it would have to reach an understanding with the nationalities, even at the expense of undisputed Russian preeminence in the empire, Maklakov worked assiduously to win over to his point of view not only the Russian Political Council in Paris, but also the White leaders in Russia. It was precisely on the nationality question that lively correspondence developed between Maklakov and his Kadet colleagues in Denikin's Special Council in the spring of 1919.

Most likely to prepare the White political leaders for the Political Council's declaration on the nationality question on 9 March, Maklakov sent two lengthy memoranda to his influential Kadet colleagues in Denikin's political apparatus outlining his views on this important issue. The astute Russian diplomat pointed out that while he was firmly convinced no territorial question pertaining to Eastern Europe could be resolved without Russia's participation, he considered it imperative to reach an understanding with the governments of the nationalities because the White movement would never grow into a force strong enough "to declare war on all the borderlands." If a more conciliatory attitude was adopted, he opined, the borderlands would choose to remain of their own accord within the framework of a Russian state because, in the end, "reason and common interests will prove more important than portfolios." Maklakov requested information on developments in Ukraine and inquired whether any contacts should be established with the forces of the UNR Directory headed by Symon Petliura.[58]

Even a slight allusion to the possibility of White contacts with the independent Ukrainian government infuriated the Kadet members of the VA's Special Council. In his reply to Maklakov, the Kadet spokesman, Stepanov, unceremoniously placed Petliura into the same category of enemies as the Bolsheviks and anarchists. He instructed Maklakov to inform the Entente governments that "the entire idea of Ukrainian independence is a tempest in a teapot, without any roots among the indigenous population," and to warn them that Bolshevism was gaining sympathizers in "Little Russia precisely because of its Russianness." Nevertheless, the legal expert in Denikin's Special Council considered it prudent to warn his colleague in Paris that if the Entente granted the Ukrainian separatists recognition, it could become impossible to correct this act in the future.[59]

In his reply, addressed to Panina, Stepanov, and Astrov, Maklakov did not try to apologize for suggesting rapprochement with the Directory. On the contrary, he pressed his point further. Until Russia recovered its strength, he advised, it was necessary to play for time by not exacerbating relations with

---

58. Maklakov's letters to Stepanov and Vinaver, 7 March 1919, Wrangel Military Archives, file 151.
59. Stepanov's letter to Maklakov, 11 April 1919, Wrangel Military Archives, file 151.

the nationalities. He warned against Russian "great-power chauvinism, which is as characteristic of us as of Napoleon on the island of St. Helena, where he insisted on maintaining all the ceremonies of the imperial court." Because it was obvious that Russia could not rise on its feet, the insistence on "maintaining the former relations with the nationalities ... in particular not wanting to conclude an agreement with them but to dictate our will to them, to give them autonomy but in no way other than by a resolution of an All-Russian Constituent Assembly—all this seems to us such a lack of understanding of our strength and our position that it only depresses us." Furthermore, Maklakov explained, if the Russians wanted to prevent what the nationalities desired most—formal recognition of their independence—they have to recognize the fact that future relations between Russia and its borderlands must be resolved through an agreement. Understanding this was of crucial importance, pointed out Maklakov, because the Entente, the French especially, favored the reconstruction of Russia on federal principles and were firmly convinced that this reconstruction would take place from below, not from above, and through the merger of independent states and not through conquests by Denikin's and Kolchak's armies. The Entente governments supported this plan not only because the White armies were obviously too weak to bring the borderlands under their control, but because such conquests were considered to be absolutely unnecessary. "The centralized structure," the right-wing Kadet admonished his left-wing colleagues, "was not the strength but the weakness of Russia; as soon as Russia is reborn—liberal and democratic and not tsarist—the nationalities will comprehend the advantage of being united with it."[60]

Maklakov's lengthy plea to endorse the Political Council's policy toward the nationalities elicited one of the most straightforward expositions of the view on the nationality question that the Kadet members of Denikin's Special Council held. First, in order to forestall criticism, the Ekaterinodar Kadets tried to correct the impression that the White movement was oversimplifying the nationality question. The VA, they acknowledged, was quite aware that it would have plenty of trouble with the borderlands. They explained the absence of a well-defined nationality program in Ekaterinodar by the vast differences between one borderland and another, which made it impossible to apply one policy toward all of them. With some borderlands such as Finland, they explained, future relations would most likely be based on an agreement, but since no one knew what the future structure of Russia would be, it was impossible to propose general rules for such an agreement. The formula of Russia's reconstruction from below was contemptuously rejected as "some

---

60. Maklakov's letter to Panina, Stepanov, and Astrov, 30 April 1919, Wrangel Military Archives, file 151.

sort of a horrid Utopia that could be deeply injurious to Russia" and as a "meaningless formula derived from Proudhon and Bakunin." What distressed the Ekaterinodar Kadets most was that the formula did "not remain a theoretical dream but is beginning to enter into the sphere of practical politics." To the most eminent leaders of Russian liberalism, federation from below was nothing but a "democratic platitude not recognizing any other [method of] state formation than self-determination, expression of will, agreement, etc." "Unfortunately," the letter continued, "state processes up to now have not conformed to these beautiful principles, and there is hardly any hope that they will ever conform to them in reality." Russia, they insisted confidently, could be reunited only from above, through the efforts of the armies led by Denikin and Kolchak. "Through Moscow, through Petrograd, this is how one should reach Kyiv in order to attain a permanent and not a temporary peace." They expressed full confidence that through its own effort, inspired by the patriotism of its armies, the White movement would reconstitute Russia, and that once the center recovered its power and former authority, it would again become "the nucleus of convergence of culture, strength, and protection and the borderlands would gravitate toward it according to their particular law of attraction." The authors of the letter were especially piqued that the French had the temerity to suggest federation as the future structure of Russia; they asked Maklakov incredulously whether he also shared this view or was simply conveying it. "We beseech you Vasilii Alekseevich," the Ekaterinodar Kadets emplored, "protest against this point of view with all the power of your unequaled eloquence, with all the zeal of your argumentation."[61]

Maklakov continued corresponding, but he rarely touched upon the question of the nationalities, knowing that his efforts would be futile. In the summer and autumn of 1919 the VA reached the peak of its military strength. If its leaders were able to withstand pressure to make concessions to the nationalities in their most trying days, they certainly would not make agreements with the borderland governments when Moscow appeared to be within reach.

Maklakov's unequivocal endorsement of the federal principle not only shocked his colleagues in Ekaterinodar, but also astonished some of his acquaintances in Paris. When Manuil S. Margulies asked him whether in the declaration on nationalities of March 1919 he, L'vov, and Sazonov had truly endorsed federation as an acceptable form of state structure for Russia, Maklakov replied without hesitation: "Oh, yes. Today we would be happy if it were possible to establish a federation, but not only the Finns, but also the Estonians, Latvians, Lithuanians, Ukrainians, and Georgians do not want to

---

61. Letter from the National Center to Maklakov, 4 June 1919, Wrangel Military Archives, file 135.

speak of it."[62] The Russian ambassador complained that the Georgian leaders Iraklii Tsereteli and Nikolai Chkheidze were in Paris but did not even deem it necessary to pay him a visit.

It was with Maklakov's approval that Margulies undertook efforts to form a Federalist League that was to consist of representatives of the Kuban, the Don, Azerbaijan, the Caucasian Mountain Peoples, Georgia, the Crimea, Ukraine, Siberia, Arkhangelsk, Estonia, Latvia, and Lithuania. These efforts found little sympathy among the delegations of the nationalities in Paris, however, and ended in total failure. Each nationality delegation was working independently and singlehandedly pursuing its objective—to gain recognition as an official delegation at the conference table. Even such a convinced federalist as Arnold D. Margolin, a member of the Ukrainian peace delegation, viewed the Russian efforts with suspicion and was far from satisfied with the Political Council's declaration on the nationalities:

> Reading the text of the project one can assume that its authors find it appropriate to transmit the solution of the question of the rebuilding of the Russian commonwealth to the All-Russian Constituent Assembly to be elected by the population of the entire former Russian Empire. The result, however, would be that the population of Great Russia would have in the Constituent Assembly twice as many representatives as the Ukraine; Ukraine four times as many as Bielorussia, and twelve times more than Kuban or Georgia. Such a proportion of votes would bring about the suppression of the will of [the] smaller nationalities by the majority of votes of more numerous nationalities. So Great Russia would be the decisive factor in such a Constituent Assembly. There is no doubt that such an Assembly would not conform to the character and essence of the principle of self-determination of peoples solemnly declared by the Allies. It is also clear that with the exception of Great Russians, who are still permeated by the thirst for hegemony and a superiority complex in regard to other nationalities, there is not even one nationality among [the] other peoples of the former Russian Empire which would freely agree to entrust its fate to the hands of the All-Russian Constituent Assembly or even to send representatives to such an assembly.[63]

Instead of the Russian Political Conference, Margolin suggested the creation of a consultative body at the Paris Peace Conference consisting of five delegates each from Russia proper, Ukraine, Estonia, and all other states formed on the territory of the former empire. "A common struggle against any dictatorial regime in Russia, the later convocation of local constituent

---

62. Quoted in Margulies, 1: 332.
63. Margolin, 193.

assemblies, the dissemination of peaceful propaganda," wrote Margolin, "these were the tasks which, in my opinion, should be the basic activities of the proposed consultative body."[64]

Maklakov expressed interest in Margolin's project but found little understanding or sympathy among his Russian colleagues. Not only the Kadets but also the Russian Socialist Revolutionaries, both at home and in Paris, refused to make any meaningful concessions to the nationalities. Margolin's negotiations with Kerenskii, Nikolai D. Avksent'ev, Mark Vishniak, and other leading Socialist Revolutionaries in Paris proved most discouraging. Pompously claiming to speak "in the name of Russian democracy," Kerenskii declared that he did not consider himself "Great Russian," but simply Russian. "This was a subconscious heritage from the era when the Czar addressed, in the name of 'All Russia,' the various national groups within the empire," commented Margolin sardonically. "'Russian democracy' seemed on Kerensky's lips to be a substitute for the Czar's 'All Russia.'"[65]

The Ukrainian Question and the Entente Intervention

The White delegation that left Jassy learned to its dismay upon arriving in Odessa, on 25 November 1918, that the French consul, Henno, had completely disregarded its instructions and published a declaration supporting the Ukrainian conservative government in Kyiv.[66] Henno had added the following statement to the declaration prepared by the Russian delegates:

> The French Consul at Kiev declares the Entente powers intend to support, with all their force, the existing authority at Kiev represented by the hetman and his government, in the hope that he will be able to maintain order in the cities and provinces until the arrival of the Allied troops in the country.... Every attack upon the existing authorities, every revolt which will render [harder] the task of the Allies, will be severely punished.[67]

Because his passage to Kyiv had been blocked by troops of the UNR Directory, Henno considered some form of moral support for Skoropads'kyi's government indispensable. Being a foreigner, he was unable to comprehend the subtler reasons for his Russian colleagues' opposition to a temporary and

---

64. Ibid., 50.
65. Ibid.
66. See supra, 91.
67. *Papers Relating to the Foreign Relations of the United States, 1919*, vol. 2 (Washington: Government Printing Office, 1934), 701.

only implicit recognition of an independent Ukrainian government, even though it was conservative.

The declaration produced great rejoicing in Kyiv. The official press reported triumphantly that finally the Entente had unequivocally declared themselves in favor of the hetman. A special welcoming committee was elected to prepare the Ukrainian capital for the arrival of the French consul.[68] Ironically, because the declaration recognized in principle the existence of Ukrainian statehood, it elicited a favorable response even among some commanders in the insurgent armies of the Directory, against whom Henno's warnings were primarily directed. Col. Petro Bolbochan, the commander of the Directory's troops in Left-Bank Ukraine, responded immediately with a message to the Entente:

> The Ukrainian people welcome the representatives of the Allies entering the territory of the independent Ukrainian state, especially after Henno's declaration that the Allies are coming as friends of the people and not as enemies and oppressors. The Ukrainian people believe in the principle of their national statehood and fully support the idea of reestablishing order in the country.... The republican [Directory's] armies are precisely those that have courageously and unrelentingly struggled against the Bolsheviks and today are defending the borders of Ukraine against Russian Bolshevism.[69]

As noted above, Henno's declaration in no way helped the hetman to stay in power. On 14 December 1918 Ukrainian insurgent troops entered the capital of Ukraine, Skoropads'kyi resigned, and the five-man Directory— Vynnychenko, Petliura, Opanas Andriiev'skyi, Fedir Shvets', and Andrii Makarenko—was installed in Kyiv.[70]

The city of Odessa, where Henno established his residence, was seriously threatened by the Directory's troops even before the fall of Skoropads'kyi's government in Kyiv. Being completely unaware of the blow his declaration had imparted to the idea of an indivisible Russia, Henno committed a second blunder, from the point of view of his Russian friends at Jassy, by initiating negotiations for a truce with the commanders of the Directory's troops near Odessa. "This was a second step dictated by the hopelessness of the situation, but which at the same time undermined the idea of the [Russian]

---

68. Newspaper reports in the Maklakov Archive, series B, box 20, Ukraine; Arnol'd Margolin, *Ukraïna i polityka Antanty* (Berlin: S. Efron, 1921), 96–8.
69. Appeal to the Allies from the commander in chief of the armies of Left-Bank Ukraine, Otaman Bolbochan, 26 November 1918, Wrangel Military Archives, file 152.
70. Khrystiuk, 3: 130, 138–41.

national struggle and distorted the meaning of Allied aid," later commented Denikin bitterly.[71]

While negotiating with the Ukrainian commanders, Henno simultaneously dispatched telegrams to Jassy and Ekaterinodar pleading for immediate aid to save the city as a base for the planned Entente intervention.[72] But the VA, which at that time was engaged in a struggle with the nationalities of northern Caucasia, was in no position to aid in the defense of Odessa. Denikin merely appealed to Franchet d'Espérey in Istanbul to expedite the dispatch of Entente troops. From Romania a message arrived from Gen. Berthelot stating that Entente forces would soon be in Odessa and that, in the meantime, Henno should inform the Bolshevik leaders, as well as Petliura and Vynnychenko, that the French Command would hold them "personally responsible for all hostile acts and all attempts tending to violate peace in the country."[73] The message was promptly published in all local papers.

The leaders of the Directory, who from the beginning of the uprising against Skoropads'kyi had tried to elicit Entente support, were careful not to arouse the ire of the first French postwar emissary through an imprudent act. Thus, although the Directory's troops were in a position to take Odessa by storm, they merely occupied one section of the city and patiently awaited the arrival of the French Military Command.[74]

In spite of this tactical restraint, the disembarkation of the first Entente detachment in Odessa on 17 December 1918 proved to be a great blow to the Ukrainian command and a victory for Henno and the White leaders. The French commander, Gen. Albert Borius, ordered the Ukrainian units to disarm, and when they refused to do so, they were forced to depart from the city. Nonetheless, because Borius's instructions specified the occupation of Odessa only, he refused to pursue the Directory's troops, even though he was urged to do so by White representatives. Thus the Ukrainians remained in control of the immediate vicinity of the city.[75]

For a brief time Henno, now aided by his close friend Shul'gin, remained master of Odessa. It was on their advice that Borius agreed to the appointment of Gen. Aleksei Grishin-Al'mazov to the post of military governor of

---

71. Denikin, *Ocherki*, 5: 9.
72. Ibid., 9–10.
73. A. G. Shlikhter, ed. *Chernaia kniga: Sbornik statei i materialov ob interventsii Antanty na Ukraine v 1918–1919 gg.* (Kharkiv: Gosizdat Ukrainy, 1925), 93; A. I. Gukovskii, *Antanta i Oktiabr'skaia revoliutsiia* (Moscow: Gosudarstvennoe sotsial'no-ekonomicheskoe izdatel'stvo, 1931), 135.
74. Margulies, 1: 75–7; Denikin, *Ocherki*, 5: 10.
75. F. Analov, "Soiuznyi desant na Ukraine," in Shlikhter, 111–13; Denikin, *Ocherki*, 5: 32.

Odessa.[76] The latter immediately informed Denikin that "nowhere, under no circumstances would he conduct any other policy except that ordered by his [Denikin's] directives."[77] The spread of Denikin's authority to Odessa led to a direct confrontation between the VA and the Directory.

Henno and Shul'gin's rule in Odessa was short-lived. Borius had little authority and no interest whatsover in the political affairs of the city. He was only too happy to follow Henno's guidance and suggestions on all nonmilitary questions during the first weeks of the Allied intervention. The situation changed radically, however, when in mid-January 1919 the long-awaited commander of the French forces in Odessa, Gen. Philippe Henri d'Anselme, arrived together with his chief of staff, Col. Henri Freydenberg. The first question d'Anselme asked Henno was whether he had already met Gen. Oleksander Hrekov, the commander of the Directory's troops in the region,[78] while Freydenberg stunned the VA representatives by announcing that the Allied Command was interested in "making use of all anti-Bolshevik forces, including the Ukrainians, in the struggle against the Bolsheviks."[79] This meant that although the VA was to receive full Entente support, it would not remain the sole recipient of French aid in the anti-Bolshevik struggle. The implication was that the principal aim of the intervention was the destruction of Bolshevism, and not, as had been understood initially in Ekaterinodar, the restoration of Russia's territorial integrity. This realization was a heavy blow to Denikin, because for him, as well as for other VA leaders, the defeat of Bolshevism was only a means to a higher end. Denikin viewed Entente attempts to establish relations with the nationalities as intolerable interference in Russia's internal affairs and a distortion of the meaning and spirit of the intervention.

What the French strove to bring about in Odessa was an agreement between the Ukrainians and the Volunteers by exacting concessions from both sides. What Freydenberg proposed to the Directory's representatives was a division of the Southwestern *krai* of the former empire into two separate zones, one Ukrainian and one Russian, with the French coordinating operations in both zones. The Directory was to organize an army of 300,000 men that would be supplied by France, but the Ukrainian government was obliged to conclude an alliance with the VA and with a small Polish legion

---

76. At the end of November 1918 Denikin dispatched Grishin-Al'mazov to Jassy to apprise Poklevskii-Kozel of political and military conditions in Siberia. On his return from Jassy, Grishin-Al'mazov remained in Odessa, where he styled himself as the VA's delegate to the Jassy Conference. Denikin, *Ocherki,* 5: 10.

77. Ibid., 11.

78. Margulies, 1: 165.

79. Azbuka report, Odessa, 1 March 1919, Maklakov Archive, series B, box 20, Ukraine.

that was in Odessa at that time.[80] The Ukrainians responded with a demand for immediate recognition of the Directory as the government of independent Ukraine and expressed readiness to participate in the anti-Bolshevik struggle, but only on Ukrainian ethnographic territory.[81]

While negotiations with the Ukrainians proceeded satisfactorily though not without difficulties, relations between the French and the VA reached a breaking point as early as mid-February. The French aroused the ire of Ekaterinodar not only by initiating negotiations with the Ukrainians, but also by their endeavors, together with conservative groups in Odessa, to establish a regional government for Ukraine. Close adherents of the VA—Shul'gin, Grishin-Al'mazov, and members of the National Center—were not the only Russian political group in Odessa. In addition to the participants in the Jassy Conference, conservatives from the Council of Russia's State Unity, and socialists from the Union of Regeneration, the city was full of émigrés of the most diverse persuasions from Petrograd, Moscow, and Kyiv.[82]

In December 1918 Odessa also became the refuge of the former supporters of Skoropads'kyi's government—wealthy landowners, conservative generals, financiers, and tsarist bureaucrats. Their attitude toward Denikin was never favorable, and they viewed the VA authority in Odessa—which after d'Anselme's arrival became only nominal—with unconcealed hostility if not contempt. What they favored instead was the establishment of a regional conservative government for Ukraine under French auspices. It appeared that the drama of Skoropads'kyi's rule in Kyiv would repeat itself in Odessa, this time under French sponsorship. It was in the milieu of Skoropads'kyi's former supporters, led by the hetman's military governor of Odessa, Gen. Biskups'kyi, that several plans for the establishment of a separate Ukrainian army and government originated.[83] Biskups'kyi was supported mainly by wealthy landowners who had gathered in Odessa and created two organizations, led by Kotov-Konoshenko and Hryhorenko. The former, a candidate for the new hetman of Ukraine, presented a scheme for a new government to the French. Although the proposal did not win French approval, Kotov-Konoshenko, as well as Hryhorenko, figured prominently on the numerous lists for a regional government endorsed by the French Command. What the conservatives aspired to was the formation of a government modeled on Skoropads'kyi's

---

80. Osyp Nazaruk, *Rik na Velykii Ukraïni: Spomyny z ukraïns'koï revoliutsiï* (Vienna: Ukraïns'kyi prapor, 1920), 119–21; S. Ostapenko, "Direktoriia i frantsuzskaia interventsiia," in Shlikhter, 260–8.
81. Ibid.
82. For a vivid description of life in Odessa in the winter and early spring of 1919, see Margulies, 1: passim.
83. Azbuka report, Odessa, 5 February 1919, Maklakov Archive, series B, box 20, Ukraine; Denikin, *Ocherki,* 5: 30.

rule that would assure the protection of the wealthy landowners' property rights in Ukraine.

Because the situation in Odessa was extremely precarious, Biskups'kyi did not limit his work to these schemes, but also worked to bring about a rapprochement between the conservative groups in Odessa and the Directory. This work was facilitated by the fact that the first representative who negotiated with the French Command on behalf of the socialist Directory was Gen. Hrekov, a former commander in Skoropads'kyi's army and one of Biskups'kyi's colleagues.[84]

That an agreement with the Directory was considered not only by Ukrainian landowners but also conservative Russian groups indicates the utter confusion and weakness of the political right during the civil war. It had neither an army nor mass support, and thus depended exclusively on foreign aid. The French seemed to have been negotiating seriously with the Directory, and it appeared that the salvation of at least part of the former empire could come through the efforts of the Ukrainians. For example, a former member of the extreme right in the State Duma, Prof. S. V. Levashov, stated at a meeting at which cooperation with the Directory was discussed that "On the basis of my activities in the past, no one can reproach me for lacking patriotism, but I declare that for the sake of Russia's salvation I am ready to reconcile myself with the yellow-and-blue [UNR] flag because I prefer to see the salvation of the country under the yellow-and-blue flag rather than a cemetery under the [Russian] tricolor."[85]

As time passed, not only members of the extreme right who never supported the VA but also moderate conservatives from the Council of Russia's State Unity, who had leaned toward Denikin at Jassy, were ready to accept the replacement of the VA authority in Odessa by an autonomous regional government. Margulies, who had supported Denikin at Jassy and authored the second appeal to the Entente—a scathing attack on the Directory—proposed a project to establish a South Russian regional government in which the Directory would be included. He argued that "Russia could be saved only through federation, without which it would not be able to survive in the future."[86] The leader of the Council of Russia's State Unity, Baron V. V. Meller-Zakomels'kii, who served as the chairman of the Jassy Conference, confided privately that if the Directory's troops proved strong enough to defend Kyiv from the Bolsheviks, he, too, would be willing to support Petliura.[87] After lengthy deliberations on this question, Margulies summed

---

84. Ibid.
85. Azbuka report, Odessa, 8 March 1919, Maklakov Archive, series B, box 18, Ukraine.
86. Margulies, 1: 164.
87. Ibid., 189. Petliura was the commander in chief of the UNR Army.

up the position of the Russian moderate right: "the minute Petliura proclaims federation without independence, all of us, with the exception of the Kadets in the National Center and Shul'gin, will cooperate to find a modus vivendi with him."[88]

The conciliatory attitude toward the Directory that the Russian moderate right evinced was prompted by dissatisfaction with VA authority in Odessa—its inability to establish order and organize a reliable military force to defend the city—and, more importantly, by French willingness, contrary to the general expectation in Jassy, to come to terms with a Ukrainian government. It is worth remembering that when the Council of Russia's State Unity was first being formed in the summer of 1918, its organizers assumed that persons harboring anti-Ukrainian sentiments would not join the association.[89] When the Entente won the war and when it appeared that Denikin would be the recipient of the bulk of Entente aid, the moderate right threw its support to the VA. In Odessa, however, when serious difficulties came to the fore between Denikin and the French Command and when an agreement between the latter and the Directory appeared probable, they again began vacillating and, while not openly working toward an agreement with the Directory, were willing to support a separate government for Ukraine that included the Directory. This would have meant in effect the establishment of a federative Russia. Not all members of the loosely organized council shared this view, of course, but the prevalent toward the Directory and federation was conciliatory rather than hostile.

No such uncertainty or vacillation was evident among members of the National Center in Odessa. In a resolution adopted unanimously at a meeting on 11 February 1919, when talks between the Ukrainians and the French were gaining momentum, they explained in great detail why cooperation with the Directory was inconceivable from the point of view of a movement striving to defend the unity of Russia. It was their firm conviction that the basic condition of all agreements between the Entente and Russia was the recognition of the inviolability of the empire's frontiers. Extension of support to Petliura and recognition of a Ukrainian state would violate this basic principle; it would constitute a hostile act toward Russia tantamount to the "revival of the annulled Brest [-Litovsk] treaty by which the Germans wanted to create a Ukrainian state" and consequently "the realization by the Allies of the former pernicious Austro-German propaganda whose aim was the partition of Russia."[90] The National Center expressed confidence that this was not the

88. Ibid., 191.
89. Brief history of the Council of Russia's State Unity, Wrangel Military Archives, file 129.
90. Resolutions of the South Russian National Center, 11 February 1919, Maklakov Archive, series B, box 20, Ukraine.

intention of the Entente and that negotiations between the French Command and the Ukrainians had one purpose only: to utilize the troops gathered by Petliura in the struggle against the Bolsheviks. This policy, warned the National Center, was mistaken and highly dangerous because the Ukrainian forces were incapable of struggling against the Bolsheviks, and yet it prevented the VA Command from introducing mobilization in territories liberated from the Bolsheviks. Moreover, the resolution claimed, if the population of the region had to choose between the Bolsheviks and the Ukrainians, it would side with the Bolsheviks.

Similar arguments directed against the Directory were repeatedly advanced by Shul'gin in his talks with the French Command. He warned d'Anselme that if the French concluded an agreement with the Ukrainians, the Russian population would have no choice but to seek protection from the Bolsheviks because the Ukrainians mercilessly persecuted Russian culture. To this the French general retorted that the Russians should keep in mind that Kyiv would be occupied by both Ukrainian and Allied forces, and thus Russian cultural interests would be protected. Moreover, d'Anselme added with unconcealed annoyance that the French should support all forces of order. "With respect to their political differences—who is for monarchy and who is against monarchy, who is for the unity of Russia and who is against a unitary Russia—is of no concern to us."[91] Shul'gin was appalled. He continued arguing passionately that the Entente should not interfere in the struggle between monarchists and republicans because it was an internal Russian problem; the struggle for the unity of Russia, however, was a different matter, and to put on the same level both the supporters and opponents of a united Russia was simply inadmissible. He called attention to the fact that both President Clemenceau and Gen. Berthelot spoke frequently of the unity of Russia.

Shul'gin's emotional plea failed to move d'Anselme. In a private conversation the Frenchman expressed annoyance that Denikin had pretensions to extending his authority over Odessa and Ukraine: "This region belongs to Petliura and not to Denikin," he remarked.[92] Shul'gin's talks with Freydenberg were conducted in a friendlier tone but had no perceptible effect on French policy in Odessa. The French chief of staff reassured Shul'gin that France was firmly committed to the idea of Russia's unity and would never recognize Ukraine's independence, but that now it was imperative to take advantage of all forces capable of struggling against the Bolsheviks. Therefore he considered a French-mediated agreement between the Russians and Ukrainians on a concerted struggle against a common enemy most advanta-

---

91. Azbuka report, Odessa, 23 February 1919, Maklakov Archive, series B, box 20, Ukraine.
92. Margulies, 1: 263.

geous. Shul'gin replied firmly that there could never be any cooperation between the Russians and Ukrainians, that Denikin's position of an uncompromising attitude toward the Directory was the only correct one, and that ultimately the Ukrainians would never agree to work with the Russians. Documents produced by Freydenberg indicating that the Directory was willing to make important concessions in order to receive French aid had no appreciable effect on Shul'gin. In the end Freydenberg could not restrain himself from asking facetiously how he was to understand the declaration of the South Russian National Center that stated that the Russians might side with the Bolsheviks if faced with the choice between the Soviet regime and the Directory. After all, the Bolsheviks, too, were considered products of German intrigue. Shul'gin replied feebly that the Ukrainians represented the same thing, and that whoever supported the Ukrainians served German interests.[93] He thought it prudent not to elaborate on this point by providing an explanation contained in one of his intelligence reports from Kyiv: "Of two evils, it is always necessary to chose the lesser one: in the Ukrainian movement one finds both class and national fanaticism. Among the Bolsheviks there exists class fanaticism only. With respect to [Russian] national-cultural matters, they do not subject the population to suppression."[94] Intelligence reports from Kyiv repeatedly emphasized that the Soviet regime—in the beginning of February 1919 Kyiv was again occupied by the Bolsheviks—was directing its persecution mainly against the Ukrainian intelligentsia and that its attitude toward Russian officers was on the whole correct.[95] "This time," one agent reported, "the Bolshevik occupation was not characterized by Red terror, and if one adds to this agitation and propaganda to the effect that only the Bolsheviks will attain an indivisible Russia, the position of the Soviets is being strengthened in Kyiv ... [and is] gaining support even among the intelligentsia."[96] For a large segment of the Russian population of the more important urban centers in Ukraine, observed another agent, the Bolsheviks thus began to represent the "standard-bearers of the idea of a united Russia."[97]

In addition to his talks with the French Command, Shul'gin also initiated a vigorous campaign in his paper, *Rossiia,* against the conclusion of a Franco-Ukrainian agreement. In this campaign he did not overlook the fact that both Freydenberg and the chief negotiator for the Directory, Margolin, were Jewish. Because of frequent anti-Semitic slurs on its pages, Shul'gin's paper

---

93. Azbuka report, 1 March 1919, Maklakov Archive, series B, box 20, Ukraine.
94. Azbuka report, Odessa, 14 February 1919, Maklakov Archive, series B, box 20, Ukraine.
95. Ibid. (notes 93–4).
96. Intelligence report no. 67, 20 February 1919, Wrangel Military Archives, file 149.
97. Azbuka report, 14 February 1919, Maklakov Archive, series B, box 20, Ukraine.

was closed for eight days on the express orders of the French Command.[98] The anti-Semitism of the VA in Odessa, a city with a large and influential Jewish population, contributed considerably to the dissatisfaction with Grishin-Al'mazov's rule there. A typical example of anti-Semitism frequently encountered in VA ranks is related by Margulies in his diary. While traveling from the Crimea to Odessa late in December 1918, he met an officer from Denikin's headquarters who was carrying a large package of leaflets printed in Ekaterinodar. The text of these leaflets was replete with derogatory Russian terms for Jews. "And you are taking this to Odessa, a city with a large [Jewish] population that is active and rich and whose support is indispensable for the army?" Margulies asked incredulously. The blank expression on the face of the officer indicated that he was incapable of comprehending the point Margulies was making.[99] Heading the VA's Political Department in Odessa was Shul'gin's close collaborator A. I. Savenko, who was well-known for his rabid anti-Semitism.[100]

Because the VA waged uncompromising war with the Directory, the local Jewish population, and subsequently the French Command, its support in Odessa quickly dwindled and became insignificant. By the end of February 1919 the little influence the Whites had on local affairs appeared to be coming to an end. In the course of that month negotiations between the French Command and the Ukrainians had proceeded at full speed. Differences encountered at their early stages were smoothed out by concessions the Directory made, such as the removal or resignation of its left-wing socialist members, their replacement with moderates, and the appointment of competent negotiators to Odessa.[101]

Especially successful as a plenipotentiary negotiator of the Directory was Arnold Margolin. He impressed the French Command by his political convictions and his government's plan for the reconstruction of Russia through "federation from below." This meant the temporary establishment of independent nation-states on the territory of the former empire that would be allies in the struggle against Bolshevism and, after its defeat, would voluntarily unite in a democratic Russian federation. For Margolin this was not a formula to be implemented sometime in the indefinite future. Upon arriving in Odessa at the end of January 1919, he took concrete steps to

---

98. Jean Xydias, *L'intervention française en Russie, 1918–1919: Souvenirs d'un témoin* (Paris: Editions de France, 1927), 251; V. Maiborodov, "S frantsuzami," *Arkhiv russkoi revoliutsii* 16: 125; Azbuka report, Odessa, 14 February 1919, Maklakov Archive, series B, box 20, Ukraine.
99. Margulies, 1: 106.
100. Ibid., 184.
101. Azbuka report, Odessa, 23 February 1919, Maklakov Archive, series B, box 20, Ukraine; Margolin, *Ukraïna i polityka Antanty*, 123–4; Vynnychenko, 3: 255–7, 264–7; Shlikhter, 267–8.

realize it by initiating negotiations with Don, Kuban, and Belarusian representatives. On 18 February a joint declaration signed on behalf of the Don Krug, the Kuban Rada, the Belarusian government, and the UNR Directory was presented to the French Command. The first part of the declaration argued persuasively in favor of federation from below:

> The most convinced adherents of a direct and immediate re-establishment of former Russian centralist commonwealth on federative foundations must agree that the events of the last eighteen months, in connection with the catastrophe which occurred in Russia after the Bolsheviks' *coup d'etat* of October 25 [November 7] 1917, have created insurmountable obstacles for the realization of a "federation from above."
>
> In general the history of the political organization of countries knows very few cases of a direct and immediate transition from a centralized and unified form of state to a federative form. Such transitions were attempted with greater or lesser success in a few South American states (Bolivia, Venezuela, etc.).
>
> Those countries, however, that are well known for their successful federative organization approached the federation not from above but from below. The United States of America and Switzerland derived from a union of separate states or of cantons.... In these cases a free agreement based on the good and free will of the separate states or cantons preceded the reorganization of federative foundations.[102]

The declaration explained that under existing circumstances, federation from above would be possible only through coercion, i.e., the use of force. It requested Entente aid to consolidate the existing national governments so that they would be in a position to struggle effectively against Bolshevism. The formation of separate regional armies, coordinated by a common general staff that would direct military operations on the basis of mutual agreement without intervening in the internal affairs of the new states, was proposed as the most effective way of combating the common enemy.

The declaration, which was signed by Margolin and Artem Halip on behalf of the Directory, Gen. Cheriachukin on behalf of the Don Krug, Luka Bych on behalf of the Kuban Rada, and Bakhanovich for Belarus, made a strong impression on the French in Odessa. By the end of February a formal agreement between the Directory and the French Command was ready to be signed. Apparently both d'Anselme and Freydenberg were prepared to break completely with the VA and, according to the terms of the proposed agreement, to recognize "the sovereign regime of the Ukrainian Democratic [i.e., People's] Republic's Directory established on 1 November 1918 on the

---

102. The full text of the memorandum is located in the Cheriachukin Papers, file 4, no. 1; the English translation is in Margolin, *From a Political Diary*, 186–8.

initiative of the Ukrainian National Union." France promised to undertake measures "for the prompt admission of the representatives of the Ukrainian Democratic Republic to the Peace Conference" and to guarantee to the Ukrainian government that no VA units would be present or participate in military operations on the territory of Ukraine. Substantial military aid in the war against the Bolsheviks was promised, but in return France demanded control over all Ukrainian railroads, assumption by Ukraine of its own share of the Russian state debt, and French supervision of all Ukrainian industrial, financial, commercial, and military policies for a five-year period.[103] A similar proposal was presented to the Directory's delegation at the Paris Peace Conference by Foreign Minister Pichon.[104] In spite of these promising developments, the Franco-Ukrainian alliance never materialized. At the end of March 1919 Freydenberg informed Margolin that he had been ordered by telegram from Paris not to sign the agreement with the Directory.[105] The negotiations, which had caused so much confusion among the Russian parties in Odessa and bitterness among the VA supporters in the city, thus came to an abrupt end.

The French decision to terminate negotiations was influenced, no doubt, by the defeats suffered by the Directory in the early spring of 1919. Bolshevik advances had forced the Directory to leave Kyiv early in February 1919. The withdrawal of the Socialist Revolutionaries and Social Democrats from the UNR government under French pressure, as well as the Directory's negotiations with d'Anselme and Freydenberg, were ably utilized by Bolshevik propaganda throughout Ukraine, and initial enthusiasm for the Directory among the troops quickly subsided. Some military units joined the Bolsheviks, while others simply melted away. By the end of March 1919 the government had evacuated to Kamianets-Podilskyi on the western border of the UNR, and Odessa was threatened with Bolshevik takeover. Just as abruptly as the French had terminated negotiations with the Directory, they decided to evacuate Odessa in the beginning of April. Neither Denikin in Ekaterinodar nor his representatives in Odessa were notified of this decision.[106] By that time relations between the VA and the French Command, because of the French negotiations with the Ukrainians and Freydenberg's attempts to organize a regional government for Odessa, appeared to be irreparably broken.

---

103. Khrystiuk, 4: 104; Margolin, *Ukraïna i polityka Antanty,* 109–24; Gukovskii, 142–3; Shlikhter, 13–135.
104. Gukovskii, 146.
105. Margolin, *Ukraïna i polityka Antanty,* 123–4; Azbuka report, 15 March 1919, Maklakov Archive, series B, box 20, Ukraine.
106. Denikin, *Ocherki,* 5: 69; *Ocherk" vzaimootnoshenii Vooruzhennykh sil iuga Rossii i predstavitelei frantsuzskago komandovaniia* (Ekaterinodar: Dobrovol'cheskaia Armiia, 1919).

During the confused first phase of the French intervention in Odessa—December 1918 to April 1919—there were no official or unofficial relations between the VA authorities in Ekaterinodar and the UNR Directory, in spite of French efforts to bring these two anti-Bolshevik forces together. Denikin flatly refused to endorse the Belarusian, Don, Kuban, and Ukrainian memorandum of 18 February.[107] He resolutely opposed any dealings with the Directory, even after the withdrawal of the socialist parties from the Ukrainian government and the assumption of leadership by men whose general outlook corresponded rather closely to that of his own advisors. Denikin's intransigence is not surprising, for the Directory stood for independence. But Denikin was a military man, and he must have taken into consideration an important asset of the Directory—which Skoropads'kyi's government had lacked—namely, a considerable army. Even by his own very conservative calculations, the hard core of the Ukrainian army consisted of 70,000 men, a figure far larger than that of the White forces in the beginning of 1919.[108] With respect to the political viability of the Directory and the reliability of its troops, intelligence reports from Kyiv varied widely. Some agents expressed surprise at the discipline and exemplary behavior of the Ukrainian troops that had entered Kyiv in December 1918: "It is necessary to bring to [your] attention that the Ukrainian armies that entered Kyiv *are truly disciplined regular armies....* Evidence indicates that the Bolsheviks will not overthrow the Directory with ease."[109] Another observer noted that "panic among the officers evident during the first days of the entrance of Petliura's armies has subsided, as in most instances they are not persecuted."[110] Other agents complained about the persecution of Russians and equated the Ukrainian troops with the Bolsheviks: "In Kyiv all power is in the hands of Konovalets', who each day is proclaiming purely Bolshevik edicts.[111] On the third day of his arrival, Konovalets' ordered that within three days all signs in Kyiv must be changed from Russian to Ukrainian. Those who refuse [to do so] will be fined 40,000 rubles."[112] Still others endeavored to downplay the Directory forces or to "unmask" the Bolshevik character of the Ukrainian

---

107. Denikin, "Navet na beloe dvizhenie," 57.
108. Denikin, *Ocherki*, 5: 11. German intelligence reports cited the same figure: 60,000 men from Right- and Left-Bank Ukraine and 10,000 Sich Riflemen from Galicia. See Hornykiewicz, 4: 232.
109. Azbuka report, 12 January 1919, Wrangel Military Archives, file 131.
110. Ibid.
111. Colonel Evhen Konovalets' commanded the Sich Riflemen, the first Ukrainian troops to enter Kyiv after the hetman's abdication. Azbuka reports noted that Konovalets' was excluded from the Directory, at the insistence of Gen. Hrekov, because he had negotiated with the VA representatives in Kyiv and tried to help the Russian officers stranded there. Report "X," February 1919, file 132; and Azbuka report, 23 January 1919, Wrangel Military Archives, file 131.
112. Azbuka report, 11 January 1919, Wrangel Military Archives, file 131.

government: "Military forces of the Directory are insignificant. One cannot think of war in the full meaning of the word.... Although there is great confusion among the Russian parties, one hears more and more often about the desirability of the Bolshevik occupation of Kyiv."[113] After news of the negotiations between the French Command and the Directory reached Kyiv, reports warned that any agreement with the Ukrainians would be a grave mistake, because it would alienate the adherents of an indivisible Russia.[114]

No amount of intelligence information could sway Denikin. His position was firm: nonalignment with any anti-Bolshevik force, irrespective of political orientation or military strength, that did not recognize the supremacy of the VA and did not accept an indivisible Russia. In spite of pressure applied by both the Russian representatives in Paris and the French Command in Odessa, he stubbornly refused to make any compromises on the question of Russia's unity. His stand was fully supported by the Kadets of the National Center, both those who were members of his Special Council and those defending VA's interests in Odessa.

The French behavior in Odessa made Denikin realize that while Russia's former Allies were willing to aid the White armies to struggle against Bolshevism, their position on the restoration of Russia's unity was highly uncertain. He had expected full and unconditional aid for the realization of both aims, and when this did not materialize, his disappointment was great. Denikin viewed even Henno's feeble attempts to come to an understanding with conservative Ukrainians as a distortion of the spirit and meaning of Entente aid, and he branded Freydenberg's efforts at reaching an agreement with the Directory in the anti-Bolshevik struggle as "a clear continuation of the German [policy] *leading not to the reestablishment but to the dismemberment of Russia.*"[115]

The misunderstanding between the French and the Volunteers in Odessa arose primarily because the Entente viewed the White movement primarily as anti-Bolshevik. They failed to comprehend that it was first and foremost a Russian national movement determined to restore the unity and power of the former empire, a movement for which both the Bolsheviks and Ukrainian nationalists were equally dangerous foes. The Allied failure to discern the essence of the White cause was at the core of the strained relations between the White leaders and the Allied intervention forces during the civil war.

---

113. Azbuka report, 13 January 1919, and an undated report of the same period, Wrangel Military Archives, file 131.
114. Azbuka report, 17 January 17, 1919, Wrangel Military Archives, file 131.
115. Denikin, *Ocherki,* 5: 34.

V

A Divided or a Bolshevik Russia: Which Was the Lesser Evil?

> With respect to cooperation with the Ukrainians, no agreement on our part with them is possible. Recognition of Petliura and cooperation with him would be recognition of the dismemberment of Russia.
>
> Neratov (Denikin) to Minister (Giers),
18 September 1919

For almost two years of its existence, the VA consistently avoided official contacts with the governments of the borderland states. Its attitude toward them tended to be negative irrespective of whether they were conservative, socialist, pro-independence, or pro-federation. Even temporary agreements with the governments of northern Caucasia and Transcaucasia, with which the VA established tenuous ties as a result of strong British pressure, did not solidify into a firm alliance because of the White movement's unbending position on Russia's indivisibility. As Denikin explained, "After all else is said, the major, indeed the only, cause of the struggle in Caucasia was the conflict between the idea of one Russia and the idea of fully independent Caucasian state formations."[1]

While the White forces were in no position militarily to oppose the centrifugal tendencies in the former empire, they exerted strenuous efforts to

---

1. Denikin, *Ocherki,* 4: 139. An excellent overview of the VA's relations with the Transcaucasian republics is presented in George A. Brinkley, *The Volunteer Army and Allied Intervention in South Russia, 1917–1921* (Notre Dame: University of Notre Dame Press, 1966), 146–82. See also A. H. Arslanian and Robert L. Nichols, "Nationalism and the Russian Civil War: The Case of Volunteer Army-Armenian Relations, 1918– 1920," *Soviet Studies* 31, no. 4 (October 1979), 559–73.

discredit the leaders of the nationalities before the diplomats and statesmen of the Entente, whose aid all anti-Bolshevik centers needed to ensure their success. First, during the Central Rada period—November 1917 to April 1918—they presented Ukrainian political leaders as Austro-German agents who, like the Bolsheviks, were hired to help dismember Russia. Subsequently, they mercilessly reviled Skoropads'kyi and the conservative members of his government as opportunists who betrayed Russia for personal interests and ambitions. During the initial months of the UNR Directory—November 1918 to January 1919—they linked the Ukrainian leaders with the Bolsheviks. Finally, when the war between the Soviets and the Directory erupted and the Ukrainian government unequivocally manifested its pro-Entente orientation, the Whites repeatedly stressed instead the weaknesses and shortcomings of the Ukrainian army.

Although shortly after the formation of the first VA advisory body, the Political Council, Gen. Alekseev was persuaded to form a Department of Nationalities headed by the Polish socialist Wendziagolski, the department disappeared along with the Political Council during the disastrous winter campaign of 1918. The Political Council's successor, the Special Council established at Shul'gin's initiative in the autumn of 1918, did not have a separate department or committee for nationalities. This lack did not seem to be a problem, because the important question of relations with the nationalities was conducted by Denikin himself:

> The question of the nationalities as well as its closely related [question]—the territorial structure of the Russian state, was resolved in full harmony by me and all members of the Special Council: the unity of Russia, regional autonomy, and broad decentralization ... [and] relations with the new [state] formations were conducted by me personally, together with the chairman of the Special Council, his office, and with the cooperation of the chief of staff of the Military Department, in particular on questions related to military matters and military representation. During the weekly meetings of the Special Council under my chairmanship, I apprised its members of the measures undertaken, frequently asking their advice, [and] never encountering any serious difference of opinion.[2]

That Denikin, in spite of his heavy load of responsibilities as the commander in chief, took it upon himself to direct relations with the nationalities without even appointing an advisory committee is indicative of the importance he imparted to this problem and of the simplicity of the principles that guided the VA's relations with the emerging states: preserving

---

2. Denikin, *Ocherki*, 4: 216–17.

the unity of Russia meant the consistent negation of all meaningful political aspirations in Russia's former borderlands.

When, at the end of 1918, the prospect of Entente aid opened new vistas for the VA and when, in December, Denikin's authority spread to Odessa, Ekaterinodar welcomed Shul'gin's initiative establishing a Provisional Commission on the Nationality Question. The commission was chaired by Shul'gin himself; Vasilii A. Stepanov was its vice-chairman. It was divided into several sections. The "Little Russian" section consisted of former professors of Odessa's New Russia University, Ivan A. Lynnychenko, M. Liapunov, Andrei D. Bilimovich (an expert in agrarian affairs), and A. I. Savenko. The work of the section was closely supervised by Shul'gin. The Caucasian and Transcaucasian section was headed by Stepanov; the Bessarabian, by A. I. Krupenskii; the Belarusian, by a former member of the State Duma, V. A. Kadygrobov; and the Russian, by E. Efimovskii. Prof. Pavel I. Novgorodtsev also actively participated in the work of the commission.[3] Its headquarters were initially located in Odessa, where the commission was founded and where most of its members were residing. Its chief task was to determine the future structure of the Russian state and to elucidate the White movement's position on the nationality question.

After the French evacuation of Odessa in early April 1919, the commission moved to Ekaterinodar, where the need for its assistance began to be acutely felt after VA's impressive military successes in the late spring and summer of 1919. From the start the commission's work was guided by the principles of the inviolability of Russia's prewar borders, with the exception of Poland, and the reconstruction of a unitary state. It unequivocally rejected federation, arguing that its juridical principles—agreement and mutual reciprocity—violated the idea of the national unity of Russia and would create dangerous precedents and insurmountable problems for any future all-Russian authority.[4] The rejection of federation meant in practice the denial of all political claims made by the nationalities. What was difficult was reconciling this rigid and uncompromising position on the nationality question with the liberal principles enunciated in the VA's political program, that is, the guarantee of full civil liberties and freedom of religion, the convocation of a National Assembly elected on the basis of universal suffrage, immediate agrarian reforms to meet the land needs of the toiling masses, and the immediate preparation of labor legislation safeguarding the working class against exploitation by capitalists or the state.

3. Azbuka report, Odessa, 14 February 1919, Maklakov Archive, series B, box 20, Ukraine; Report of meeting, 10 January 1919, Wrangel Military Archives, file 130; Denikin, *Ocherki,* 4: 217 and 5: 139; D. Kin, *Denikinshchina* (Leningrad: Priboi, 1927), 240.
4. Denikin, *Ocherki,* 5: 138.

The solution found was substituting regional autonomy for national autonomy. Thus article four of the political program promised broad decentralization of power through the establishment of regional autonomy and local self-government.[5] It was the task of the nationality commission to assure that this regional autonomy would be specifically designed to weaken the centrifugal forces in the former multinational empire. The criteria by which the autonomous regions (*oblasti*) would be delimited varied widely and were generally approached from the point of view of what was best for Russia's unity.[6] Thus Northern Caucasia, whose numerous Muslim ethnic groups tended toward unification with each other, an inclination viewed as potentially dangerous and hostile to Russia, was divided into small units based on ethnographic criteria. These territorial units, Dagestan, Ossetia, Ingushetia, Kabarda, and Chechnia, were to be amalgamated into a large North Caucasian *oblast'* together with former Stavropol *krai* and the southern part of Astrakhan gubernia, regions populated predominantly by Russians. In Ukraine, which was inhabited by the largest ethnic minority in the empire, the opposite principle was to be applied: the ethnic boundaries established by the Central Rada and the hetman's government were to be erased; instead, the territory was to be divided into three separate, autonomous regions: Kyiv, Kharkiv, and New Russia.[7] While the division of territories occupied by the VA into separate *oblasti* was partly realized in Caucasia and Ukraine, the implementation of regional autonomy was never even begun. Because most of the land under VA control remained a zone of military operations throughout the civil war, it was governed according to extraordinary, provisional measures by an appointed governor-general who had virtually unlimited authority.

By the spring of 1919 the nationalities of Northern Caucasia had been brought under the secure control of the White authorities. This control enabled Denikin to move his troops in the direction of Tsaritsyn (now Volgograd) and northwest into Ukraine. Instead of concentrating his forces on the northeastern front—as he was strongly urged to do by one of his better commanders, Gen. Wrangel—so that the Volunteers could join the Siberian forces advancing at this time toward the Russian heartland, Denikin chose instead to move his best troops, the core of the VA commanded by Gen. Mai-Maevskii, into Ukraine.[8] By the end of summer the VA had advanced as far as Kyiv.

5. Ibid., 4: 215–16, n. 2.
6. Ibid., 5: 141.
7. Ibid., 5: 140.
8. Denikin's military strategies and tactics in the spring and summer of 1919 are described in detail in his *Ocherki*, 5: 72–84, 104–37. For criticism of Denikin's strategy, see P. N. Wrangel, *Always with Honor* (New York: Robert Speller and Sons, 1957), 70–99.

On the eve of entering the Ukrainian capital, the VA leaders published a memorandum outlining their nationality program for Ukraine. This document, which was addressed "To the Inhabitants of Little Russia," was prepared by the Special Council's Department of Education. At the end of August 1919 it appeared in all newspapers published in VA-occupied territories.[9] The chief aim of the VA, the memorandum announced, was the restoration of Russia's unity, which was presented as indispensable for the preservation of the state's independence and for the normal functioning and full development of its economic life. Russia's enemies, the document proceeded to explain, desired to weaken the Russian state and therefore promoted a movement that had as its aim the separation from Russia of its nine southern gubernias into a formation called the Ukrainian State. "The desire to sever the Little Russian branch of the Russian people from Russia has not been abandoned even today," the memorandum warned. "The former German appointees, Petliura and his partisans, having laid the foundations for the dismemberment of Russia, are continuing even now to promote the evil cause—the establishment of an independent 'Ukrainian State.'" But this dangerous movement directed against the resurrection of Russia, the memorandum explained, should be clearly differentiated from local efforts "inspired by the love of the native land, its peculiarities, its local antiquity, and its local vernacular language." Therefore full respect was promised for the "peculiarities of the local way of life," including the use of the "Little Russian" language, but the "Great Russian" language was to be reinstituted as the state language in all governmental institutions and public schools. People desiring to use the local language in the local courts and institutions of self-government would be permitted to do so.

Similarly, private schools were to be permitted to conduct lectures in whichever language they desired. In addition, during the first years of elementary education in state-supported schools, the "Little Russian" language was to be permitted in order to make it easier for children to become acquainted with the first principles of learning. Full freedom of the press was promised. While the division of Ukraine into three separate regions was not mentioned, broad decentralization and the establishment of local self-government institutions was promised. In conclusion Denikin exhorted all inhabitants of the "South Russian regions" to support the VA cause:

> According to God's will, the South Russian regions have been invested with the honor and great responsibility to be the support and source of reinforcement for the armies marching confidently toward the restoration of *One*

---

9. Denikin, *Ocherki*, 5: 142–3; "K naseleniiu Malorossii," *Velikaia Rossiia*, 15 (28) August 1919.

Russia. In the struggle for *Russia One and Indivisible*, I am appealing to all faithful sons of the Motherland to support actively the army bringing salvation to the masses suffering under the Bolshevik yoke. Let all for whom the happiness and greatness of the Motherland and the success of our armies in their forward march toward the heart of *Russia—Moscow*[10]—is dear work indefatigably for the formation and reinforcement of the rear and support the brave men suffering at the front for the greatness and unity of Russia.[11]

No other document promulgated by the White leaders recalled the tone and the spirit of the bygone era as vividly as this appeal. It had little in common with the succinct and rather staid pronouncement usually issued by VA Headquarters. That the reserved and self-effacing Denikin chose at this time to assume the pose of a benevolent tsar addressing his faithful subjects in "Little Russia" is astonishing, even if one takes into consideration the purely propagandistic intent of the proclamation. Such theatricality was atypical of Denikin.

Of course, the commander in chief of the White forces, who was at the time preoccupied with one of his most ambitious military campaigns, did not author the appeal. It was put together by two illustrious Kadets, I. I. Malinin, the head of the Department of Education in the Special Council, and Novgorodtsev, the eminent jurist and distinguished scholar of Moscow University. The appeal was obviously addressed primarily to the unsophisticated peasant masses constituting the bulk of Ukraine's population and to the apolitical, conservative landed gentry still deeply attached to the local language and folklore but out of sympathy with the radical politics of the Ukrainian independence movement. It was hoped that the limited cultural rights promised in the appeal would win the confidence of the former and assure the enthusiastic support of the latter.

It is important to point out that underneath the bombastic and inflated patriotic verbiage of the document lay hidden the most widely accepted view on the nationality question held by the Western-oriented Russian intelligentsia. It was customarily argued in progressive circles both before and after the 1917 revolution that in a multinational state undergoing rapid socioeconomic changes, the national development of the minorities was doomed. All manifestations of nationalism in Russia's borderlands were interpreted as either an echo of nineteenth-century romanticism or the consequence of the highly oppressive tsarist nationality policy. It was the unenlightened, humiliating

---

10. On 3 July 1919 Denikin announced his ambitious plan to march on Moscow. In the fall of that year the VA advanced as far as Tula.

11. Denikin, *Ocherki*, 5: 142–3.

treatment of the nationalities by reactionary tsarist authorities that was primarily responsible for the emergence of political nationalism among the non-Russians. Consequently it was taken for granted that once the most oppressive restrictions that had been imposed on the national minorities were lifted, nationalism in the border regions would fade away. This was a great oversimplification of an important and complicated issue, but Denikin's political advisors were not the only ones blindly holding to this interpretation.

The token cultural rights promised to the Ukrainians in the appeal were contradicted by the overzealous efforts of the newly appointed White administrators to destroy all manifestations of "Ukrainian conspiracy." Consequently the first weeks of Denikin's rule in Ukraine were marked by a chilling wave of White terror. Thousands of people, primarily members of the Ukrainian intelligentsia, were imprisoned, tortured, and even executed. In Odessa alone, 3,000 men were summarily shot, while in Katerynoslav and Kharkiv executed victims were left to hang for days from gallows constructed in the central squares to instill fear among the masses.[12] Busts of highly revered Ukrainian poets were desecrated, and Ukrainian reading rooms, libraries, and cultural institutions were demolished.

Even though at the time the memorandum on the Ukrainian question was promulgated the Bolsheviks still occupied Kyiv, the document mentioned them only in passing. The entire thrust of the attack in the declaration was against the Directory, in particular against its leader Petliura, because in the summer of 1919 the UNR Army, and not the Bolsheviks, represented the greatest threat to Denikin in Ukraine. At the same time that the VA approached Kyiv from the east, the forces of the Directory were rapidly advancing from the west while clearing Right-Bank Ukraine of the Bolsheviks. The declaration was promulgated precisely when the two armies were about to meet.

Denikin and the UNR Directory

VA Headquarters in Ekaterinodar were supplied through a wide net of intelligence agents with detailed data not only about the fighting ability of the UNR Army and the work of the Directory's emissaries in the West, but also about the mood in the Ukrainian countryside.[13] Even though Denikin and his political advisors tended to minimize the social and economic aspects of the struggle, they could not completely overlook them, especially when it became

---

12. A. D. Skaba et al, eds, *Ukraïns'ka RSR v period hromadianskoï viiny 1917–1920 rr.,* vol. 2 (Kyiv: Vydavnytstvo politichnoï literatury Ukraïny, 1968), 343–4; Kin, 241.
13. Intelligence reports, Wrangel Military Archives, files 131, 145, 148, 151, 166.

obvious that the support of the local population was the decisive factor in the outcome of the war. When reporting on the political currents in the villages, most agents tended to agree that in Ukraine, as in other parts of the former empire, the peasants were primarily interested in land. As to everything else, great confusion prevailed in the peasant mind. It was clear, however, that the slogan of "Russia One and Indivisible" was not popular among the masses because, as one agent pointed out, "it is always connected either with the Bolsheviks or the Black Hundreds."[14] The question of an independent Ukraine also did not seem to be important to the rural inhabitants: "the masses are more or less indifferent to this question: it is something they understand little, [and] it is something that involves their interests to a very small degree."[15] The typical reasoning in the rural communities seemed to be: "We should not separate from Russia, but a border must be established for we are being mercilessly plundered."[16]

In the early spring of 1919 widespread peasant dissatisfaction with the Bolshevik regime was reported. "In Ukraine the Bolsheviks rule only in the large cities. In the smaller towns they are being sporadically overthrown. In the villages there is no trace of their rule."[17] Nonetheless, certain rural communities, some agents reported, considered themselves Bolshevik but were careful to distinguish themselves as "Ukrainian Bolsheviks." "Bolshevism" they understood as full freedom to own and dispose of land.[18] By the summer of 1919 peasant uprisings against the Soviet authorities became widespread, and sizable peasant armies began roaming the countryside. The leaders of these guerrilla bands emerged from the village and had pronounced anarchistic tendencies. What VA agents found disturbing was that nationally conscious local Ukrainian intelligentsia, primarily those with socialist leanings, were joining the guerrillas and becoming their leaders. The latter were primarily responsible for the drive to unify the diverse anarchist peasant bands under the slogan of an "Independent Soviet Ukrainian Republic," and their considerable success in this regard was reported already in spring of 1919.[19] According to information provided by VA agents within the UPSR, the party most actively involved in the peasant insurgency, there were approximately 250,000 rural guerrillas in Ukraine.[20] Although no evidence of a direct connection between the peasant insurgents and the Directory had been

---

14. Intelligence report, Spring 1919, Wrangel Military Archives, file 145.
15. Azbuka report, Kyiv, 22 April 1919, Wrangel Military Archives, file 151.
16. Ibid.
17. Azbuka report, Kyiv, 5 May 1919, ibid.
18. Azbuka report, Kyiv, 22 April 1919, ibid.
19. Ibid.
20. Report from Romania on the Ukrainian Insurgent Army, Wrangel Military Archives, file 148.

reported, according to one agent the possibility could not be excluded because of the excellently organized propaganda and agitation apparatus of the Ukrainians. The agent warned that if the VA's propaganda did not reach the village, "the Ukrainians will become the masters in Kyiv."[21]

While intelligence on the military strength of the Directory's army was on the whole negative in the spring of 1919, definite improvement was reported during the summer of that year. Estimates provided by Denikin's agents ranged from 45,000 to 120,000 men.[22] Morale among the officers and rank and file was low even though, as Denikin's agents reported, "dedication, discipline, and obedience is considered the pride of Petliura's army." The agent assured Denikin that if the peasants in the Ukrainian army were given the opportunity to return to their villages, they would abandon Petliura.[23]

Denikin tended to believe the reports stressing the weaknesses rather than strength of the Ukrainian troops. In his discussions with representatives of the Entente military missions, he spoke disparagingly of the Directory's troops, emphasizing their unreliability and isolation. This prompted two British agents visiting VA Headquarters to comment that Denikin was misinformed largely because the information his local agents provided was faulty and, owing to poor communications, impossible to verify. *"Petliura is much stronger than he [Denikin] imagines,"* emphasized British intelligence.[24] According to French intelligence, the Ukrainian army had approximately 55,000 regular troops.[25]

It was primarily because of the rapid rise of the VA in the spring and summer of 1919 and the military successes of the Directory's troops that both Britain and France renewed their efforts to bring about a rapprochement between Denikin and Petliura.

Although after the evacuation of Odessa in April 1919 relations between France and the VA were at a breaking point, they were never completely severed. France continued to evince interest in both the VA and developments in Ukraine. In Ekaterinodar the chief of the French military mission maintained most cordial relations with Denikin,[26] while the French Foreign

---

21. Intelligence report, Spring 1919.
22. Material and moral condition of the Ukrainian army, Summer 1919, Wrangel Military Archives, file 148; Intelligence report, 14 September 1919, Kharkiv, ibid.; Political currents in Little Russia, 14 September 1919, ibid; Intelligence report, 15 November 1919, ibid., file 145.
23. Material and moral condition of the Ukrainian army.
24. A secret British intelligence report intercepted by Russians in Istanbul, in G.H.Q. General Staff, "Intelligence," Constantinople, no. 4794/16 "I", Wrangel Military Archives, file 148.
25. Report from the military representative in Romania, 6 October 1919, ibid.
26. Denikin, *Ocherki,* 5: 169.

Ministry promised the representatives of the Directory in Paris to send a military mission to Kamianets-Podilskyi, the seat of the UNR government.[27]

The task of bringing about cooperation between Denikin and Petliura was entrusted to the French military representative in Romania, Gen. Philippe Pétain, on the direct orders of Clemenceau.[28] Two factors, in addition to the pressure of France and Britain, induced the Ukrainians, who had initiated the negotiations, to undertake this step. First, the Ukrainian army, though not inconsiderable, was in no position to wage war on two fronts, i.e., against the Bolsheviks and the advancing White troops. The second, most important, and new factor was the presence in Kamianets-Podilskyi in the summer of 1919 of the Ukrainian Galician Army (UHA).[29]

The Ukrainian military consisted of two forces: the UNR Army east of the Zbruch River on the territories of the former Russian Empire; and the UHA, which had been struggling with the Poles since November 1918 for the control of Eastern Galicia, formerly a part of the Austro-Hungarian Empire. Both armies operated under separate commands but had Petliura as their commander in chief. The Galicians also had their own government and had proclaimed their own state, the Western Ukrainian People's Republic (ZUNR), which was united in January 1919 with the UNR but retained a broad measure of autonomy. At that time Evhen Petrushevych, the head of the Western Ukrainian government since November 1918, became a member of the Directory. In mid-July 1919, after nine months of heavy fighting with the Poles, the UHA and Petrushevych's government had to retreat into territory east of the Zbruch River. While the Polish victory was a heavy blow, the cessation of hostilities on the Polish-Ukrainian front enabled the Ukrainians to direct their combined forces against the Bolsheviks and thus to clear them from Right-Bank Ukraine during the summer of 1919.

Although their anti-Bolshevik offensive was going well, differences between the two Ukrainian armies soon arose. The Galicians were bitterly disappointed that Petliura had decided to end the war with Poland and were uneasy about the possibility of an alliance between Petliura and Józef Piłsudski at the expense of Eastern Galicia. To forestall such a possibility, they pressured the UNR government to seek an anti-Bolshevik alliance with the VA. Cooperation between the Ukrainians and Denikin was precisely what France and Britain had been trying to achieve since the end of the First World War. Because the future of Eastern Galicia, now that Ukrainian military operations against Poland had ended, hinged on the decision of the Paris Peace Conference, an alliance with Denikin would create a favorable

---

27. Margolin, *Ukraïna i polityka Antanty,* 145–6, 372–4.
28. Denikin, *Ocherki,* 5: 255.
29. I. Mazepa, *Ukraïna v ohni i buri revoliutsiï, 1917–1921,* v. 2 (Munich: Prometei, 1951), 3.

impression on the representatives of the Great Powers who would determine the fate of Eastern Galicia. According to the prime minister of the UNR, Isaak Mazepa, it was primarily Galician pressure that prompted the Directory to seek reconciliation with Denikin.[30]

Intelligence reports from the Directory's agents in Ekaterinodar consistently emphasized that anti-Ukrainian feelings at VA Headquarters were strong, the attitude there toward the Directory was uncompromisingly hostile, and therefore the ground was not ready for sending an official delegation to Denikin.[31] The UNR government decided, therefore, to approach the VA indirectly through its diplomatic mission in Bucharest. It was in the Romanian capital that Gen. Pétain mediated a meeting between Col. Stryzhevs'kyi, a member of the Ukrainian mission, and Gen. A. Gerua, the VA representative in Romania. Stryzhevs'kyi presented the Directory's proposal: the Ukrainians were willing to participate in the formation of a united anti-Bolshevik offensive under Denikin's command; all political questions were to be suspended for the duration of the anti-Bolshevik war, with the understanding that the Volunteers would march under the slogan of "Russia One and Indivisible," and the Directory, under the flag of an independent Ukraine; but after the victory over Bolshevism hostilities between the two anti-Bolshevik camps would resume.[32] To this proposal Gerua responded that the VA would not undertake any hostile action against the UNR Army provided there was a united command.[33] This reply was interpreted at UNR Army Headquarters as a positive sign, and orders were immediately issued by the Ukrainian General Staff to cease hostile activities against the VA and, if possible, to reach an agreement with it based on demarcated zones of separate activities.[34]

It was largely because of this directive that the VA was able to enter Kyiv on 31 August 1919 unopposed by the Ukrainian troops already in the city.[35] In fact, the latter complied with the demand of the VA commander, Gen. N. Bredov, to evacuate Kyiv and withdraw southwest of the city. That Gen. Antin Kravs, the commander of Ukrainian military operations in Kyiv, was from the UHA facilitated matters greatly, and the Ukrainians agreed to withdraw on the understanding that negotiations for an agreement between representatives of the two armies would immediately commence. Shortly

30. Ibid.
31. Ibid.
32. Ibid., 63–4; Denikin, *Ocherki,* 5: 255.
33. Mazepa, 64.
34. M. Kapustians'kyi, *Pokhid ukraïnskykh armii na Kyïv–Odesu v 1919 rotsi (Korotkyi voienno-istorychnyi ohliad),* 2d ed., vol. 2 (Munich: S. Sliusarchuk, 1946), 161; Mazepa, 64.
35. Mazepa, 67–8; Intelligence report from Lt. Rashevskii, Wrangel Military Archives, file 183.

thereafter, however, an official delegation of the Ukrainian General Staff headed by Gen. Mykhailo Omelianovych-Pavlenko was bluntly informed by Bredov that no negotiations were possible.[36] A meeting between Omelianovych-Pavlenko and Gen. Nepenin of the VA did take place, however, with Bredov's knowledge and approval. On behalf of the Ukrainian General Staff, Omelianovych-Pavlenko proposed an agreement on joint military operations against the Bolsheviks based on zones of activity for the two armies. Negotiations were soon prorogued pending new directives from VA Headquarters.[37] They were never resumed, and at the end of September hostilities between the Ukrainians and the White forces broke out.[38]

While it is clear that Denikin wished to avoid hostilities with Petliura's forces at this juncture, he had no intention of concluding a military alliance with the Directory. Shortly after the occupation of the Ukrainian capital, the VA commander in chief's directives to his field commanders were as firm and unrelenting as before the Kyiv interlude:

> An independent Ukraine is not recognized. Petliura's men either can remain neutral, in which case they should immediately lay down their arms and disperse, or they should join us, recognizing our slogans, one of which is broad autonomy for the borderlands. If they will not accept these conditions, they should be considered enemies just as the Bolsheviks.[39]

Denikin continued to maintain this uncompromising attitude toward the Ukrainians in spite of continuing external pressure. At the end of August 1919 Winston Churchill, the British war minister, appealed by telegram to Denikin to exercise great caution with respect to the Ukrainian movement for independence and "to meet, as far as possible, the Ukrainian separatist strivings half way,"[40] and two British visitors at VA Headquarters, Gens. Heroys and Keyes, discussed this matter thoroughly with the White commander. Similarly, the representative of the United States Military Mission in Warsaw, Edgar Jadwin, worked energetically to bring about an alliance between Denikin and Petliura. Maklakov too, in his frequent messages from Paris, urged that all conflicts with the Ukrainians be avoided because, according to rumors, the Directory had concluded a military alliance with the Poles against the Bolsheviks. Although the Russian ambassador doubted that

---

36. Ibid.
37. Denikin, *Ocherki*, 5: 257.
38. Mazepa, 81–3; Denikin, *Ocherki*, 5: 254.
39. Denikin, *Ocherki*, 5: 257.
40. Telegram, Tatishchev (Denikin) to Giers (Rome), 29 August 1919, Giers Archives, box 40, file 97, Ukraine; Denikin, *Ocherki*, 5: 255.

in the event of conflict between the VA and Petliura the Poles would side with the Ukrainians, he considered it prudent to bring such a possibility to Denikin's attention.[41] The indefatigable Russian diplomat once again tried to influence Denikin indirectly through his colleagues, this time right-wing Kadets who had some connections with Ekaterinodar. Early in September 1919 he sent a personal letter through Margolin, the former Ukrainian foreign minister, to Mikhail V. Chelnokov and Fedor I. Rodichev asking the two eminent Kadets to use their influence in persuading Denikin to meet some of the demands of the Directory and to open negotiations with Petliura.[42] In his reply Chelnokov informed Maklakov that an alliance with Petliura or any separatist government was unthinkable. Experience had proven, confidently asserted the Kadet leader, that Denikin's nationality policy was the only correct one. After all, the Bolsheviks were able to defeat the Ukrainians in February 1919 "solely because they raised the banner of 'Great Russia—One and Indivisible.'" In any case, there was no cause for concern, pointed out Chelnokov. Both he and Rodichev were confident that "Denikin, under the guidance of Astrov, Fedorov, [N. N.] Chebyshev, and [Viktor N.] Chelishev [all members of the Kadet party], would find a way to assure the *khokhly* [a derogatory term for the Ukrainians] the right to use their own language [and have] their own schools, theater, folk dancing, etc., which is known as 'cultural self-determination.'"[43]

Offensive epithets were not reserved for the Ukrainians only. What appeared to upset the respected Russian liberals was not only Maklakov's importunate suggestion that he would mediate between the VA and Petliura, but also the Russian ambassador's choice of an intermediary. Margolin, a former diplomat of the Directory, was a prominent Jewish lawyer in prerevolutionary Ukraine. It was on him that Chelnokov vented his spleen: "I personally would advise you" he wrote to Maklakov, "that negotiations be conducted by persons resembling, at least, Little Russians, and not by Petersburg lawyers, Galician doctors, Moscow shopkeepers, and Jews fond of ministerial portfolios and automobiles who now parade under the guise of 'Ukrainians.'"[44] Several days later, perhaps on Rodichev's advice, Chelnokov attempted to soften the vitriolic tone of his reply, but as the following postscript indicates, with little success:

---

41. Maklakov (Paris) to Neratov (Denikin), 3 September 1919; Maklakov (Paris) to Omsk (Kolchak), 8 September 1919, Giers Archives, box 40, file 97, Ukraine.
42. Letter, M. V. Chelnokov (Belgrade) to Maklakov (Paris), 17 September 1919, Maklakov Archive, series B, box 20, Ukraine.
43. Ibid.
44. Ibid.

After rereading the letter, I fear that you may interpret my outburst against Petliura and the separatists as applicable to our Little Russians in general. We all here recognize the need to meet the legitimate demands of the Little Russians, but we do not want to play into the hands of the Galician masters of intrigue of the Austrian school and of various business dealers who agreed in Odessa to form an independent government for Odessa. For these gentlemen [an allusion to Protofis] it makes no difference what kind of government it is: Ukrainian, Estonian, Latvian, Georgian, or Odessan, so long as they have an automobile and a ministerial visiting card.... All of them have repeatedly made slighting remarks regarding Denikin: that he is a reactionary, that he kills the Jews, etc. Margolin too began to sing a similar tune here.[45]

In the beginning of September, pressure on the VA Command to cooperate with the Ukrainian anti-Bolshevik forces came from unexpected quarters—from Admiral Kolchak, since June 1919 Denikin's nominal superior. In a telegram sent on 3 September 1919 Kolchak explained that he was fully aware of the harmful nature of Petliura's separatist activities but advised that "at this time the aim of our work is to unite all elements capable of helping in the struggle against the Bolsheviks, and for this purpose it is considered desirable in all cases to establish local cooperation not predetermining the future structure of Russia."[46] Kolchak proposed that a demarcation line be drawn designating separate zones of operations between the VA and Petliura's forces in accordance with the territories occupied by the two armies. Although Petliura's claims to territories occupied by the VA should not be recognized, instructed Kolchak, the Volunteers should not attempt to occupy cities already in Petliura's hands. Such a policy would win the support of the Entente while not violating the principle of the unity of Russia.[47]

No amount of persuasion and pressure could move Denikin. In his talks with the British emissaries he stressed the unreliability of the Ukrainian forces, noting that while Petliura was of no practical use to him, he could prove dangerous to the VA's rear. Therefore he urged the Entente states to withdraw their support from the Ukrainian cause and to inform Petliura once and for all that he would not receive any aid from them.[48] The Ukrainian leader, Denikin maintained, was a chauvinist and an unscrupulous opportunist who, with Romanian support, German money, and an aura of importance

---

45. Ibid.
46. Sukin (Omsk) to Minister (Rome), 3 September 1919, Giers Archives, box 40, file 97, Ukraine.
47. Ibid.
48. Secret report of British intelligence intercepted by the Russians in Istanbul.

given to him by French recognition, had gathered in one corner of Ukraine what amounted to little more than a rabble. For the sake of peace in Europe, Denikin stressed, Petliura's movement should not be encouraged.[49]

In reply to Kolchak and Maklakov's urging to come to terms with Petliura, Denikin stressed neither the weakness nor the opportunism of the Ukrainian movement. His explanation for rejecting any form of joint action was much more direct: "With respect to cooperation with the Ukrainians, no agreement on our part with them is possible. Recognition of Petliura and cooperation with him would be recognition of the dismemberment of Russia.[50]"

That definite advantage could be derived from a concerted joint anti-Bolshevik struggle of the VA and UNR Army was obvious not only to the Entente leaders and to Kolchak and Maklakov in Paris, but also to some individuals closer to Ekaterinodar. When hostilities between the Volunteers and the Ukrainians erupted, P. M. Ageev, the vice-president of the Don Cossack Krug, exclaimed in desperation:

> Petliura's troops, officially known as the Ukrainian Republican Armies, had fought against the Bolsheviks and had driven them out of Podillia, Volynia, and part of Kyiv gubernia.... That means that in the struggle against the Bolsheviks we had an ally who had diverted part of the Soviet armies against itself. That means that one should have made an agreement with it in order to struggle together against the principal enemy, the Bolsheviks. Instead of that, what do we see? General Shtakel'berg was ordered to attack the Ukrainians if they refused to subordinate themselves to the VA Command. And horror! Instead of an ally, a new, unnecessary front has opened—to the rejoicing of the Bolsheviks and to our misfortune.[51]

The lowest figure cited by VA intelligence regarding Petliura's troops was 45,000 men. In view of new information regarding direct ties between the Directory and Ukrainian peasant insurgent leaders, the Ukrainian army was a force to be reckoned with.[52] Yet Denikin continued to be adamant in his refusal to consider an alliance with it. His inflexibility at this critical juncture

---

49. Ibid.
50. Neratov (Denikin) to Minister (Giers), 18 September 1919, Giers Archives, box 40, file 97, Ukraine.
51. Quoted in Pokrovskii, 237–8. Ageev's letter, which was read at the opening ceremonies of the Kuban Rada, was met with enthusiastic applause. Thousands of copies were distributed throughout the Kuban.
52. Political currents in Little Russia, 10 September 1919, Wrangel Military Archives, file 148; Report on the Makhno movement, 31 October 1919, ibid., file 166.

for the White struggle can be explained by the fact that since the summer of 1919 White leaders had persistently tried to weaken the Ukrainian army by estranging from it its better part, the UHA.[53]

Denikin and the Ukrainian Galician Army: An Unholy Alliance

All intelligence reports, no matter how uncomplimentary they were about the Ukrainians' fighting ability, stressed the discipline and excellent training of the UHA troops. At the same time they mentioned the serious friction between the two Ukrainian armies stemming from the Galician leaders's suspicion that Petliura might sacrifice their homeland, Eastern Galicia, to gain an alliance with Poland. Rumors of such an alliance were rampant by September 1919,[54] precisely at a time that Denikin thought it most opportune to deprive Petliura of his best troops. Denikin issued orders to the VA field commanders in Ukraine to "establish friendly relations with the Galicians with the aim of drawing them away from subordination to Petliura."[55] This new course was adopted only after considerable soul-searching by the VA General Command, which reviled the UHA as inveterate Russophobes. Many White officers considered an agreement with the UHA politically unacceptable, no matter how advantageous it was from a military point of view. Shul'gin used all the influence he could muster to try to prevent this alliance, and when it finally materialized, he discerned in it a "German plan to exacerbate relations between the Russians and Poles."[56] Similar sentiments were expressed by Gen. Gerua, the VA representative in Bucharest; he warned Denikin that an alliance with the UHA could seriously aggravate the White movement's relations with the Poles.[57]

Denikin, no doubt, must have given these warnings serious consideration, because precisely when secret talks between the VA and UHA were gaining momentum, a Polish trade and military mission was visiting his headquarters. At this time Poland, too, was at war with the Bolsheviks, and an alliance with

---

53. Material and moral condition of the Ukrainian Army.
54. Report from Warsaw, Dolgov, 14 September 1919, Wrangel Military Archives, file 158; Maklakov (Paris) to Washington (Bekhmeteff), 30 August 1919, Giers Archives, box 40, file 97, Ukraine. Maklakov received the news of Petliura's impending alliance with Poland from members of the ZUNR delegation in Paris.
55. Denikin, *Ocherki*, 5: 257. The first order was issued on 21 August 1919. Several others followed in the early autumn.
56. V. Shul'gin, "Korolevstvo Russkoe," *Velikaiia Rossiia*, 2 (15) November 1919.
57. Report from the military representative in Romania, 6 October 1919, Wrangel Military Archives, file 148.

the newly established state, which was generously subsidized by France, would have been most welcomed by the VA. Denikin cordially greeted the Polish mission headed by Gen. Aleksander Karnicki, his former colleague from the Russian Military Academy, but their talks proved most disappointing. The main stumbling block to military cooperation was the question of the Russo-Polish frontier. While the Polish representatives insisted that an agreement on borders must be concluded before the conclusion of an alliance, Denikin was not willing to make any commitments beyond the recognition of Poland within its ethnic frontiers as designated by the Curzon Line, arguing once again that he had no authority to make any decisions on this matter and that only a future all-Russian government could resolve it.[58]

The arrogance of some members of the Polish mission while in Ekaterinodar, the inactivity on the Polish-Bolshevik front, the silence from Warsaw after Karnicki's departure, and the intelligence reports warning of a secret Polish-Ukrainian alliance[59] led Denikin to believe that no anti-Bolshevik agreement with Poland was possible. Shortly after the news of a de facto armistice between Poland and the Soviets reached Ekaterinodar early in November 1919,[60] the VA commander went ahead with his plans to conclude an agreement with the UHA.

Denikin demanded from the Galicians neither the acceptance of an indivisible Russia nor complete incorporation into his army—terms he had unconditionally demanded from the Directory. According to the agreement concluded in November 1919, the UHA recognized Denikin as the commander in chief but was able to maintain its autonomy; the head of the ZUNR government, Petrushevych, retained authority over the UHA. Political relations between the ZUNR government and the VA, as well as the fate of Eastern Galicia, were to be resolved through political negotiations. The UHA was given assurances that it would not be used against the forces of Petliura.[61]

The agreement was most advantageous militarily to Denikin—without the UHA Petliura could hardly withstand attacks from both the Bolsheviks and the

---

58. Gen. Karnicki, "Pierwsze kroki u Denikina i sprawa mjr. Przezdieckiego," Akty Adiutantury Generalnej Naczelnego Dowództwa, file 20, no. 1827/T2, Józef Piłsudski Institute of America, New York; Denikin, *Ocherki,* 5: 175–7.
59. Report from Paris, 29 September 1919, Wrangel Military Archives, file 148.
60. Piotr S. Wandycz, "Secret Soviet-Polish Peace Talks in 1919," *Slavic Review* 24, no. 3 (September 1965), 425–49.
61. For the text of the agreement, see Osyp Levyts'kyi, "Viiskovyi dohovir Ukraïns'koï Halyts'koï Armiï z Dobrarmieiu hen. Denikina," in *Ukraïnska Halyts'ka Armiia u 40-richchia ïï uchasty u vyzvol'nykh zmahanniakh (materiialy do istoriï),* ed. Myron Dol'nyts'kyi et al, vol. 1 (Winnipeg: Dmytro Mykytiuk, 1958), 484–514; or Mykhailo Lozyns'kyi, *Halychyna v r. 1918–1920* (Vienna: Institut Sociologique Ukrainien, 1922), 198–200; a brief summary is in Denikin, *Ocherki,* 5: 258.

Volunteers—and it did not impinge in any way on the founding principles of the White cause. Though the UHA was fighting for the same objective as Petliura's troops—an independent Ukraine—it was in a different political category. Eastern Galicia had never been part of the Russian Empire except during the wartime occupation of 1914–15. Even though annexation of this territory had constituted one of imperial Russia's war aims, Denikin's principal concern was the restoration of Russia's territorial unity as it existed before the war except for ethnic Poland, whose independence had been recognized by the Provisional Government. Thus provisional recognition of the ZUNR under Petrushevych and a military alliance with the UHA did not violate the principle of Russia's territorial integrity.

It has been argued by leaders of the Directory that the UHA abandoned it precisely when, according to the plan of operations of the UNR Army's General Staff, the joint Ukrainian forces had every chance of surrounding and destroying the VA.[62] After the UHA defected, the UNR Army never fully recovered. Not long thereafter its General Staff had to issue orders to close its regular front and to replace it with a segmental, insurrectionary front under Gen. Omelianovych-Pavlenko in Denikin's rear. In the beginning of December Petliura left for Warsaw, where the ground for an alliance with Piłsudski had been in preparation since the late summer.

Even after the outbreak of hostilities between the Volunteers and the Directory's forces, hopes for a reconciliation between Denikin and Petliura were not given up by either the Russian or Ukrainian diplomats in Paris. It was still considered desirable by the Russian representatives because even though the VA occupied a large part of Ukrainian territory, its control was not secure; it was continually plagued by peasant guerrillas in the southeast and by Omelianovych-Pavlenko's troops in the southwest. In early November 1919 Boris Savinkov, a member of the Russian Political Conference, attempted, through French mediation, to find out from a member of the UNR delegation, Artem Halip, the conditions under which an agreement with the Volunteers would be possible. While Halip indicated that the climate for negotiations was far from favorable and that the Directory's attitude toward Denikin was resolutely hostile, he enumerated three principles that could constitute the basis for a future agreement: (1) Denikin's recognition of the Directory as the legitimate government of Ukraine; (2) the immediate evacuation by the VA from Ukrainian territory; and (3) initiation of the negotiations by the Entente.[63]

While Count Mykhailo Tyshkevych, the head of the UNR delegation in

---

62. Oleksander Lotots'kyi, *Symon Petliura* (Warsaw: Komitet dlia vshanuvannia X richnytsi smerty Symona Petliury, 1936), 23.

63. Report from Paris, 6 November 1919, Wrangel Military Archives, file 172.

Paris, was unequivocally in favor of an alliance with Poland, the other members of the delegation were divided on this issue. Vasyl' Paneiko, a representative of the ZUNR government, and Halip worked energetically to bring about a reconciliation with Denikin and were prepared to accept federation with Russia. According to an intelligence report from Paris, Paneiko was instrumental in bringing about the agreement between the UHA and the White movement.[64] Halip, a close friend of Petliura, exerted strong pressure on the head of the Directory to prevent the eruption of hostilities with the Volunteers. When fierce clashes between the two forces commenced, he pleaded with Petliura to authorize him to begin negotiations with the VA mission in Paris.[65]

By this time Petliura was categorically opposed to reconciliation with the Whites because, in the first place, he felt that the atrocities perpetrated by the White authorities against the Ukrainians in Odessa and Kyiv had made his troops so indignant that "now they do not even want to hear of any agreements with the *moskali*";[66] and secondly, because the UPSR, the party with the largest following in Ukraine, threatened to join the Bolsheviks if an alliance was concluded with Denikin.[67] Instead of working toward a rapprochement with Denikin, Petliura urged Halip to initiate a press campaign to convince the French public that in the future, because of the economic and political forces operating in Europe, the Russians, and not the Ukrainians, would be the natural allies of Germany.[68] On 28 October, through a letter to his friend Jean Pélissier, Petliura appealed to the French people to urge their government to support the Ukrainian movement. The VA, Petliura charged, was the Directory's most dangerous adversary, for instead of fighting the Bolsheviks it had turned against the Ukrainians the artillery and rifles it had received from the Entente, and was applying the same terror as the Soviets against the Ukrainians, thus playing into Bolshevik hands.[69]

Petliura's irreconcilable hostility toward Denikin prevented all attempts at reconciliation between the Ukrainians and Russians even in Paris, even

---

64. Report no. 14, 8 November 1919, Wrangel Military Archives, file 114; Report from Paris, 8 December 1919, ibid., file 172.
65. Report from Paris, 18 October 1919, ibid., file 148; Report from Paris, 4 November 1919, ibid., file 172.
66. Report from Paris, 18 October 1919, ibid., file 148. "*Moskali'*" is a Ukrainian vernacular term for Russians, particularly Russian soldiers.
67. Report from Paris, 4 November 1919, ibid., file 172. A VA agent, Capt. Marynovych, had access to the correspondence between Petliura and Ukrainian diplomats.
68. Report from Paris, 18 October 1919, ibid., file 148.
69. Un appel du président Petlioura a la démocratie française (letter to Jean Pélissier, 22 October 1919), Hoover Institution; *Symon Petliura: Statti, lysty, dokumenty*, vol. 1, ed. L. Drazhevs'ka et al (New York: Ukrainian Academy of Arts and Sciences in the U.S., 1956), 236–8.

though the diplomats' mood was rather conciliatory. Because of Denikin's military reverses, by mid-November even those Ukrainians in Paris who had strongly urged cooperation with the Volunteers were inclined to favor an alliance with Poland and Romania.[70] In November 1919 Denikin's agents in Warsaw observed increased contacts between the Polish government and the Ukrainian diplomats as the Polish attitude toward the Russians became more arrogant and hostile. "The Russians in Warsaw have *no rights*," complained one agent. "The position adopted by the government and those in authority toward Russia is the following: 'We want the Bolsheviks to struggle against Denikin, and Denikin to struggle against the Bolsheviks.' Taking advantage of the civil war in Russia, they want to derive as much benefit as possible."[71]

By this time it was sufficiently clear to the Russian agents in Warsaw that a powerful and united Russia was not viewed as advantageous by Poland. Poland regarded a chain of buffer states between it and Russia over which it could maintain influence as much more expedient. An independent Ukraine figured prominently in this plan, and thus an alliance between Piłsudski and Petliura was a logical step in Poland's designs in Eastern Europe. What was most disturbing, one report observed, was that a Polish-Ukrainian alliance had the full backing of France.[72] The latter, having lost influence at Denikin's Headquarters and faith in the success of the Volunteer cause, wanted at least to salvage its interests in Southern Ukraine.

By the late fall of 1919 France was in favor of terminating its intervention. Instead it wanted to concentrate on aiding Poland and other states on Russia's western frontier "in order to dam up the Russian flood and to provide a check to Germany."[73] A strong stand against continuing aid to the White cause was also taken by Lloyd George in the House of Commons. The British prime minister openly questioned whether a White "Russia One and Indivisible" was in the interest of Great Britain.[74] Privately he confided that he was in favor of Russia's dismemberment and the recognition of the border states.[75]

The danger of the withdrawal of Entente aid, no matter how insignificant it was, and the possibility of a Polish-Ukrainian alliance against Russia were heavy blows to the White cause at a time when (the late autumn and early

---

70. Reports from Paris, 8 and 10 November 1919, Wrangel Military Archives, file 172.
71. Reports from Warsaw, 19 and 24 November 1919, Wrangel Military Archives, file 158.
72. Report from Warsaw, 12 September 1919, ibid.
73. E. L. Woodward et al., eds. *Documents on British Foreign Policy, 1919–1939*, vol. 2 (London: H. M. Stationery Office, 1949), 744–5.
74. Great Britain, *Parliamentary Debates,* 5th series, House of Commons, vol. 121, 721–4; Denikin, *Ocherki,* 5: 171.
75. Cited in Brinkley, 220.

winter of 1919) Denikin suffered his most crushing defeats. The VA's hold over Ukraine was brief. Under heavy attacks by the Bolshevik armies in Left-Bank Ukraine and eastern Volynia and suffering heavy casualties and reverses as a result of peasant uprisings and attacks by Omelianovych-Pavlenko's troops in their rear, the Volunteers were compelled to retreat in the direction of their base at Novorossiisk in the winter of 1919–20.

Denikin's outright rejection of a truce with the Directory, which would have enabled him to direct his troops against the Bolsheviks instead of being embroiled in a simultaneous struggle with the Red and UNR armies, was only one factor that contributed to his defeat in Ukraine. Of major importance were his social, economic, and administrative policies. Yet, as already pointed out, one would look in vain for the restoration of the monarchy or political reaction in the VA's social and economic program. Indeed, with the exception of denying the non-Russian peoples of the former empire the right of self-determination, the VA's political objectives coincided rather closely with the Provisional Government's. In spite of strong pressure from the right to proclaim the restoration of the monarchy as one of the VA's aims, Denikin consistently refused to do so, to the great chagrin of his opponents and even some of his close colleagues.

With respect to the agrarian question, which was of major significance in Ukraine, not only was a committee of the Special Council working on a reform that transferred land to smallholders, but Denikin issued provisional orders protecting the peasants against the seizure of their land by former owners.[76] Similarly, labor legislation introduced an eight-hour workday, workers' insurance, labor unions, health and safety inspections, programs to improve living conditions, measures to end unemployment, and institutions to arbitrate labor-management disputes in July 1919.[77] As soon as the VA entered Ukraine, its Department of Internal Affairs broadly publicized its intention to establish organs of self-government and to make special efforts to assure that the new administrative posts would be occupied by individuals "with broad worldviews who enjoy the confidence of the people" and whose careers were untainted by association with the tsarist bureaucratic regime.[78]

What sounded most promising in theory failed completely in practice. No Ukrainian territory was occupied by the VA long enough for it to establish peace and order. Thus in spite of Denikin's orders, previous landlords hastened to reclaim their possessions; because of the general chaos, they were

76. Denikin, *Ocherki*, 4: 212, 223.
77. Ibid.
78. *Velikaia Rossiia*, 15 (28) August 1919.

able to do so with impunity.[79] Similarly, the shortage of administrative personnel compelled the Department of Internal Affairs to turn to former tsarist bureaucrats who, as Denikin admits, "were tied to the past and tried to recreate this past in both form and spirit."[80]

Even the token cultural rights guaranteed in Denikin's widely publicized "Appeal to the Little Russian People" were not respected. Instead, White administrators zealously uprooted all manifestations of "Ukrainian conspiracy," and the closing of Ukrainian cultural societies, clubs, and cooperatives became widespread in the territories under VA control. With the appointment of Gen. Dragomirov, Shul'gin's close friend, as governor-general of the Kyiv region, and of Savenko, a notorious Ukrainophobe, as head of the Department of Propaganda in Kyiv, persecution of everything Ukrainian was, if not condoned, at least tolerated by the authorities. Shul'gin's group in Kyiv—the Bloc of Russian Voters—demanded that the VA authorities "ignore completely all peculiarities of the Little Russian land." Their objective was the eradication of Ukrainian culture, and they urged a most resolute and uncompromising struggle to that end.[81] Consequently all Ukrainian schools and papers and journals, irrespective of their content or political orientation, were shut down, and the sale of Ukrainian books, including titles permitted under the tsarist regime, was prohibited. Proprietors were ordered to replace the Ukrainian signs on their storefronts with Russian signs, and were fined heavily if they did not do so. The well-known writer Vladimir Korolenko described the arrogant and insulting manner in which this order was implemented: "on the streets of Poltava the following episode became a frequent occurence. A Volunteer would approach a group of local inhabitants and ask them to help him take down a sign in the 'language of dogs.' The offended bystanders do not make a move. The Volunteer then brings down the sign with the aid of his rifle, angrily banging with it on the [sign's] tin plate. The tin plate responds with subversive resistance."[82]

Such practices could not but elicit widespread criticism both in the occupied territories and abroad. The school board of Poltava gubernia resolved to ignore the VA authorities' directives to reintroduce Russian as the language of instruction in local schools, arguing that Denikin's order was "contrary to the principles of autonomy, was disrupting school activity, [and] demoralizing both teachers and students because it contradicted the basic principles of peda-

---

79. G. N. Rakovskii, *V stane belykh: Grazhdanskaia voina na iuge Rossii* (Istanbul: Pressa, 1920), 1–13.
80. Denikin, *Ocherki*, 4: 218.
81. Kin, 241; Denikin, *Ocherki*, 5: 243–4; Skaba, 2: 348–9.
82. Quoted in Skaba, 2: 349.

gogy."[83] The Poltava Central Committee of the Kadet party issued an appeal to the Special Council strongly urging the continuation of state support for Ukrainian schools and cultural institutions, arguing that only the free development of the Ukrainian language would draw the Russian and Ukrainian cultures closer together and win the confidence of the local intelligentsia. Otherwise Ukrainian cultural endeavors would be driven underground, where the differences rather than similarities between the two cultures would be emphasized.[84]

The VA's policies in Ukraine mobilized opposition even among the relatively passive Ukrainian clergy. The governor of Katerynoslav gubernia accused all clerics, including Archbishop Ahapit Vyshnevs'kyi, of actively opposing the White authorities and demanded that the archbishop and his associates be removed from the eparchy because they inspired others to pursue the ideals guiding the Ukrainian movement.[85]

While local organizations' protests against the indiscriminate persecution of Ukrainian culture were generally ignored, the White authorities, always sensitive about their reputation in France and Great Britain, could not ignore similar protests from abroad. Thus, as early as August 1919, the Special Council's Department of Foreign Affairs issued a declaration to the Russian ambassadors in the Western capitals that the charges that VA authorities were persecuting the Ukrainian language were unfounded. "It has been resolved to reestablish the former Russian schools existing prior to the Bolshevik uprising and to withdraw from the newly founded Ukrainian schools the government subsidies they were receiving both from the Hetman's and Petliura's government."[86] As evidence of the VA's leniency toward the Ukrainian language, an article from a local paper was enclosed together with a note explaining that Gen. Mai-Maievskii, the governor-general of Kharkiv gubernia, had postponed the eviction of a Ukrainian school from a state-owned building at the request of a committee of parents and teachers.[87]

Denikin's nationality policy in Ukraine provoked anger and indignation even among Ukrainian conservative intellectuals and landowners, who, while not opposed to the principle of the empire's reunification, defended Ukraine's right to autonomy. But the White movement's intolerance of every expression of Ukrainian cultural identity provoked the greatest discontent among that intelligentsia within which nationalist tendencies were firmly rooted—village

83. Denikin, *Ocherki,* 5: 244.
84. Panina Papers, box 3, file 22.
85. Kin, 243.
86. Tatishchev (Denikin) to Minister (Giers), 16 August 1919, Giers Archives, box 40, file 97, Ukraine.
87. *Taganrogskii vestnik,* 3 (16) August 1919, ibid.

teachers, cooperative workers, and railroad, postal, and telegraph employees—i.e., precisely those who became leaders of the peasant guerrillas creating so much havoc in Denikin's rear. To them White restrictions on the development of Ukrainian culture and language recalled the old regime's policies during the darkest days of reaction. Coupled with the reappearance of tsarist landlords and bureaucrats, the restrictions gave Denikin's regime a restorationist image. Not much effort or ingenuity was required on the part of the Bolsheviks to depict the Volunteers as bands of Black Hundreds intent on restoring tsarist reaction.[88]

As early as September 1919, one of Denikin's agents reported that "the peasant insurgent leaders are resolutely in favor of Ukrainian independence within the framework of a Ukrainian socialist republic. [Their] attitude toward the VA and Russians in general is hostile."[89] The Bolsheviks, while agitating against Denikin in the summer of 1919, were careful not to arouse the suspicion of the local population by denigrating the Directory. Even in the highly industrialized Donets Basin, which had a large Russian population, an agent observed the Bolsheviks operating under the slogan "through Petliura to the return of the Reds."[90] The indiscriminate White struggle against the Ukrainian cultural and political rebirth undoubtedly played a significant role in the collapse of Denikin's authority and control over Ukraine. "Warring with Petliura's regular units and with the nationalistic guerrillas brought considerable harm to Denikin," points out an early Soviet work.[91] While for ordinary peasant insurgents the question of land may have been of utmost importance, for their leaders it was the question of both land and national freedom. The Bolsheviks promised both, and it is hardly surprising, therefore, that many guerrilla leaders joined the Red Army against Denikin, thus facilitating the Bolshevik advance into Ukraine in the winter months of 1919–20.

Denikin acknowledged that overzealous VA administrators had committed many blunders in Ukraine by persecuting even the most innocent manifestation of Ukrainian "particularism." He maintained, however, that the principles and general direction of the White movement's nationality policy were correct. He found it preposterous that Russian had been categorized a foreign language in Kyiv or in any other borderland capital. He viewed Ukrainian

88. Report, Summer 1919, Wrangel Military Archives, file 145.
89. Report on the Ukrainian Insurgent Army, September 1919, ibid., file 148.
90. "Political currents in Little Russia," report of 10 September 1919, ibid. The tactics were necessary because of Bolshevik weakness in Ukraine. Leon Trotsky admitted to the Politburo in November 1920 that "Soviet power in Ukraine has held out so far (and held out feebly) mainly thanks to the authority of Moscow, the Great Russian Communists, and the Russian Army." The Trotsky Papers, quoted in Ewan Mawdsley, *The Russian Civil War* (Boston: Allen and Unwin, 1987), 266.
91. Kin, 243.

schools and cultural institutions as political instruments directed against Russia; therefore he considered their elimination fully justified. He felt that no matter how broad the framework of cultural freedom would have been, it would have been of little consequence in Ukraine because it would not have satisfied the Ukrainian nationalists; meanwhile, the federalists there, he believed, were weak and without influence.[92] What Denikin did not acknowledge in his attempt to justify the VA's nationality policy, however, was that the White movement was as resolutely opposed to federation as it was to separatism.

Opposition to the idea of federation was at the root of Denikin's refusal to come to terms with the Directory or any other borderland government. From numerous reports by Russian ambassadors and agents in the Western capitals, as well as from assurances by Entente emissaries at VA Headquarters, Denikin knew that Russia's former allies were generally in favor of autonomy for the nationalities but were resolutely opposed to the empire's partition. He knew, therefore, that the strivings of the Ukrainian nationalists were futile because there was little prospect for their success without Entente military assistance or recognition. An alliance with the Directory, especially if arranged through Entente mediation, could have significantly strengthened the federalists among the Ukrainians. Of course, a special status for Ukraine in a Russian federation would have been recognized because of the Directory's efforts in the anti-Bolshevik struggle, but Ukraine's claim to complete independence would have been compromised if it had allied with Denikin. Because of the firm White stand on the empire's territorial integrity, only the federalists had the best prospects of success, provided they found support in the White milieu.

For Denikin and the Kadets in the Special Council—the principal architects of the White nationality program—federation, especially "federation from below," whereby each component of "Russia" would be united with the center on the principle of full equality, signified the first step toward "Russia's" disintegration. The right of each nationality to full cultural development under a liberal regime at the center would sooner or later lead to the replacement of Russian culture—the bond holding the empire together—by its nationality counterparts, and thus undermine the empire. It would also lead to the emergence of nationality intelligentsias that would not be satisfied with purely cultural rights. Denikin and his political advisors faced the same dilemma that plagued the Russian liberals before the revolution: the desire to construct a democratic yet united Russia. Both Denikin and his Kadet advisors were convinced that this objective could be

---

92. Denikin, *Ocherki,* 5: 144.

achieved only at the expense of the political rights of the nationalities.

By January 1920 Denikin was aware that the movement he had been heading for almost two years was rapidly collapsing.[93] His armies were beaten on all fronts, and thus there was little prospect of further Entente support. In the middle of the month Maklakov reported from Paris that the Entente had reached the conclusion that the effort to regenerate Russia through the VA alone had irretrievably failed and that therefore they had resolved to concentrate on aiding the East European states and new borderland republics. At this eleventh hour of the White struggle, the Russian ambassador once again urgently pleaded to the VA to endorse federation as a concession to the nationalities and accept, in principle, the possibility of territorial concessions to Poland and Romania.[94]

It was only then that Denikin bowed to the inevitable. After it was brought to his attention that the Entente resolved to grant de facto recognition to the Transcaucasian states, and after he himself became aware that Transcaucasia might be the only place his rapidly retreating troops could seek refuge, he agreed to extend de facto White recognition to those republics.[95] In a proclamation issued on 14 January, the Denikin announced that he recognized the de facto independence of the border governments fighting against the Bolsheviks and that future relations between the border states and Russia would be determined by an agreement.[96]

Had this proclamation been issued a few months earlier, one could have assumed that the obdurate White leader actually endorsed the principle of federation as the last resort for saving Russia. By January 1920, however, all White hopes for reaching Moscow were irretrievably lost. It is more than likely that Denikin issued the proclamation only to save the battered remnants of his army. In March 1920 part of the VA was forced to seek refuge in Transcaucaisia, from where it was subsequently transported with Entente aid to its remaining stronghold, the Crimean Peninsula.

---

93. This period is vividly portrayed in Peter Kenez's *Civil War in South Russia, 1919–1920: The Defeat of the Whites* (Berkeley: University of California Press, 1977).

94. Letters from Maklakov to Neratov, 12 and 21 January 1920, Denikin Papers, box 2.

95. On 10 January 1920 the Allied Council of Foreign Ministers resolved to grant de facto recognition to Georgia and Azerbaijan. *Documents on British Foreign Policy,* 3 (1949): 700–2; On the relations between the VA and the Transcaucasian republics, see Peter Kenez, "The Relations between the Volunteer Army and Georgia, 1918–1920: A Case Study in Disunity," *The Slavonic and East European Review* 48, no. 112 (July 1970), 403–23; and Artin H. Arslanian and Robert L. Nichols, "Nationalism and the Russian Civil War: The Case of Volunteer Army-Armenian Relations, 1918–1920," *Soviet Studies* 31, no. 4 (October 1979), 559–73.

96. *Documents on British Policy,* 3: 792–3; Denikin, *Ocherki,* 5: 245–7.

VI

The Crimean Experiment: General Wrangel and The Nationality Question

Denikin's distress over the defeats suffered by his troops in the winter months of 1919–1920 was compounded by political dissension within the VA, which was emboldened by the military setbacks. The monarchist bloc headed by one of Denikin's most outspoken critics, Gen. Petr N. Wrangel (Vrangel'), consisted of a number of prominent military men, including Gens. Lukomskii, Iakov A. Slashchev, and Pavel Shatilov, and Adms. Neniukov and A. D. Bubnov.[1]

Wrangel attracted the support not only of conservative officers and former tsarist bureaucrats but also of adventurers, whose number increased steadily as the demoralized White troops retreated into the Crimea. Early in 1920 a Capt. Orlov organized a revolt against the VA authorities in the Crimea; the rebels carried a banner emblazoned with Wrangel's name.[2] Although Wrangel publicly repudiated any connection between himself and the rebels, this incident exacerbated further the ill feelings that existed between the monarchist opposition and Denikin. Subsequently, when Lukomskii urged Denikin to put Wrangel in charge of the Crimea so that the VA Command could deal more effectively with the revolt, Denikin responded by relieving the officers who opposed him, including Lukomskii and Wrangel, of their posts.[3] As agitation in favor of Wrangel continued, in mid-March Denikin ordered his rival to leave the territory occupied by the VA. Wrangel, deeply offended and

---

1. For an account of the opposition, see P. S. Makhrov, "V Beloi armii generala Denikina," 481–3, Bakhmeteff Archive; P. Shatilov, "Zapiski," 868–75, Bakhmeteff Archive; and Ia. A. Slashchev-Krymskii, *Trebuiu suda obshchestva i glasnosti: Oborona i sdacha Kryma; memuary i dokumenty* (Istanbul: M. Shul'man, 1921), 5–7.
2. Ia. Shafir, "Orlovshchina," in *Antanta i Vrangel': Sbornik statei* (Moscow: Gosizdat, 1923), 125–37.
3. P. N. Vrangel', *Vospominaniia*, vol. 1 (Frankfurt am Main: Posev, 1969), 292–4.

embittered, complied and left for Istanbul.⁴

While Denikin was eliminating the leading figures on the right, he was, at the same time, compelled to make a number of far-reaching concessions to his opponents at General Headquarters. Of these the most important was the removal of Gen. Romanovskii from the post of chief of staff. Among the conservative officers hostility toward Romanovskii, Denikin's closest friend and confidant, had existed since the beginning of the civil war. The VA's monarchist circles considered him a socialist, "the evil influence on Denikin," and many held him personally responsible for the defeat of the White cause. A group of officers even threatened to assassinate Romanovskii if he did not resign.⁵ As a result, he was forced to flee to Istanbul.

The removal of the leading rightists and Romanovskii did not suffice to stem the tide of opposition. Soon after Wrangel's departure from the Crimea, a public conference was organized for the beginning of April by Gen. Slashchev clearly for the purpose of demonstrating the all-pervasive opposition to Denikin.⁶ Slashchev was so certain that public pressure would compel Denikin to resign that he even wrote to Wrangel not to leave Istanbul, but to await news from his adherents in Sevastopol.⁷

By this time Denikin had resolved to part from his army. On 31 March the embittered commander in chief issued orders for the convocation of a secret military conference at which the senior officers were to select the new leader of the White cause.⁸ Several factors may have influenced the proud and headstrong commander in making this decision. One may have been his recognition of the magnitude of the opposition, but this could not have been the crucial factor. Opposition from the right was something that Denikin had had to face from the very beginning of his leadership. No matter how strong the opposition—at times it was reported that eighty percent of the VA officers were monarchists—Denikin was able to cope with it, his strongest asset being the White movement's reliance on Entente aid. That France and Britain were willing to support their former Russian ally only if the White movement maintained a democratic profile prevented the monarchist officers from assuming leadership. So long as the VA depended on Entente aid or so long as France and Britain were willing to extend support to the White cause, Denikin's position was secure. The possibility of complete withdrawal of

---

4. Ibid., 300–1; V. A. Obolenskii, "Krym pri Vrangele," *Na chuzhoi storone* (Berlin and Prague) 9: (1925): 5–6.
5. Georgii Shavel'skii, "Vospominaniia," 422–34, Bakhmeteff Archive; Denikin, *Ocherki,* 5: 355–6.
6. Makhrov, 685–6; Denikin, *Ocherki,* 5: 355–6.
7. Vrangel', 1: 303.
8. Ibid., 304.

Entente aid was something VA leaders were forced to take into account from the late autumn of 1919. Yet it was not until the end of March 1920 that Denikin was informed by the British foreign secretary, Lord George Curzon, that in London the anti-Bolshevik struggle was considered finished. The only thing that Britain could offer now was to use its influence to make peace between the White forces and the Soviets and to assure the safety of the VA and its adherents while they retreated from Russia.[9] Even though Denikin denied emphatically that Curzon had any influence on his decision to resign, there is little doubt that Britain's determination to terminate the struggle against Bolshevism made the White leader realize the precariousness of his position.[10] Without Entente backing he was powerless to face the agitation of the monarchists within the VA.

Other factors, too, might have contributed to Denikin's decision to part from his army. If the aim of reaching Moscow seemed to have been abandoned by everyone, the hope of retaining at least the Crimea and perhaps the Cossack territories had not been altogether lost. But even this modest objective could not be attained without the cooperation of the Cossacks and the nationalities. It was primarily to their support that Denikin's energetic and politically alert new chief of staff, Gen. Petr S. Makhrov, prepared a draft for an all-embracing reform.[11] By this time, however, Denikin's name was so discredited among the people that the word "*denikinets*", according to a contemporary observer, "was pronounced with hatred and aversion."[12] So long as Denikin headed the VA, the people would view the White cause with suspicion, no matter how thorough the reforms. Denikin's resignation was therefore necessary if the White movement hoped to retain at least a foothold in the former empire, and even some of his supporters favored a change in leadership.[13] The last and perhaps crucial factor that influenced Denikin to resign was the changing character of the White movement. It should be remembered that Denikin, together with Gens. Kornilov and Alekseev, had undertaken the cause of restoring the territorial integrity and political power of Russia. From this point of view, fighting for a foothold in the southwestern tip of the former empire must have appeared utterly futile and meaningless.

When Wrangel read Denikin's telegram in Istanbul regarding the secret military conference, the recently exiled general no longer had doubt that he

---

9. Curzon to Chicherin, 11 April 1920. *Documents on British Foreign Policy*, 12 (1962): 693–99.
10. Denikin, *Ocherki*, 5: 347–8.
11. Report of the chief of staff of the Armed Forces of South Russia, 19 March 1920, P. S. Makhrov Papers, Bakhmeteff Archive.
12. Obolenskii, 5.
13. Ibid.

was destined to lead the White cause. In this belief he was reassured by the British high commissioner in Istanbul, Adm. Sir John de Robeck, who was so certain that the ambitious general was destined to be the new VA commander that he communicated to Wrangel the contents of a telegram from the British government to Denikin.[14] The message from London was anything but encouraging for the prospective White leader. It was a fomal statement that Britain considered the struggle against Bolshevism ended and that if the VA continued the war, the British goverment would be obliged to disclaim all responsibility for the conflict and would cease immediately to furnish any assistance to the White cause. If, however, the VA agreed to cease fighting, Britain offered to mediate in the negotiations for peace between the VA and the Bolsheviks.[15]

Immediately after his formal appointment as commander in chief by Denikin, Wrangel prepared a reply to the British ultimatum. He expressed readiness to comply with the British wish to end the war, but requested at least a two-month period after the conclusion of peace with the Bolsheviks for the liquidation of the White administrative, military, and civil organs in the Crimea. During this time Wrangel expected Britain to continue supplying him with the necessary aid.[16]

To Wrangel's surprise and, no doubt, relief, he soon learned that Gen. Charles Mangin, the head of the French mission at VA Headquarters, now located in Sevastopol, knew nothing of the British ultimatum.[17] It soon became widely known that the French, unlike the British, still refused to consider the struggle against Bolshevism ended and thus were resolutely opposed to any negotiations with the Soviet regime. Even though the government in Paris placed its hopes mainly on Poland and the new border republics, since the autumn of 1919 it had been logical to assume that the French favored the continuation of the White struggle so long as Poland was at war against the Bolsheviks. In fact, shortly after Wrangel's assumption of power, Mangin and the head of the American mission in Sevastopol, Adm. Newton H. McCully, urged Wrangel to prepare a public statement outlining the new leader's aims and objectives.[18] Obviously both France and the United States were not yet ready to accept the idea that the war against the Bolsheviks should be terminated.

One of the first steps Wrangel undertook with respect to the White movement's internal structure was to root out the Kadet influence at the VA's

---

14. Vrangel', 1: 304–5.
15. Ibid.
16. *Documents on British Policy,* 12: 696–7; Vrangel', 2: 13–4.
17. Vrangel', 2: 23.
18. Ibid., 42.

center. Before long, of Denikin's political apparatus only A. A. Neratov, the head of the foreign administration, his assistant B. A. Tatishchev, and the head of the finance department, Mikhail V. Bernatskii, remained at VA Headquarters. Even these officials were stripped of whatever influence they might have had, and they were never part of Wrangel's intimate circle. The new commander in chief preferred to discuss matters of policy with his close friend P. B. Struve, the prerevolutionary liberal leader whom the upheaval of 1905 and the civil war had converted to conservatism, and with the moderate zemstvo activist Prince Vladimir A. Obolenskii. On specific political issues their opinions varied widely, but on broader questions they reached a general consensus that "an attempt should be made to end the civil war, provided that a South Russian government was preserved and that [the concept] of Russia's unity be considered not as the foundation of the program, as it was under Denikin, but as the crowning of a slowly constructed edifice."[19] This consensus was of crucial significance, because it meant that the new leaders were prepared to see the transformation of the White movement from a drive to save Russia's unity and indivisibility into an anti-Bolshevik cause first and foremost. The struggle for the reunification of the empire was not to be abandoned, but it was to be viewed now as the end result of a gradual process of Russia's reconstruction from below through the concerted effort of all forces opposed to Bolshevism. This reorientation had important implications for the new leaders' relations with the Allies and the nationalities.

Nationality Policy in the Rightists' Hands

While these discussions were taking place, Wrangel's chief of staff, Makhrov, was preparing general guidelines for an official announcement of the new political goals. In a long, detailed memorandum submitted to Wrangel on 21 April, Makhrov proposed a thoroughly revised political program and suggested some radical changes in the VA's relations with the new borderland states. In line with the leaders' endorsement of the idea of Russia's reconstruction "from below," the cornerstone of the new nationality program was to be the principle of federation. All of the new states on the territory of the former Russian Empire were to be invited to join a "federal and united Russia" as equal members. They were to be induced to participate in the struggle against Bolshevism by the assurance that after their territories were liberated from the Red troops, only military formations organized by their governments would remain within the boundaries of their republics. The VA

19. Obolenskii, 8.

commander was to exercise supreme authority in military, naval, and foreign relations, but no longer than for the duration of the anti-Bolshevik war. Because it was envisaged that Ukraine would constitute one of the principal regions of military operations against the Bolsheviks, Makhrov urged that an alliance be concluded with Petliura and that aid be extended to the UNR troops in the form of arms, ammunition, and money. The Dnieper River was to serve as a dividing line between the zones of operations of the UNR Army and the VA, the former operating on the Right Bank and the latter, on the Left Bank. Closely tied with the nationality question was the issue of the VA's relations with the East-Central European states. Here, too, Makhrov urged close cooperation, considering it of primary importance to establish close ties with pro-Russian individuals and groups in Serbia, Czechoslovakia, Poland, and particularly Eastern Galicia.[20]

In short, Makhrov urged the adoption of principles favored by the Entente since the beginning of the civil war as the basis for rapprochement with the nationalities. And if the new leaders were indeed determined to transform the White movement into an exclusively anti-Bolshevik cause, it appeared that Makhrov's draft would be readily endorsed. Yet when Wrangel announced the VA objectives to the press, he made very little use of Makhrov's suggestions. What the announcement amounted to was a scathing condemnation of his predecessor's program. Wrangel criticized Denikin for not maintaining the White movement "above politics" and for considering as enemies all who did not bear a "Volunteer Army stamp." Above all Wrangel attacked Denikin and his political entourage for not uniting all anti-Bolshevik forces in the struggle against the Soviets: "They fought against the Bolsheviks, they fought against the Ukrainians, against Georgia and Azerbaijan, [and] very little was needed to start fighting the Cossacks who made up half of our army."[21] Yet, instead of unveiling a new nationality program, the new leader limited himself to announcing that an agreement had been concluded with the representatives of the Don, Kuban, Terek, and Astrakhan Cossacks, in which they were promised local autonomy in return for subordinating their military forces to the VA commander in chief.[22] What this meant was that other nationalities that joined the VA's struggle against Bolshevism could expect an agreement based on similar principles. Ironically, the agreement with the Cossacks differed little from the one concluded between the VA and the Kuban leaders in the early stages of the war; moreover, the fact that in the spring of 1920 all Cossack territories were under Bolshevik control rendered the agreement

20. Report of the Chief of Staff, Commander in Chief of the Armed Forces of South Russia, 21 April 1920, Makhrov Papers.
21. Vrangel', 2: 43–4.
22. Ibid.

to grant them local autonomy meaningless for all practical purposes. Thus Wrangel's announcement was a very weak inducement for the nationalities to join the anti-Bolshevik cause.

Although Wrangel's statement left much to be desired for the nationalities, the energy and zeal with which he set out to restore order and discipline in his demoralized army and the speed with which he initiated agrarian and local-government reforms was truly remarkable. As early as 24 April Wrangel proclaimed the formation of a commission for the elaboration of a land-reform program under the chairmanship of Grigorii V. Glinka, a former assistant to the tsarist minister of agriculture A. V. Krivoshein. The commission, consisting largely of wealthy landowners and former imperial bureaucrats, procrastinated in its work, but at Wrangel's express orders a draft of the new agrarian program was ready for publication at the end of May.[23] The reform, while enlightened, by no means rallied the peasants to join the VA. Wrangel's propaganda apparatus, like Denikin's, was poorly organized and inefficient. In many regions the peasants were ignorant of the land law and greeted the reform with suspicion and apathy.[24] Even though the agrarian program was a failure in practice, the fact that an energetic effort had been made to implement it in the territories under White control did create a favorable impression abroad and on Entente representatives in the Crimea.

The speed with which the reforms were inaugurated, however, indicated that Wrangel entertained plans other than an immediate evacuation from the Crimea. While he confided to some of his closest associates that he by no means considered the struggle ended,[25] in his public statements he gave the general impression that the VA Command would fully comply with the British ultimatum. It was not until 2 June, when Wrangel issued a highly patriotic appeal to the people to help the VA to liberate Russia from the "Red yoke," that it became generally known that the White struggle would continue.[26] To the British, Wrangel had cautiously intimated his intentions somewhat earlier. While not rejecting directly the British offer for mediation between the Bolshevik and White forces, on 2 May he wrote to Gen. J. S. J. Percy, the head of the British mission in Sevastopol, that it was his deep conviction that peace with Bolshevik Russia was impossible because the people themselves could not tolerate Soviet rule. "The sole method of putting an end to the continuing anarchy in Russia," explained Wrangel, "was to preserve a healthy nucleus around which all the elemental movements which have broken away

23. Obolenskii, 14; Vrangel', 2: 60–9.
24. A. A. Valentinov, "Krymskaia epopeia," *Arkhiv russkoi revoliutsii* 5 (1922): 15; see also Nikolai Ross, *Vrangel' v Krymu* (Frankfurt am Main: Posev, 1982).
25. P. S. Makhrov, "General Vrangel' i B. Savinkov," 8, Makhrov Papers.
26. Obolenskii, 17; Vrangel', 2: 76.

from the tyranny of Bolshevism would regroup themselves."[27] It was at this time that Wrangel openly proposed what had been his secret intention from the beginning, namely, that the Volunteer Army become the center of anti-Bolshevik resistance, a center that would be joined by the armies of the nationalities and by any other anti-Soviet force that would emerge on the territory of the former empire. He failed to specify, however, what steps he planned to undertake in order to achieve this end. Nonetheless, a joint Polish-Ukrainian offensive against the Bolsheviks launched at the end of April 1920 opened new possibilities for cooperation between the nationalities and the White cause.

The Polish-Ukrainian Alliance

The Polish-Ukrainian offensive did not surprise Wrangel. VA agents in Warsaw and Paris had reported the possibility of a Polish-Ukrainian alliance as early as the beginning of the autumn of 1919. Reports continued throughout the winter months of 1919–20.[28] It was not until 22 April 1920, however, that Piłsudski and Petliura signed a formal treaty according to which Poland recognized the Directory as the supreme government of the UNR, while the Directory conceded that the Zbruch River would be the border between Poland and Ukraine and thereby surrendered Eastern Galicia and Western Volynia, regions inhabited predominantly by Ukrainians, to Poland. In addition to this political agreement, they signed a military convention that gave the Poles wide powers with regard to the army, finances, administration, and railroads of Ukraine.[29] Three days after the conclusion of the first agreement, a joint Polish-Ukrainian force advanced on Kyiv.[30]

Shortly after the opening of the offensive, Maklakov telegraphed Wrangel from Paris to inform him that the French government was resolutely opposed to any agreement with the Bolsheviks and would therefore not exert any pressure on the White leaders to evacuate the Crimea nor agree to mediate between the Bolsheviks and the VA. Maklakov assured Wrangel that while the French were in favor of the Polish advance into Ukraine, the thought of Poland's annexation of Right-Bank Ukraine was inconceivable to them;

---

27. Vrangel', 2: 48–9.
28. Intelligence Report, 12 January 1920, Paris, Wrangel Military Archives, file 172; Report from Paris, 9 February 1920, Giers Archives, file 97, Ukraine; Gorlov's report, 30 April 1920, Maklakov Archive, box 20, Ukraine.
29. Mazepa, *Ukraïna v ohni*, 3: 8–9, 204–5.
30. Oleksander Udovychenko, *Ukraïna u viini za derzhavnist': Istoriia orhanizatsiï i boiovykh dii Ukraïns'kykh Zbroinykh Syl, 1917–1921* (Winnipeg: Dmytro Mykytiuk, 1954), 142–3.

moreover, any Ukrainian government established in the territories liberated from the Bolsheviks would receive only de facto recognition from Paris.[31]

As the success of the Polish-Ukrainian offensive mounted—on 7 May Petliura's troops entered Kyiv—the French hastened to pressure the VA to coordinate its activities with Piłsudski and Petliura. In Paris Marshal Ferdinand Foch, a staunch supporter of the anti-Bolshevik offensive, insisted that the VA commissioner in Paris, Gen. Shcherbachev, urge Wrangel to begin operations immediately against the Bolsheviks. Shcherbachev was not the right man to serve as an intermediary in this urgent matter. The patriotic White officer, who was closely tied with Denikin's cause at the beginning of the White struggle, was of the opinion that any White involvement in an anti-Bolshevik offensive during the Polish-Ukrainian march on Kyiv would be deeply injurious to Russia. His feelings on this matter were so strong that he preferred to resign rather than convey Foch's message to Wrangel. Together with his resignation note he submitted a lengthy memorandum on the Ukrainian question to the new VA Command. Cooperation with the Polish-Ukrainian offensive could lead to negotiations with the Ukrainians, and it was this eventuality that Shcherbachev wanted to prevent above all else. Such negotiations, explained Shcherbachev, would give the Entente states a moral right to recognize Ukraine's independence. During the peace negotiations in Paris, the general pointed out with emphasis, such recognition was withheld only because "*all* Russian parties had adopted a negative stand on the question of Ukraine's independence." Furthermore, explained the departing commissioner, any cooperation with the Ukrainians would be a severe moral blow to the all-Russian national movement and would provide the Bolsheviks with an opportunity to style themselves as the bearers of the Russian national ideal of the unification of all Russian lands.[32]

The VA leaders, outwardly at least, did not seem to heed Shcherbachev's warnings. When Mangin inquired in Sevastopol about Wrangel's feelings on cooperation with the Poles and Ukrainians, he received a positive response from Wrangel's Department of Foreign Affairs. Prince Evgenii N. Trubetskoi, the acting foreign minister, replied on 17 May that while Wrangel did not wish to discuss political questions nor comment on the political agreement between the Poles and the Ukrainians, he was willing to coordinate his

---

31. Maklakov to Struve, 1 May 1920, Wrangel Military Archives, Diplomatic Correspondence, case 1, file 5; Vrangel', 2: 48. The policy of the French government is discussed in Michael Jabara Carley, "The Politics of Anti-Bolshevism: The French Government and the Russo-Polish War, December 1919–May 1920," *Historical Journal* 19, no. 1 (March 1976), 163–89.

32. Report of the military representative of the Russian armies at the Allied missions and the Allied Supreme Command to the Supreme Command of the Armed Forces of South Russia, 8 June 1920, Giers Archives, box 97, Ukraine; Val', *K istorii belago dvizheniia*, 150–6.

activities with the Polish and Ukrainian forces. "Because the single aim of the [White] Armed Forces of South Russia" was "the struggle against Bolshevism," explained Trubetskoi, the VA commander was ready to accept all military formations that would help him defeat the Soviets. In order to assure the best possible results in the war against the Bolsheviks, the note suggested that the region east of the Dnieper River and south of Katerynoslav be designated the zone of VA operations, while the Poles and Ukrainians should concentrate their activities in the Right Bank.[33] Mangin, although undoubtedly pleased with this encouraging response from Wrangel, pressed for a more concrete plan of coordinated action. He wished to know in particular how Wrangel saw the question of a united command. Wrangel's response was cautious and reserved. Only the future, he stated, would show how to resolve the question of a united command, but on "Russian" soil, the White leader asserted firmly, no foreign command would be tolerated.[34]

Shortly after this exchange of views, the VA received from its intelligence agents detailed plans of the Bolshevik counteroffensive against the Polish-Ukrainian armies. The reports convinced the White leaders that strategically it would have been most advantageous to attack the southern flank of the Bolshevik advance. Such an attack would have required the VA to cross into Right-Bank Ukraine, an action the White leaders were not willing to take because it would have compromised the idea of Russia's territorial integrity. By crossing the Dnieper, explained Wrangel, the VA Command could not limit itself to merely a military alliance with Poland, because it would then be operating in a territory that Warsaw recognized as part of an independent Ukraine. While Wrangel was willing to recognize broad autonomy for "Little Russia," he considered, as did Denikin, the region an indivisible part of the empire; on this question serious complications would be inevitable in any negotiations with the Poles. The all-important issue of Russia's integrity precluded the possibility of a united effort against the Bolsheviks.[35]

The anticipated coordination of activities between the White and Polish-Ukrainian armies was therefore never realized. Instead of rejecting from the outset any thought of cooperation with forces whose activities in one way or another promised to violate the integrity of Russia—as did Denikin—Wrangel preferred to show readiness to comply with the wishes of his benefactors, knowing in advance that he could always find an excuse to back out. France, after all, was the only ally still willing to support the White cause, and this, no doubt, prompted the VA leader to exercise great caution while discussing

---

33. Vrangel', 2: 84–5.
34. Ibid., 85–6.
35. Ibid.

plans put forth by Paris. When finally Wrangel did launch an offensive in mid-June 1920, the Polish-Ukrainian forces were already retreating from a Bolshevik offensive. From 7 June Kyiv was in Soviet hands.[36] Although even at this time it was not yet too late to coordinate VA operations with the retreating Polish-Ukrainian forces, Wrangel showed no desire to do so. Although the new command endorsed the idea of federation in principle, the White leaders continued to hold sacred the empire's territorial integrity. Thus no cooperation with the Polish-Ukrainian offensive was possible even at this most critical juncture for the White struggle.

The failure of the Polish-Ukrainian offensive did not dampen French interest in the VA. In fact, the French concern for the developments in the former empire intensified because it soon appeared that Poland itself might be threatened by the Bolshevik advance. In June Wrangel's newly appointed foreign minister, Petr Struve, was received in Paris by Premier Alexandre Millerand. On this occasion Struve presented a detailed note on the new White political and economic objectives, expounding with special care the VA's nationality program. The new White leaders, Struve's note emphasized, endorsed without any reservations the principle of "federation from below," and though the VA had not abandoned the drive for the reunification of Russia, it would never try to bring about reunification by force. The future Russian federation was to be based on freely concluded agreements derived from common interests and mutual economic needs. The future structure of both the federation and its constituent parts was to be determined by the "free expression of the will of the people by means of representative assemblies elected on democratic principles."[37]

While Struve was trying strenuously to enlighten the French government and public about the liberal nature of Wrangel's nationality program, only insignificant steps were being undertaken in the Crimea to implement the program's principles. Wrangel and his political advisers did not even deem it necessary to appoint a separate commission to formulate a consistent nationality policy. Relations with the nationalities were, in most instances, resolved piecemeal and haphazardly, depending on circumstances.

36. Udovychenko, 143–5.
37. Vrangel', 2: 107–9.

The Implementation of the New Nationality Program

The Transcaucasian republics were far removed from Wrangel's immediate theater of operations, and thus they attracted little of his concern. Aside from petty trade with Georgia, the VA's relations with Transcaucasia were practically nonexistent. The situation was quite different with respect to the Tatars and Ukrainians. When Wrangel took over the command in the Crimea, the indigenous population in the southwest corner of the peninsula was in a state of revolutionary upheaval. The excesses perpetrated by Denikin's retreating troops—pillaging, forced requisitioning of food and horses—induced many Tatars to join the insurgent forces in the Crimean Mountains. To soften the ever-growing hostility of the local people, as early as April 1920 Wrangel ordered D. D. Perlik, the chairman of his civil administration, to convoke a Tatar National Congress. The congress took place during the last days of May; forty-two delegates attended. To show his good will toward the national minorities, Wrangel addressed the congress. He assured the Tatars of his deep respect for their local traditions, customs, and religion, but pointed out that only after Bolshevism was defeated would the time come to discuss such issues as autonomy and the right of self-determination. Suspecting that Wrangel's promises—cautious and ill-defined as they were—might arouse undue hopes among the Tatars for political autonomy, Perlik, as chairman of the congress, thought it prudent to explain in his concluding remarks that if the local population fulfilled its duty toward Russia by supporting the White cause, it would be guaranteed cultural and religious self-rule. Aside from that, stated Perlik flatly, the VA leaders would make no commitments.[38]

The only notable outcome of the congress was the establishment of a special commission for working out the principles of Tatar self-government. One of its first acts was the dismissal of the conservative mufti appointed during Denikin's brief rule in the Crimea, but it failed to ensure that the vacant position was filled within a reasonable period of time. Throughout the spring and summer its work stagnated, and the project for Tatar self-government was continually shelved. The apathy with which the commission approached the project and the absence of a new mufti contributed further to the local unrest. Impatient with the commission's procrastination, the Tatar leaders sent a delegation to Wrangel headed by the Kipchak *murza* Mustafa to request expediting the introduction of Tatar self-rule in the region.[39] The delegation's visit, as well as the arrival on 19 October of a new French commissioner at VA Headquarters, Damien Charles Comte de Martel, who

---

38. Grigor'ev (Genker). "Tatarskii vropros v Krymu," in *Antanta i Vrangel': Sbornik statei* (Moscow: Gosizdat, 1923), 234.
39. Ibid., 237–8.

from the beginning showed special interest in the nationality question, prompted the commission to resume its work. Late in October, on the eve of the collapse of Wrangel's army and five months after the establishment of the commission, the project for Tatar self-government was finally completed and approved by Wrangel. But there was no chance of implementing it or even making it public.

Next to the Tatar question in terms of immediate concern to the VA was the smoothing out of relations with the Ukrainians. Any larger VA campaign would inevitably involve operations on Ukrainian territory, where the cooperation of the Ukrainian military formations and population in general would be of crucial significance. Yet Wrangel, like Denikin before him, ruled out military collaboration with the Directory and its sizable army because they pursued separatist goals.[40] Instead he favored the establishment of ties with the insurgent anti-Bolshevik Ukrainian irregular units operating in the Crimea and even with the anarchist peasant guerrillas led by Nestor Makhno, because negotiations with them would not lead to the violation of the principle of Russia's unity. Moreover, concessions made to the insurgents would not be as binding as those made to the Ukrainian government through French mediators. Thus, while Wrangel systematically avoided relations with the Entente-backed Directory, he sought contacts with the peasant anarchists. These adventurous moves proved to have the most unfortunate consequences. Demonstrating his unmitigated hatred and disdain for the White movement, Makhno unceremoniously executed two of Wrangel's highest-ranking emissaries, who had been sent to negotiate an alliance.[41]

Even though Wrangel viewed cooperation with the Ukrainian insurgents as most advantageous, especially after he launched an offensive in the beginning of June, the White center made no concrete effort in this direction. It was on the Ukrainians' initiative that contact was established between the two anti-Bolshevik forces at the end of July. Of primary concern to the Ukrainians was the consolidation of all partisan units in Ukraine and the reestablishment of a Ukrainian regular army to fight against Bolshevism. They were also interested in the formation of a Ukrainian political center in Sevastopol that would surpervise civil administration in the regions cleared of the Bolsheviks. While Wrangel received the Ukrainians very cordially and assured them that he agreed with their proposals "in principle," he instructed them to address all military matters to VA Headquarters through Gen. Kirei, who was in charge of information on the insurgent movement. When, three

---

40. Vrangel', 2: 178.
41. Piontkovskii, *Grazhdanskaia voina v Rossii,* 637. On the Makhno movement, see Michael Palij, *The Anarchism of Nestor Makhno, 1918–1921: An Aspect of the Ukrainian Revolution* (Seattle: University of Washington Press, 1976).

days later, the Ukrainian delegation presented a detailed plan for the implementation of the two proposals to Wrangel through Kirei, it was curtly rejected by Wrangel's newly appointed chief of staff, Gen. Shatilov.[42]

At the beginning of September another delegation from the Ukrainian insurgent army, headed by its leader Gen. Omelianovych-Pavlenko, again visited Wrangel. Even though the VA commander appeared to be favorably impressed by the delegation, nothing of substance evolved from their meeting beyond the White center extending some aid in the form of arms, ammunition, and money to the insurgents.[43] Yet although Wrangel's equivocation did not lead to a firm alliance, it did neutralize the hostility toward the White forces that had been virtually universal within the Ukrainian military since Denikin's time.

Struve's declarations in Paris regarding the reconstruction of Russia on federal principles bolstered the profederalist diplomatic representatives of the nationalities in the French capital. In the summer of 1920 a Ukrainian National Committee was formed in Paris to disseminate propaganda abroad and in Ukraine in favor of Ukraine's federation with Russia.[44] The committee sent a delegation to Wrangel headed by its chairman, Markotun, in the second half of September. Even though the VA commander was convinced that the committee had no real power behind it and thus could be of little use in the struggle against the Bolsheviks, its delegation was greeted with great pomp and ceremony because, as Wrangel explained, it was a friendly organization with some connection both in Western capitals and Ukraine and because it might be useful as a foil to the Ukrainian separatists.[45]

Wrangel's conference with Markotun took place in the presence of Struve, Krivoshein, and Shatilov. In response to the delegation's proposal regarding the reconstruction of Russia on federal principles, Wrangel most courteously replied that he agreed with the committee's program "in principle" and, because his chief objective was the unification of all Russian forces struggling against Bolshevism, was willing to conclude an agreement with the newly established states on the same principles as the agreement with the Cossacks.[46] In a lengthy speech delivered at a banquet organized in the delegation's honor by the Cossack leaders, Wrangel avoided the nationality question altogether and addressed instead matters of a broader nature. He spoke of Bolshevism as a worldwide threat, calling attention to the fact that

---

42. Slashchev-Krymskii, 57–9.
43. Vrangel', 2: 178.
44. Report on the activities of the Ukrainian National Committee, Summer 1920, Giers Archives, file 97, Ukraine.
45. Vrangel', 2: 178.
46. Telegram, Neratov to Giers, 2 October 1920, Giers Archives, file 97, Ukraine; Vrangel', 2: 194.

the press in Warsaw often pointed out that the Poles were fighting not against the Russian people but against the representatives of the Communist International. The White leader expressed the hope that the Poles would not abandon the forces still struggling against the Bolshevik menace.[47]

Wrangel's preoccupation with Poland on this occasion reflected the nervousness at VA Headquarters caused by the opening of negotiations for peace between the Poles and the Soviets at the beginning of September 1920. The possibility of such a peace was viewed with alarm because the Bolsheviks could then throw the bulk of their troops against the remnants of the VA in the Crimea. To explore the various avenues for averting the conclusion of a Polish-Bolshevik peace, Wrangel dispatched Gen. Makhrov as his special envoy to Warsaw.

Upon arriving in the Polish capital, Makhrov was astonished to learn that he was one of many emissaries there claiming to speak on behalf of anti-Bolshevik Russia. Of the numerous Russian organizations in the Polish capital, the most important was the Russian Political Council headed by Boris Savinkov and composed primarily of moderate socialists, including the well-known poet Dmitrii Merezhkovskii and the former minister for Russian affairs in the Ukrainian government, Dmitrii Odinets. Because the council's existence depended entirely on French support and on the good graces of Poland, it is not surprising that its political program conformed fully to the principles endorsed by the governments in Warsaw and Paris. It called for the convocation of a constituent assembly, distribution of land to the peasants, a democratic form of government, and the reconstruction of Russia on federal principles.[48] One of the council's most important activities consisted of organizing an army made up of the Russian troops stranded in Poland, principally from the Northwestern Front of Gen. Nikolai Iudenich, and of prisoners of war who had served in the Red Army. Since July 1920 Savinkov had been in Warsaw working energetically on the formation of what later became known as the Russian Third Army. The Polish Ministry of War was cooperating fully in this endeavor. In fact, it was Piłsudski who had invited Savinkov to Warsaw to supervise the organization of the army.[49]

Having become aware of Savinkov's influence—the chairman of the Russian Political Council was an intimate friend of Piłsudski with direct access to the marshal—Makhrov prudently decided not to challenge his claim to represent anti-Bolshevik Russia or to interfere in the organization of the

---

47. Vrangel', 2: 193.
48. Declaration of the Russian Political Council, Miliukov Personal Archive, box 1.6.6.1., pt. 2, file 18. On Savinkov's activities, see reports 4768-9, file 27, Akty Adjutantury Generalnej Naczelnego Dowództwa, Józef Piłsudski Institute of America, New York.
49. *Ispoved' Savinkova: Protsess Borisa Savinkova, August 1924* (Berlin: "Russkoe ekho," 1924), 82.

Russian Third Army. Instead he tried to reach some form of an agreement with his influential compatriot. Together with Capt. V. M. Gorlov, the VA intelligence agent in Poland, Makhrov attended meetings of the Russian Political Council to gather information and to show the VA's readiness to cooperate with the Russian socialist group. One of the first questions Savinkov raised at his meeting with Makhrov was the issue of Wrangel's attitude toward the Directory. He considered an agreement with the Ukrainians of crucial importance irrespective of whether the Polish government decided to continue the war with the Bolsheviks or to make peace with the Soviet regime. Savinkov's position was strongly supported by Odinets, who claimed that the Ukrainians were favorably disposed toward an agreement with Wrangel, that they were only reluctant partners in the Polish-Soviet war, and that if Petliura wished to avoid complete isolation in the event the Poles concluded peace with the Bolsheviks, Petliura had no choice but to conclude an alliance with Wrangel. By this time, on the basis of his own experience—Makhrov was a strong advocate of an alliance with Petliura—Wrangel's envoy must have had strong misgivings about the possibility of an agreement between the VA and the Ukrainians. Nonetheless he replied diplomatically that Wrangel had agreed in principle, shortly after his assumption of power, to form an alliance with the Ukrainian anti-Bolshevik forces.[50]

While in Warsaw Makhrov conferred with Eustachy Sapieha, the Polish foreign minister, Gen. Tadeusz Rozwadowski, the Polish chief of staff, and Piłsudski. During these talks the VA envoy was assured that the Poles were doing everything possible to prolong the negotiations with the Bolsheviks, but that even if the Polish government concluded a peace agreement with the Soviets, the Whites still had time to organize their forces in Poland. During these talks the Polish marshal very frankly expressed his views about Russia. While admitting openly that he did not consider the Soviet regime legitimate, Piłsudski did not conceal his dislike of the Russia of Kolchak and Denikin because both White leaders were reactionaries desiring to bring back the old, oppressive order. Piłsudski looked forward, however, to the emergence of a third, democratic Russia that would not be oppressive. It was with this Russia that he would welcome as an ally. While discussing the military and political situation in the Crimea, Piłsudski did not hide his scepticism regarding Wrangel's widely publicized democratic goals. "Could the White leader's liberal declarations be really taken at face value when he surrounded himself with such well-known reactionaries as the former tsarist ministers Krivoshein and Glinka?" the Polish leader asked.[51]

---

50. Makhrov, "General Vrangel' i B. Savinkov," 292.
51. Makhrov's report to Wrangel, 12 September 1920, no. 350, Makhrov Papers; Makhrov, "General Vrangel' i B. Savinkov," 231, 343-4.

Shortly after these talks Makhrov dispatched a report to Wrangel urging him to approve Savinkov's project on the formation of the Russian Third Army and requesting immediate authorization to begin negotiations with Petliura, who had an army of about 15,000 in Poland. The representatives of the Directory, wrote Makhrov, had already intimated to him that they were ready to open negotiations with the Russians, but he could not initiate these talks until he received official authorization from Wrangel.[52] Wrangel promptly authorized the formation of the Third Army on the condition that it be concentrated on the right flank of the Ukrainians on the Polish front, but he failed to make any reference to what was considered the most urgent matter in the Polish capital, namely, an alliance with Petliura.[53] This perplexed Makhrov considerably, because by this time he was being pressured from all sides to open talks with the Ukrainian delegates in Warsaw. The head of the French mission in the Polish capital, Gen. Henri Niessel, who was well acquainted with prerevolutionary Russia, could not understand what difficulties could result from an agreement among the parties, especially because under existing conditions all sides would be inclined to make concessions.[54] Piłsudski was visibly annoyed that Wrangel chose to remain silent on the Ukrainian question. Savinkov angrily announced that he would no longer wait for Wrangel's decision regarding talks with the Ukrainians and that the Russian Political Council would proceed on its own to conclude an agreement with Petliura. Negotiations with the Ukrainians, Savinkov explained, already had the full approval of all the council members.[55]

The need for a speedy agreement with the Directory appeared even more urgent after the Poles concluded a truce with the Bolsheviks on 12 October that was to go into effect within six days. In spite of this development, Gen. Rozwadowski continued to press Makhrov for a political agreement between Wrangel and Poland according to which the Poles would send volunteers for the Russian armies and exert pressure on Petliura to conclude an alliance with Wrangel on the basis of federation. Since no reply was forthcoming from Wrangel, Makhrov, exasperated by his own helplessness in the Polish capital, welcomed an opportunity to go to Paris, where a conference was to take place between the representatives of Poland, the VA, and France on the question of the establishment of a council under Gen. Foch's staff to coordinate operations against the Bolsheviks.[56]

52. Makhrov's report to Wrangel.
53. Makhrov, "General Vrangel' i B. Savinkov," 347.
54. Ibid., 346.
55. Ibid., 349.
56. Makhrov, "General Vrangel' i B. Savinkov," 352, 360.

When Makhrov arrived in Paris on 24 October, he learned the conference had been called off. This development did not discourage him, however, and he immediately took steps to win the support of the Russian diplomats in Paris for an alliance with the Directory. On his initiative a meeting of the Russian Political Conference was called to discuss this urgent issue. To Makhrov's disappointment, however, his proposal was supported only by Vasilii Maklakov and the new VA commissioner in Paris, Gen. Evgenii K. Miller. The chairman of the meeting, N. N. Giers, Russia's former ambassador to Rome, appeared to be considerably perplexed by the political consequences that might result from an agreement with the Ukrainians. The dominant figure at the meeting was Wrangel's foreign minister, Struve, who, to Makhrov's annoyance, was entirely uninterested in the military advantages that could result from the alliance with Petliura. Instead of directly addressing the urgent issue under consideration, Struve opened a meandering discussion on the economic and ethnographic aspects of the Ukrainian question. It was only under Maklakov's pressure that he promised to send a telegram to Wrangel and to notify Makhrov immediately about the White leader's position on this issue. In spite of Struve's reluctance to discuss the practical aspects of the Ukrainian question, Makhrov, to his surprise and, no doubt, relief, on the following day shortly before his return trip to Warsaw, received a message from Wrangel's foreign minister that he could proceed to negotiate with the representatives of the Directory in Poland even before getting formal authorization from the Crimea.[57]

Meanwhile, in Warsaw, Savinkov had reached an agreement with the Ukrainians according to which the Russian Political Council recognized Ukraine as an independent state and subordinated the Russian Third Army to the Ukrainian Military Command in return for an anti-Bolshevik alliance. In the second week of November 1920 a joint offensive of the Russian and Ukrainian forces was launched.[58] It was during this ill-fated offensive—the Russian and Ukrainian troops were almost immediately routed by the Red Army—that Makhrov received Wrangel's long-awaited approval to open negotiations with the Directory. The message from the VA commander, which was conveyed through Struve, expressed his government's readiness "to recognize the right of Ukraine to complete self-determination under the condition of the formation of one front and a unified supreme command."[59] Makhrov was provided with detailed guidelines for the talks with the Directory:

---

57. Ibid., 360–77.
58. Ibid., 385.
59. Telegram from Struve to Makhrov, 2 (15) November 1920, Makhrov Papers.

(1) The Supreme Command of the [White] Government of South Russia agrees that the future fate of Ukraine and its structure [should] be determined by a freely elected Ukrainian Constituent Assembly.

(2) Until that moment, the Supreme Command and the government will recognize that de facto government in Ukraine willing to join us in the struggle against the Bolsheviks and not recognizing the Soviet regime.

(3) Russian military units that have already entered the territory of Ukraine or plan to advance there from Poland should form a separate Russian Army.

(4) With respect to military operations, the Russian Army can be subordinated to the Ukrainian Command provided that a united front is formed and all active armed forces, both Russian and Ukrainian, at this front are subordinated to the Supreme Command of Gen. Wrangel.

(5) The financing of the Ukrainian and Russian armed forces on the Ukrainian front should be based on an agreement between the two armies.[60]

The concessions the VA leaders were willing to make to the Directory must have astounded even Makhrov, the most consistent proponent of the White movement's alliance with the nationalities. Not only was Wrangel willing to recognize the Directory, but he also acknowledged Ukraine's right to self-determination through the convocation of a Ukrainian Constituent Assembly—a far-reaching concession that hitherto no Russian government or political group was willing to make. Makhrov did not have to wait long for an explanation for this unprecedented step. Almost simultaneously with Struve's instructions, he received a telegram from Istanbul informing him about the collapse of the White struggle and the imminent evacuation of the VA from the Crimea.[61]

In this respect, Wrangel's behavior was not unlike Denikin's. Only at times of extreme adversity, when the entire movement was at the brink of total collapse, either out of desperation or utter dejection were both White leaders willing to make concessions that would impair the idea of the former empire's territorial integrity. In spite of his scathing criticism of Denikin's nationality policy and his widely publicized declarations of friendship toward the nationalities, it was only after the VA suffered its crushing defeat that Wrangel was willing to deal with a former national minority of the Russian Empire as an equal.

This does not imply that Wrangel's nationality program was identical to Denikin's. Wrangel geniunely tried to change the image the West and the nationalities had of the White movement. While Denikin unequivocally rejected federation and the concept of Russia's reconstruction "from below," Wrangel unhesitatingly endorsed both of these ideas; judging from his vague

60. Ibid.
61. Makhrov, "General Vrangel' i B. Savinkov," 386.

and ill-defined declaration and rather naive and often self-contradictory speeches, however, it is doubtful that he had a clear understanding of the full implication of these two closely related concepts. Wrangel was first and foremost a military man who prior to becoming the leader of the VA had little contact with or interest in politics. Neither his formal education in a technical school nor his career as a chemical engineer and Guards officer prepared him to comprehend fully the political intricacies unleashed by the revolution and the civil war. He criticized Denikin so severely because he failed to understand that military matters and political questions were closely intertwined. Declarations of friendship and elaborate and colorful receptions in honor of the minority delegations, while useful in softening somewhat the animosity the nationalities generally felt toward the White cause, were not sufficient for forging a solid anti-Bolshevik bloc. Military alliances and agreements negotiated on the basis of equality had to be made, and this was a step the new leader was not willing to take so long as there was hope that the White struggle had any chance of success on its own.

Thus, even though in practice Wrangel's nationality policy differed but little from that of his predecessor, the fact remains that the new commander in chief did include in his program the the principle of federation. This was a marked departure from the policy pursued by Denikin and his Kadet entourage, who envisioned Russia as a democratic, territorially decentralized, but, from the point of view of the nationality question, rigidly unified state. Wrangel's readiness to accept the principle of federation reflected rather clearly the right-wing ideology of the new men in the White political apparatus—men who felt that a federal structure based on the nationality principle would not impair the idea of Russia's unity once a strong monarch, the symbol of the empire's unity, was reinstated.

VII

Conclusions

> The essence and birthmark of the Russian Revolution is its anti-national character; its aims were directed toward the destruction of Russia—toward the political suicide of a great nation. The very essence of the revolution shows the way toward salvation.... This means that the only organizing and spiritual force of that new Russia that will rise from the ashes of the revolution can be found only in *nationalism*.
>
> Petr Struve, "Natsionalizm," *Velikaia Rossiia*

In numerous studies dealing with the great upheaval that swept through the territory of the former Russian Empire from 1917 to 1920, the White movement has been presented as a military effort organized by eminent generals of the imperial army to overthrow the Bolshevik regime. The achievements and failures of the White armies and the strategy and tactics of their leaders have been examined, analyzed, and evaluated chiefly as if the White struggle had been exclusively an anti-Bolshevik cause. What has been largely overlooked or ignored is that although the White generals were vigorously opposed to Bolshevism, they put forward an ideology that was far from being merely anti in its conception and application. The chief task of the movement they were heading was, in accordance with its origins, the preservation or reestablishment of Russia's territorial unity and integrity. The White armies strove for neither the restoration of the former political order nor the economic and social structure of the empire, but rather for the regeneration of the political power, international prestige, and territorial cohesiveness of a rapidly disintegrating empire. They fought the Bolsheviks first and foremost because they believed that the Soviet leaders, as hired agents of Germany—Russia's foremost enemy—were responsible for the dissolution of Russia.

From the point of view of the White leaders, the Bolsheviks were not the only ones responsible for the breakup of the Russian Empire; equally responsible were the leaders of the borderland nationalities who, before the Bolshevik coup, "were pretending to be struggling for the *Russian* revolution, but who, when this revolution destroyed Russia, very quickly and adroitly turned away from Russia and became the most ardent propagators or, if convenient, most zealous fellow travellers of the German idea of the dismemberment of Russia."[1]

In principle the White leaders made little distinction between the nationalists in the borderlands and the Bolsheviks in the center. They considered both to be traitors and "aliens" and their governments' chief shortcoming to be, as Denikin pointed out with emphasis, that they were *"not national,"* i.e., non-Russian.[2] There was a major difference between the two, however: the military formations of the nationalities did not pose an immediate threat to the VA so long as the White armies remained outside the borders of the newly established states, whereas the Bolsheviks were a constant menace to the VA and, at the same time, the strongest single opponent of the White cause. In the long run, however, the White movement perceived both forces as equally dangerous to the state interests of Russia. A message of greetings to Denikin from the People's Freedom party stated characteristically that the VA, from its very inception, was considered the only force "capable of saving Russia as one, indivisible entity from both oppressive Bolshevik dominance and the perfidious treachery of the separatists."[3]

Nonetheless, the chief agents responsible for the catastrophe that befell Russia, according to the White leaders, were neither the Bolsheviks in the capital nor the separatists on the periphery, but the Germans. Of this the White leaders were certain, and they never doubted that the principal aim Germany pursued singlemindedly during the First World War was the complete destruction of Russia. From the White viewpoint the Bolsheviks and separatists were merely carrying out the grand design of Russia's dismemberment prepared in Berlin. The White leaders' hostility toward Germany was implacable even during the darkest hours of the VA's existence, when it was clear that only the German forces occupying Ukraine could provide the VA with the necessary military aid to withstand the Bolshevik attacks. The position of the White generals could not have been different. As its political program and military strategy during the early period of the civil war clearly

---

1. Petr" Struve, *Razmyshleniia o russkoi revoliutsii* (Sofia: Rossiisko-bolgarskoe knigoizdatel'stvo, 1921), 7. It consists of two lectures delivered by Struve in November 1919 in Rostov.
2. Denikin, *Ocherki,* 3: 6.
3. Greetings of the South Russian Conference of the People's Freedom party (29–30 June 1919) to Gen. Denikin in Ekaterinodar, Panina Papers, box 3, file 18.

indicate, the VA was established primarily to keep alive the idea of Russia's struggle with the Central Powers until an Allied victory was achieved, and not merely to dislodge the Bolsheviks from power. The steadfast White loyalty to the Allies was founded on the firm belief that only the victorious Entente states would provide the necessary aid for the reestablishment of the power and unity of Russia. If Germany had won the war, the ousting of the Bolsheviks at the center would have mattered little, considering the principal goals of the VA.

The small corps of volunteers answering Alekseev's call for the salvation of Russia was hardly in a position to wage war simultaneously against the Germans, the Bolsheviks, and the armies of the newly established national republics on the periphery of the former empire. During the first year of its existence the VA confined its activities to self-defense, its chief immediate objective being to preserve a nucleus of the Russian army that was unswervingly loyal to the Allies.

After the defeat of Germany, the fall of the Bolshevik and borderland governments appeared imminent to the Whites. Subsequent events revealed, however, that the Bolsheviks were not simply Germany's agents without the means to maintain power, and that the leaders of the nationalities were not mere puppets of the Central Powers without roots among their people. In spite of this revelation, the attitude of the White generals remained unchanged. From the vantage point of Ekaterinodar, the Bolsheviks and especially the borderlands' nationalists were continuing Germany's aim of dismembering Russia. Uncompromising White hostility toward the nationalities was maintained even after it became clear that, contrary to expectations, the number of volunteers eager to fight for the unity of Russia was deplorably small and that the intervening powers, whose aid was of crucial significance to the success of the White movement, were interested primarily in the defeat of Bolshevism and were ready to attain this defeat at the expense of Russia's indivisibility. All Allied efforts to deal separately with the governments of the borderlands and to effect some form of cooperation between the military forces of the nationalities and the White armies were interpreted by the latter as flagrant interference in Russia's internal affairs, as the direct continuation of Germany's goal to dismember Russia, and thus as gross distortions of the spirit and meaning of Allied aid. The Whites were appalled at the ease with which the Entente states became accustomed to what Struve called the "Brest-Litovsk point of view."[4]

Considering the origins and aims of the White movement, the VA leaders' implacable attitude toward the newly independent governments on the

---

4. Struve, *Razmyshleniia*, 6.

periphery of the former Russian Empire was inevitable. No matter how promising cooperation with the armies of the nationalities was for the anti-Bolshevik cause, and no matter how strongly the Entente exerted pressure to bring about a united military offensive, the White movement tenaciously adhered to the view that the slightest, informal contacts with "separatists" would irretrievably compromise the idea of Russia's unity. The White generals' position on this question was fully supported by all major non-Bolshevik Russian parties and groups, with the exception of the right.

But the leaders of the nationalities were not exclusively adherents of full independence for the newly established states. In each Ukrainian government, irrespective of whether it was conservative, liberal, or socialist, there were currents favoring the establishment of federal ties with all nations of the former empire, including the Russians. Some leaders, especially in the socialist governments, appear to have been convinced that the reconstruction of the former empire on federative principles would represent a "higher form of state formation." Others, even though they were disillusioned with the abstract idea of federalism promoted by the progressive intelligentsia before the 1917 Revolution, reluctantly accepted federation because it became quite clear in the course of the civil war that the Entente states were in favor of federation but were resolutely opposed to Ukraine's complete separation from Russia. And without outside aid and Entente recognition—considering the simultaneous military pressure from the Bolsheviks, the White armies, and the Poles—it was doubtful that an independent Ukrainian state could have been maintained.

The White leaders were made fully aware of the existence of these profederalist currents not only through their numerous intelligence agents but also through the overtures of the Ukrainian governments, on a number of occasions, to reach an understanding with the White armies. Skoropads'kyi's conservative government even proclaimed federation of the Ukrainian State with Russia. Yet cooperation with a party or a government advocating a federative platform—irrespective of its political complexion—was most resolutely rejected by the VA leaders. In fact it was Skoropads'kyi's government that became the object of the most scathing White diatribes both during and after the civil war.[5] The White generals' adamant refusal to endorse the federative principle earned them the earmark of conservatism and reaction, especially abroad, where the establishment of a unitary Russia was associated with the restoration of tsarism and the old regime. Yet at home, ironically, in its stubborn rejection of federation the VA was most steadfastly and consistently supported by the liberals in the National Center. Both the

---

5. A. Denikin, "Okrainnyi vopros," *Posledniia novosti,* 7, 8, 28 December 1932; copies in the B. I. Nikolaevsky Collection, Hoover Institution.

ultraconservatives in the monarchist bloc and the leading members of the moderate right in the Council of Russia's State Unity were willing to cooperate with the borderland governments, and strongly criticized Denikin for his stubborn refusal to do the same. The National Center, however, not only unequivocally supported Denikin in his militant opposition to federalism, but also advised the White leader to exercise great caution and vigilance in dealing with the nationalities and especially not to take any steps that could facilitate recognition of the newly established states in the future or be interpreted as acknowledgement that relations between Russia and the borderlands could be settled through negotiations. Skoropads'kyi's edict on federation was greeted by the Kadets with apprehension because, as Miliukov admitted candidly, it made the recognition of Ukraine's separate status within Russia more acceptable to the Allies.[6]

The Russian liberals' opposition to federation predated the revolution. It increased during the period of Russia's disintegration especially among those party leaders who were caught in the whirlwind of the war and personally witnessed the intensity and growth of nationalism in the borderlands. It was rooted primarily in the fear that the introduction of civil liberties throughout the empire would endanger the unity of Russia, as well as in the conviction that this unity could be safeguarded only if Russian cultural hegemony remained intact throughout the vast multinational state. The preservation of Russian political and cultural supremacy was the central idea concealed behind the slogan of "Russia One and Indivisible," and it was the reinstitution of Russian power both at the center and in the borderlands that the White movement considered to be its principal task.

Denikin found it inconceivable to think of placing the Russians and the Russian language in Kyiv in the category of a national minority.[7] What was true of Kyiv was also true of Tbilisi, Mahileu, and Tashkent because, as Struve pointed out before the war, the Russians and Russian culture also enjoyed undisputed superiority there.[8] The semiofficial organ of the VA, *Velikaia Rossiia*, proclaimed during Denikin's Moscow campaign that "it is just as impossible to think of Russia without Turkistan and the Transcaspia as it is to think of it without its heart, Moscow."[9] To assure the continuing preeminence of the Russians in the periphery of the former empire, both political and broader cultural rights had to be withheld from the nationalities. A federated Russia with a constitutional regime at the center was viewed as a prelude to the empire's disintegration.

6. Miliukov, "Dnevnik," 18 November 1918, 299.
7. Denikin, *Ocherki*, 5: 144.
8. Struve, "Chto takoe Rossiia," *Russkaia mysl'*, January 1911, 185.
9. "O Turkestane i Zakaspii," *Velikaia Rossiia*, 12 (25) September 1919.

The White generals considered the defense of Russia's unity a sacred duty, an obligation based on the military oath they had taken before the revolution. To the Russian liberals it was a lofty cause fought in the name of human progress. Their emotional attachment to the greatness of Russia—which many may have become fully aware of only during the revolution and the civil war—injected a new vibrant element into their crusade for the unity of the empire. They were convinced that a democratic Russia held together not by a police regime but by Russian culture would provide the shortest and most efficient road to progress and would benefit all inhabitants. Their nationalism was supported by the ideas of one of the most highly respected ideologies of the day, and it forged them into the most consistent and ardent crusaders for the cause of an indivisible Russia.

Because the VA was under the strong influence of the Russian liberals and because its political objectives were modeled on the Kadet program, it was destined to assume an inflexibly hostile attitude toward federation. It was, therefore, not the counterrevolutionary nature of the VA that dictated an outright rejection of federation, but the categorical rejection of federation that imparted a counterrevolutionary character to the VA. In the West, largely through the energetic efforts of the numerous delegations of the borderland governments at the Paris Peace Conference, the nationality policy of the White movement attracted wide publicity. From the nationalities' point of view, the policies of the tsarist regime and those pursued by the VA differed but little. It was clear that behind the facade of "no predetermination" with respect to Russia's state structure, and behind the continuous postponement of the question of reconstructing Russia until a constituent or national assembly was convoked, lay the design for reasserting Russian dominance throughout the former empire. Because the principle of "Russia One and Indivisible" overshadowed all the other objectives the VA pursued, in the West the White movement was generally associated with tsarist restoration even though it fought under the banner of the Kadet program and never adopted, in spite of strenuous internal and external pressure, the monarchist slogan.

It should be noted that by the summer of 1919 the Kadets in Denikin's council constituted only a minority. The majority of this advisory body consisted either of nonparty members or moderate conservatives. Yet Denikin points out that many of the moderate conservatives were appointed at the suggestion of his Kadet advisers in Ekaterinodar. There is no question that the influence of the Russian liberals on Denikin was overwhelming. The program of no other Russian political party or group coincided so closely with the objectives pursued by the VA leaders, and no other party supported the VA's policies, especially with respect to foreign affairs and the nationalities, as consistently and steadfastly as the Central Committee of the People's Freedom party. The Kadet founding members of the Special Council, N. I. Astrov, V.

A. Stepanov, and K. N. Sokolov, remained at Denikin's side through all the vicissitudes the VA commander experienced during the civil war. When, at the end of 1919, Denikin decided to institute a formal government in place of the Special Council, he based the new structure on a model proposed by his Kadet advisers.[10] Significantly, there was no place for a minister of nationalities in the new cabinet.

It is true that with respect to the formulation of the VA's nationality policy, a strong influence was exerted by V. V. Shul'gin. The former editor of *Kievlianin* was not a liberal, but a conservative and a confirmed monarchist. What prompted Shul'gin to desert the monarchist bloc was its pro-German orientation. What provided a unifying bond between him and the liberals in the National Center was the Kadets' firm stand on the unity and indivisibility of Russia. Shul'gin's and the Kadets' views on the nationality question did not differ in principle. What the Kadets in Denikin's Special Council did not share with Shul'gin was his almost pathological hatred of all Jews and Ukrainians. For Shul'gin a Jew was synonymous with a Bolshevik,[11] and a Ukrainian, with a traitor. Both had to be combatted for the sake of preserving the might and indivisibility of Russia. Shul'gin's presence and influence within the Special Council was responsible to no small degree for the strong anti-Semitism and Ukrainophobia that prevailed at Ekaterinodar.

If the Russian Kadets at Denikin's Headquarters did not condone the acts of violence perpetrated against the Jews and the Ukrainians by the White armies, they did remarkably little to soften the rabid chauvinism that prevailed in Ekaterinodar in spite of protests by colleagues from abroad[12] and by local Jewish party members.[13] On the contrary, V. A. Stepanov's and P. B. Struve's articles in *Velikaia Rossiia* called for the intensification of Russian nationalism among the people. A typical article by Struve reads:

---

10. Denikin, *Ocherki*, 5: 282–4.
11. Shortly after the civil war Shul'gin strongly attacked Maklakov for not mentioning the word "Jew" even once in an article about Bolshevism published in a French journal. Shul'gin tried to demonstrate by concrete examples that Maklakov could easily have used the word "Jew" in place of "Bolshevik" throughout the article without changing its meaning. Shul'gin's unpublished article is in the Maklakov Personal Archive, box 2, file B.
12. Telegram from Burtsev and Miliukov to Denikin regarding Jewish pogroms, 8 October 1919, Miliukov Personal Archives, box 1.6.6.1., file 13.
13. At a Kadet Central Committee meeting, a Jewish party member, Mandelshtam, strongly censured discrimination against the Jews in the Propaganda Section of the Special Council, which was headed by a Kadet. Mandelshtam's protest was unheeded by the other party members in Ekaterinodar. See Minutes of Central Committee Meetings, 12 May 1919, Panina Papers, box 3, supplement.

> [T]he only organizing and spiritual force of that Russia that will rise from the ashes of the revolution can be found only in *nationalism*.... There are many of those who only yesterday were blind and immature. There are so many of them that if they organize themselves they will become an invincible force. This very day already, throughout the entire organism of the nation great, reinvigorating currents of national awakening are becoming visible. To comprehend, establish, and strengthen them is one of the most important tasks of our time.[14]

Cooperation between the liberals and the moderate conservatives in the Special Council and in the National Center shows the shift to the right among those Kadet party members who remained in Russia during the civil war. Struve described this metamorphosis:

> The long-lasting hostility of Western democratic elements to "tsarism" very lightheartedly and swiftly was applied to Russia as a great state after the dissolution of the Russian state. These circles reasoned in the following manner: the fall of Russia is the fall of tsarism, and [they] accepted this as a positive development. Many of us Russians, on the other hand, thought the exact opposite. Because for the Russians the fall of the monarchy meant the fall of Russia, many educated Russians, not being monarchists, became monarchists out of Russian patriotism. And certainly, from the point of view of Russian patriotism, this was the only correct decision.[15]

Although the Kadets in Denikin's Special Council did not advocate the monarchist principle, they did indeed become to a certain extent conservatives "out of Russian patriotism," as Astrov's, Panina's, Stepankov's, and Sokolov's correspondence with Maklakov indicate. Since Russian patriotism was at the root of the liberals' shift to the right, conservatism naturally left the strongest imprint on their attitude toward the nationalities. During the civil war no other party, whether conservative or socialist, defended the principle of Russia's unity and indivisibility as steadfastly and consistently as the People's Freedom party, and no other political group opposed federation as unflinchingly as the liberals in Denikin's council.

The VA's refusal to reach an agreement with the governments of the nationalities on the basis of federation was an important factor in the failure of the White struggle against Bolshevism. One Western scholar has assigned to it prime importance: "Denikin could not execute a land reform in chaos, and he could not force the Allies to secure his supply lines, but he might have

---

14. P. B. Struve, "Natsionalizm," *Velikaia Rossiia,* 1 (14) November 1919.
15. Ibid., 7.

filled the gap to some extent by adopting a policy of joint cooperation with all borderland governments on the basis of federation."[16]

Several years after the civil war ended, Denikin was somewhat ambivalent in his evaluation of the VA's categorical rejection of federation. In addition to pointing out the serious consequences that federation might have posed to the preservation of the empire's unity, Denikin doubted that concessions to the borderland governments would have improved the VA's chances for success. If federation had been proclaimed, he asked, "Would the new state armies, poisoned by the sweet venom of dreams of full independence, have closed their ranks with us sincerely and unselfishly?... [W]ould the morale of the Russian army have been buoyed up [by] going into battle for a 'Federal Republic'?"[17] To these rhetorical musings Denikin unequivocally replied, "Of course not! The wheel of history has not been turned by declarations and formulas." Twenty years after the revolution he still strongly defended the VA's avoidance of cooperation with the borderland governments. The widely divergent interests pursued by the White movement and the borderland states, as well as what he saw as the opportunism of the nationalities' leaders, precluded any form of common effort in the borderlands, from his point of view.[18]

At one point in one of the last volumes of his monumental *Ocherki russkoi smuty*, however, Denikin conceded that the VA might have been a bit too rigid in its attitude toward federation. It might have neglected to see that the federal principle did not necessarily predetermine Russia's internal structure, "which could have been fully rational and equitable without violating the state interests of Russia."[19] Perhaps the White generals had failed to perceive that "The state ties of Russia with its borderlands are predetermined by history, the economy, markets, the direction of the railroads, communications, the defense of boundaries, the psychology of Russian society, by the entire array of the cultural-economic forces of the *mutual* interests of *both* parties."[20] The reestablishment of ties between the center and the borderlands either through an agreement or by force was inevitable and would have been accomplished, Denikin claimed, by "*any* Russia."[21] Writing in the mid-1920s, Denikin most certainly underestimated the degree of force that would be required to keep the empire together during the Soviet period. His more astute Kadet advisers were aware that it was doubtful that

16. Brinkley, 289.
17. Denikin, *Ocherki*, 4: 245.
18. Denikin, "Navet na beloe dvizhenie," 48–62.
19. Denikin, *Ocherki*, 5: 138.
20. Ibid., 139.
21. Ibid.

the unity of a multinational state could be preserved by a democratic Russia that, by its very nature, would be obliged to outlaw the use of force.

The two extremes of the Russian political spectrum, the Bolsheviks and the ultra-right, were confident that reunification would take place once the regimes they were promoting were firmly established at the center. In the intervening period they were willing to extend broad concessions to the nationalities. Whether reunification would have been attainable under a liberal government is subject to speculation. It was in part the Russian liberals' realization that a constitutional government, at this stage of Russia's historical development, could not safeguard the unity of the empire, and in part their conviction that even the slightest concession to the nationalities—especially if granted as a result of Allied mediation by a weak and prostrated Russia—could serve as a precedent for further steps toward the loosening of the cohesiveness of the state, that prompted them to insist on a most rigid and uncompromising policy toward the political aspirations of the nationalities.

History has destined the White generals to bear the brunt of responsibility for both the military defeats and political mistakes of the White cause. Their lack of political acumen and tact is often cited as an explanation for their intractability concerning the idea of Russia's unity and indivisibility in regions where such slogans were tantamount to political suicide. Yet the political leaders in and outside Denikin's Special Council who were responsible for the elaboration of the White political programs have not been scathed by historians. This absence of criticism has resulted partly because it is much easier to accuse a military man of political callousness and chauvinism than a leading intellectual of the Central Committee of the Kadet party, and partly because the Russian liberals tended to shift the blame for their own mistakes on others. Even during the civil war Maklakov foresaw that if the White movement failed, his Kadet colleagues would whitewash their participation in the VA. For the failure of the Provisional Government it was Prince L'vov who was blamed and not the Kadets, "and tomorrow the same Kadets," sardonically observed Maklakov, "will say 'Denikin is to blame and not the Kadets.'"[22]

Denikin and his political advisers were convinced that the VA could not have adopted a conciliatory attitude toward the political aspirations of the nationalities without, at the same time, changing its principal objectives. To the end of Denikin's leadership, the White movement in the South remained first and foremost a drive for the reunification of Russia. In one of his last instructions to the Special Council, at the end of 1919, Denikin again reaffirmed that the reestablishment of "One, Great, Undivided Russia" was the

---

22. Letter from V. A. Maklakov to I. I. Petrunkevich, 15 September 1919, Panina Papers, box 3, file 27.

VA's principal task.[23] Only under Denikin's successor Gen. Wrangel, after the VA leadership, both political and military, had been completely revamped and the liberals of Denikin's council had been replaced by conservatives from "the old school of statesmen" who were not "ready to throw in their lot with the Revolution,"[24] did the struggle against Bolshevism emerge as the White movement's principal goal. After this transformation, cooperation with the nationalities against the Bolsheviks was sought, and the formula of federation, in principle at least, was endorsed. Yet by this time it was too late to speak of any meaningful cooperation. The pro-federalist currents among the nationalities had become virtually extinct. Moreover, the White movement, even when confined to the Crimean peninsula, could not divest itself of great-power chauvinism. It was great-power chauvinism, which was at times blurred by the lofty, enlightened slogans in the progressive political programs of the Western-oriented Russian intelligentsia and was often not discernible, that was a determining factor in the nationality policies of the Provisional Government and the Volunteer Army.

23. Denikin, *Ocherki*, 5: 280–1.
24. Wrangel, *Always with Honor*, 272.

Bibliography

MANUSCRIPTS and ARCHIVES

The Hoover Institution, Stanford University, California

Cheriachukin, A. V. Papers of the Don Envoy.
Denikin, A. I. "Navet na beloe dvizhenie." Microfilm.
Dratsenko, P. D. Documents.
N. N. Giers Archives.
V. A. Maklakov Personal Archive. 2d series.
V. A. Maklakov Archive of the Russian Embassy in Paris, 1918–23.
B. I. Nikolaevsky Collection.
D. G. Shcherbachev Papers.
Vatatsi, M. P. "The White Movement, 1917–1920: Memoirs."
P. N. Wrangel Military Archives.

The Bakhmeteff Archive of Russian and East European History and Culture, Columbia University, New York

A. I. and K. V. Denikin Papers.
Kazanovich, B. "Ataka Ekaterinodara i smert' Kornilova."
Makhrov, P. S., "General Vrangel' i B. Savinkov."
P. S. Makhrov Papers.
Makhrov, P. S., "V Beloi armii generala Denikina."
Miliukov, P. N., "Dnevnik." May 1918–April 1920.
P. N. Miliukov Personal Archive.
S. V. Panina Papers.
Poliakov, I. A. "General Kornilov."
Shatilov, P. "Zapiski."
Shavel'skii, Georgii. "Vospominaniia."
Svechin, M. A. "Dopolnenie k vospominaniiam."

The Józef Piłsudski Institute of America, New York

Akty Adjutantury Generalnej Naczelnego Dowództwa, 1918–1922.

Archives of the United States of America, Washington

German Foreign Office Archives. Microfilm no. 110.

Dissertations and Theses

Berk, Stephen Michael. "The Coup d'État of Admiral Kolchak: The Counterrevolution in Siberia and East Russia, 1917–1918." Ph.D. diss., Columbia University, 1971.
Priest, L. W. "The Cordon Sanitaire, 1918–1922." Ph.D. diss., Stanford University, 1954.
———. "The French Intervention in South Russia, 1918–1919." M.A. thesis, Stanford University, 1947.
Procyk, Anna. "The Ukrainian Treaty of Brest-Litovsk, February 1918." Russian Institute Essay, Columbia University, 1967.
Rosenberg, William G. "A. I. Denikin and the Anti-Bolshevik Movement in South Russia." Amherst College Honors Thesis No. 7, 1961.

PRINTED DOCUMENTS

Belov, G. A., et al, eds. *Iz istorii grazhdanskoi voiny v SSSR: Sbornik dokumentov i materialov.* 3 vols. Moscow: Institut marksizma-leninizma pri TsK KPSS, 1960–1.
Browder, R. P., and A. F. Kerensky, eds. *The Russian Provisional Government, 1917: Documents.* 3 vols. Stanford: Stanford University Press, 1961.
Bunyan, James, ed. *Intervention, Civil War and Communism in Russia, April–December 1918: Documents and Materials.* Baltimore: Johns Hopkins Press, 1936.
Bunyan, James, and Harold H. Fisher, eds. *The Bolshevik Revolution, 1917–1918.* Stanford: Stanford University Press, 1934.
Declaration Addressed to the President of the Peace Conference by the Russian Political Conference in Paris, 9 March 1919. Delegation Propaganda (Authenticated): Russia (Anti-Bolshevik Documents Presented to the Peace Conference—Memoranda). Hoover Institution.
France, Assemblée Nationale. *Annales de la Chambre des Députés, débats parlementaires, 1917–1921.*
Great Britain, Foreign Office. *Documents on British Foreign Policy, 1919–1939.* Vols. 2–3, 12. Edited by E. L. Woodward, R. Butler, and J. P. T. Bury. London: H. M. Stationery Office, 1949, 1962.
Great Britain. *Parliamentary Debates.* 5th Series. House of Commons, vol. 121.
Hornykiewicz, Theophil, ed. *Ereignisse in der Ukraine, 1914–1922, deren Bedeutung und historische Hintergründe.* 4 vols. Philadelphia: W. K. Lypynsky East European Institute, 1969.
Ispoved' Savinkova: Protsess Borisa Savinkova, August 1924. Berlin: "Russkoe ekho," 1924.

Kapustians'kyi, M. *Pokhid ukraïns'kykh armii na Kyïv–Odesu v 1919 rotsi (Korotkyi voienno-istorychnyi ohliad).* 2 vols. Munich: V–vo Khvylovoho and S. Sliusarchuk, 1946.

Khrystiuk, Pavlo. *Zamitky i materiialy do istoriï ukraïnskoï revoliutsiï. 1917–1920 rr.* 4 vols. Vienna: Ukraïns'kyi sotsiol'ogichnyi instytut, 1921–2. Reprint, New York: Vydavnytstvo Chartoryis'kykh, 1969.

Korolenko, P. P., ed. *Pereselenie kazakov za Kuban'; Russkaia kolonizatsiia na Zapadnom Kavkaz'e; materialy dlia istorii Kubanskoi oblasti.* Ekaterinodar: Kubanskoe oblastnoe pravlenie, 1910.

Korolivskii, S. M., et al, eds. *Grazhdanskaia voina na Ukraine: Sbornik dokumentov i materialov.* 3 vols. in 4 books. Kyiv: Naukova dumka, 1967.

Lenin, V. I. *Sochineniia.* Vol. 16. 3d ed. Moscow: Gosudarstvennoe izdatel'stvo, 1935.

Lisovoi, Ia. M., ed. *Belyi arkhiv: Sbornik materialov po istorii i literature voiny, revoliutsii, bol'shevizma, belago dvizheniia i t. p.* 3 vols. Paris: n. p., 1926–8.

Manilov, V., ed. *1917 god na Kievshchine: Khronika sobytii.* Kyiv: Gosudarstvennoe izdatel'stvo Ukrainy, 1928.

Petliura, Symon. *Statti, lysty, dokumenty.* Vol. 1. Edited by L. Drazhevs'ka et al. New York: Ukrainian Academy of Arts and Sciences in the U.S., 1956.

Piontkovskii, S. A., ed. *Grazhdanskia voina v Rossii, 1918–1921 gg.: Khrestomatiia.* Moscow: Izdatel'stvo Kommunisticheskogo universiteta im. Ia. M. Sverdlova, 1925.

Protokoly Pervago s"ezda Partii sotsialistov-revoliutsionerov. St. Petersburg, 1905.

Shliapnikov, A. *Semnadtsatyi god.* 4 vols. Moscow and Petrograd: Gosizdat, 1925.

Shlikhter, A. G., ed. *Chernaia kniga: Sbornik statei i materialov ob interventsii Antanty na Ukraine v 1918–1919 gg.* Kharkiv: Gosizdat Ukrainy, 1925.

Texts of the Ukraine "Peace." Washington: United States Department of State, 1918.

Troinitskii, N. A., ed. *Pervaia vseobshchaia perepis' naseleniia Rossiiskoi Imperii, 1897 g.: Obshchii svod.* Vol. 2. St. Petersburg, 1905.

Un appel du président Petlioura à la démocratie française (letter to Jean Pélissier, 22 October 1919). Hoover Institution.

United States, Department of State. *Papers Relating to the Foreign Relations of the United States, 1918, Russia.* Vol. 2. Washington: United States Government Printing Office, 1931.

———. *Papers Relating to the Foreign Relations of the United States: The Paris Peace Conference, 1919.* 13 vols. Washington: Government Printing Office, 1942–7.

CONTEMPORARY PAMPHLETS

Alekseev, A. A. *Avtonomiia i federatsiia*. Rostov, 1917.
Denikin, A. I. *Za chto my boremsia?* N. p., n. d.
Dolgorukov, P. D. *Natsional'naia politika i Partiia narodnoi svobody*. Rostov: Svobodnaia rech, 1919.
Kokoshkin, F. F. *Oblastnaia avtonomiia i edinstvo Rossii*. Moscow, 1906.
———. *Avtonomiia i federatsiia*. Petrograd, 1917.
Kto takoi Denikin? N. p.: Narodnaia biblioteka, 1919.
Losskii, N. O. *Chego khochet Partiia narodnoi svobody (Konstitutsionno-demokraticheskaia)*. Petrograd, 1917.
Mel'gunov, S. P. *Edinaia ili raschlenennaia Rossiia?* Paris [194?].
Nol'de, B. *Avtonomiia Ukraïny z istorychnoho pohliadu*. Translated by M. Zalizniak. Lviv: Ivan Aikhel'berger, 1912.
———. *Natsional'nyi vopros v Rossii*. Petrograd: Novoe vremia, 1917.
Rostov, B. *Pochemu i kak sozdalas Dobrovol'cheskaia armiia i za chto ona boretsia*. Rostov: Biblioteka Dobrovol'cheskoi armii, 1919.
Shchepkin, G. *General-leitenant A. I. Denikin*. Novocherkassk, 1919.
Struve, Petr". *Razmyshleniia o russkoi revoliutsii*. Sofia: Rossiisko–bolgarskoe knigoizdatel'stvo, 1921.
Volunteer Army. *Kratkaia zapiska istorii vzaimootnoshenii Dobrovol'cheskoi armii s Ukrainoi*. Rostov: Delo, 1919.
———. *Ocherk" vzaimootnoshenii Vooruzhennykh sil Iuga Rossii i predstavitelei frantsuzskago komandovaniia*. Ekaterinodar, 1919.
———. *The Volunteer Army as a National Factor in the Renaissance of Great Russia, One and Indivisible*. Ekaterinodar, 1919.
Volkonskii, P. M. *The Volunteer Army of Alexeiev and Denikin*. London: Russian Liberation Committee, n. d.
Zakonodatel'nyia proekty i predlozheniia Partii narodnoi svobody, 1904–1907 gg. St. Petersburg, 1907.

MEMOIRS and DIARIES

Alekseev, S. A., ed. *Denikin, Iudenich, Vrangel'*. Moscow: Gosizdat, 1927.
———. *Nachalo grazhdanskoi voiny*. Moscow: Gosizdat, 1926.
———. *Revoliutsiia na Ukraine po memuaram belykh*. Moscow: Gosizdat, 1930.
Andriievs'kyi, Viktor. *Z mynuloho*. 2 vols. Berlin: Ukraïns'ke slovo, 1923. Reprint, New York: Hoverlia, 1963.
Chernov, V. M. *Rozhdenie revoliutsionnoi Rossii: Fevral'skaia revoliutsiia*. Paris: Iubileinyi komitet po izdaniiu trudov V. M. Chernova, 1934.
Denikin, Anton I. *The Career of a Tsarist Officer: Memoirs, 1872–1916*. Minneapolis: University of Minnesota Press, 1975.
———. *Ocherki russkoi smuty*. 4 vols in 5 bks. Paris: J. Povolozky et cie., 1921–2 (vols. 1–2); Berlin: Slovo, 1924–6 (vols. 2–4).
———. *Put' russkogo ofitsera*. New York: Izdatel'stvo im. Chekhova, 1953.
———. *The Russian Turmoil: Memoirs Military, Social, and Political* London: Hutchinson, 1922.
———. *The White Army*. London: Jonathan Cape, 1930. Reprint, Gulf Breeze: Academic International Press, 1973.
Denisov, S. V. *Zapiski: Grazhdanskaiia voina na iuge Rossii, 1918–1920 gg.* Istanbul: the author, 1921.
Ivanys, Vasyl'. *Stezhkamy zhyttia: Spohady*. Neu-Ulm: Ukraïns'ki visti, 1959.
Kerensky, A. F. *Russia and History's Turning Point*. New York: Duell, Sloan and Pearce, 1965.
Lotots'kyi, O. *Storinky mynuloho*. 3 vols. Warsaw: Ukraïnskyi naukovyi instytut, 1932–4. Reprint, South Bound Brook: Ukrainian Orthodox Church of USA, 1966.
Loukomsky [Lukomskii], A. S. *Memoirs of the Russian Revolution*. London: T. F. Unwin, 1922.
———. *Vospominaiia*. 2 vols. Berlin: Otto Kirchner, 1922.
Margolin, Arnold D. *From a Political Diary: Russia, the Ukraine, and America, 1905–1945*. New York: Columbia University Press, 1946.
———. *Ukraina i politika Antanty*. Berlin: S. Efron, 1921. Translated as *Ukraine and Policy of the Entente*. Washington(?): L. A. Margolena, 1977.
Margulies, M. S. *God interventsii*. 3 vols. Berlin: Z. I. Grzhebin, 1923.
Miliukov, P. N. *Vospominaniia*. 2 vols. New York: Izdatel'stvo im. Chekhova, 1955.
Nazaruk, Osyp. *Rik na Velykii Ukraïni: spomyny z Ukraïnskoï revoliutsiï*. Vienna: Ukraïnskyi prapor, 1920.
Nesterovich-Berg, M. A. *V bor'be s bol'shevikami*. Paris: Imprimerie de Navarre, 1931.
Pavlov, V. E., ed. *Markovtsy v boiakh i pokhodakh za Rossiiu v osvoboditel'- noi voine, 1917–1921*. Paris: n. p., 1922.

Rakovskii, G. N. *V stane belykh: Grazhdanskaia voina na iuge Rossii.* Istanbul: Pressa, 1920.
Shchegolev, P. E., ed. *Frantsuzy v Odesse: Iz belykh memuarov gen. A. I. Denikina, M. S. Margulies, M. V. Braikevicha.* Leningrad: Krasnaia gazeta, 1928.
Shul'gin, V. V. *Dni.* Belgrade: M. A. Suverin i ko., Novoe vremia, 1925.
―――. *1920 g.: Ocherki.* Sofia: Rossiisko–bolgarskoe knigoizdatel'stvo, 1921.
Slashchev-Krymskii, Ia. A. *Trebuiu suda obshchestva i glasnosti: Oborona i sdacha Kryma; memuary i dokumenty.* Istanbul: M. Shul'man, 1921.
Sokolov, K. N. *Pravlenie generala Denikina.* Sofia: Rossiisko–bolgarskoe knigoizdatel'stvo, 1921.
Stankevich, V. B. *Vospominaniia, 1914–1919.* Berlin: I. P. Ladyshnikov, 1920.
Suvorin, B. *Za rodinoi: Geroicheskaia epokha Dobrovol'cheskoi armii, 1917–1918 gg.* Paris: O. D. i ko. 1922.
Vrangel' (Wrangel), P. N. *Always with Honor.* New York: Robert Speller and Sons, 1957.
―――. *Memoirs.* London: William and Norgate, 1929.
―――. "Zapiski." In *Beloe delo: Letopis' beloi bor'by.* Edited by A. A. von Lampe. Vol. 5: 9–306; vol. 6: 5–261. Berlin: Russkoe natsional'noe knigoizdatel'stvo, 1926, 1928. Reissued as *Vospominaniia.* 2 vols. Frankfurt am Main: Posev, 1969.
Williamson, H. N. H. *Farewell to the Don.* New York: John Day, 1971.

SECONDARY WORKS

Books

Aleksachenko, A. P. *Krakh denikinshchiny.* Moscow: Izdatel'stvo Moskovskogo universiteta, 1966.
Allworth, Edward, ed. *Central Asia: A Century of Russian Rule.* New York: Columbia University Press, 1967.
―――. *Soviet Nationality Problems.* New York: Columbia University Press, 1971.
Avalov (Avalishvili), Z. D. *The Independence of Georgia in International Politics, 1918–1921.* London: Headley Brothers, 1940.
Bechhofer-Roberts, C. E. *In Denikin's Russia and the Caucasus, 1919–1920.* London: W. Collin's Sons and Co., 1921.
Beliaevskii, V. A. *Pravda o gen. Denikine: Prichiny prekrashcheniia belogo dvizheniia na iuge Rossii v 1920 g.* San Francisco: n.p., 1959.

Berger, J. N. *Zur Lösung der österreichischen Verfassungsfrage*. Vienna, 1861.
Borshchak, Elie. *L'Ukraine à la conférence de la Paix, 1919*. Paris: n. p., 1938.
Bradley, John. *Allied Intervention in Russia*. New York: Basic Books, 1968.
———. *Civil War in Russia, 1917–1920*. London: Bedford, 1975.
Brinkley, George A. *The Volunteer Army and Allied Intervention in South Russia, 1917–1921*. Notre Dame: University of Notre Dame Press, 1966.
Chmielewski, Edward. *The Polish Question in the Russian State Duma*. Knoxville: University of Tennessee Press, 1970.
Carley, Michael Jabara. *Revolution and Intervention: The French Government and the Russian Civil War, 1917–1919*. Kingston: McGill-Queens University Press, 1983.
Choulguine, Alexandre [Shul'hyn, Oleksander]. *L'Ukraine contre Moscow*. Paris: F. Alcan, 1935.
———. *L'Ukraine, la Russie et les puissances de L'Entente*. Bern: Imprimeries Réunies S. A. Lausanne, 1918.
Davies, Norman. *White Eagle, Red Star: The Polish-Soviet War, 1919–1920*. New York: St. Martin's Press, 1972.
Denikin, A. I. *Kto spas sovetskuiu vlast' ot gibeli*. Paris: Soiuz dobrovol'tsev, 1937.
———. *Ofitsery*. Paris: n. p., 1928.
———. *Staraia armiia*. 2 vols. Paris: Rodnik, 1929–31.
———. *World Events and the Russian Problem*. Paris: Imprimerie Rapide, 1939.
Denisov, S. V., ed. *Belaia Rossiia*. New York: Izdatel'stvo Glavnago pravleniia Zarubezhnago soiuza russkikh voennykh invalidov, 1935.
Dnistrianskyi, Stanislaus. *Ukraina and the Peace Conference*. N. p., 1919.
Dobrynin, V. *Bor'ba s bol'shevizmom na iuge Rossii: Uchastie v bor'be donskago kazachestva*. Prague: Slavianskoe izdatel'stvo, 1921.
Dolenha, Sviatoslav. *Skoropadshchyna*. Warsaw: M. Kunyts'kyi, 1934.
Doroshenko, Dmytro. *Istoriia Ukraïny, 1917–1923 rr.* 2 vols. Uzhhorod: Osyp Tsiupka, 1930. Reprint, New York: Bulava, 1954.
Dol'nytskyi, Myron, et al, eds. *Ukraïns'ka Halyts'ka Armiia u 40-richchia iï uchasty u vyzvol'nykh zmahanniakh (materiialy do istoriï)*. Vols. 1–3. Winnipeg: Dmytro Mykytiuk, 1958–66.
Dotsenko, Oleksander. *Litopys ukraïns'koï revoliutsii*. Lviv: the author, 1923. Reprint, Philadelphia: Doslidchyi instytut modernoï ukraïns'koï istoriï, 1988.
Dumova, N. G. *Kadetskaia kontrrevoliutsiia i ee razgrom: Oktiabr 1917–1920 gg.* Moscow: Nauka, 1982.
———. *Kadetskaia partiia v period Pervoi mirovoi voiny i Fevral'skoi revoliutsii*. Moscow: Nauka, 1988.

Fedenko, Panas. *Ukraïns'kyi hromads'kyi rukh.* Poděbrady: n. p., 1934.
Fedyshyn, Oleh S. *Germany's Drive to the East and the Ukrainian Revolution, 1917–1918.* New Brunswick: Rutgers University Press, 1971.
Fisher, George. *Russian Liberalism: From Gentry to Intelligentsia.* Cambridge: Harvard University Press, 1958.
Filippov, N. *Ukrainskaia kontrrevoliutsiia na sluzhbe u Anglii, Frantsii i Pol'shi.* Moscow: Moskovskii rabochii, 1937.
Footman, David. *Civil War in Russia.* London: Faber and Faber, 1961.
Golovin, N. N. *Rossiiskaia kontrrevoliutsiia v 1917–1918 gg.* 5 vols. Paris: Biblioteka "Illiustrirovannoi Rossii," 1937.
———. *The Russian Army in the World War.* New Haven: Yale University Press, 1931.
Gukovskii, A. I. *Antanta i Oktiabr'skaia revoliutsiia.* Moscow: Gosudarstvennoe sotsial'no-ekonomicheskoe izdatel'stvo, 1931.
Horak, Stephan M. *The First Treaty of World War I: Ukraine's Treaty with the Central Powers of February 9, 1918.* Boulder: East European Monographs, 1988.
Ioffe, G. Z. *"Beloe delo": General Kornilov.* Moscow: Nauka, 1989.
Ivanov, N. Ia. *Kornilovshchina i ee razgrom: Iz istorii bor'by s kontrrevoliutsiei v 1917 g.* Leningrad: Izdatel'stvo Leningradskogo universiteta, 1965.
Juzwenko, Adolf. *Polska a "Biała" Rosja: Od listopada 1918 do kwietnia 1920 r.* Wrocław, Warsaw, Cracow, and Gdańsk: Zakład Narodowy im. Ossolińskich, Wydawnictwo Polskiej Akademii Nauk, 1973.
Kantorovich, V. A. *Frantsuzy v Odesse.* Petrograd: Byloe, 1922.
Kapustin, M. I. *Zagovor generalov (iz istorii kornilovshchiny i ee razgroma).* Moscow: Mysl', 1968.
Katkov, George. *Russia, 1917: The February Revolution.* New York: Harper and Row, 1967.
———. *Russia 1917: The Kornilov Affair; Kerensky and the Breakup of the Russian Army.* London and New York: Longman, 1980.
Kennan, George F. *Russia and the West under Lenin and Stalin.* Vol. 1. *Russia Leaves the War.* Princeton: Princeton University Press, 1956.
Kenez, Peter. *Civil War in South Russia, 1918: The First Year of the Volunteer Army.* Berkeley: University of California Press, 1971.
———. *Civil War in South Russia, 1919–1920: The Defeat of the Whites.* Berkeley: University of California Press, 1977.
Kerensky, A. F. *The Prelude to Bolshevism: The Kornilov Rebellion.* London: T. Fisher Unwin, 1919.
Kin, D. *Denikinshchina.* Leningrad: Priboi, 1927.
Krypiakevych, I., et al. *Istoriia ukraïns'koho viiska.* Winnipeg: Ivan Tyktor, 1953.
Lampe, A. A. von, ed. *Beloe delo: Letopis' beloi bor'by.* 7 vols. Berlin: Russkoe natsional'noe knigoizdatel'stvo Mednyi vsadnik, 1926–8.

Lehovich, Dimitry V. *White against Red: The Life of General Anton Denikin.* New York: W. W. Norton, 1974.
Leontovitsch, Viktor. *Geschichte des Liberalismus in Russland.* Frankfurt am Main: V. Klosterman, 1959.
Lincoln, W. Bruce. *Red Victory: A History of the Russian Civil War.* New York: Simon and Schuster, 1989.
Lotots'kyi, Oleksander. *Symon Petliura.* Warsaw: Komitet dlia vshanuvannia X richnytsi smerty Symona Petliury, 1936.
Lozyns'kyi, Mykhailo. *Halychyna v r. 1918–1920.* Vienna: Institut Sociologique Ukrainien, 1922. Reprint, New York: Chervona kalyna, 1970.
Luckett, Richard. *The White Generals: An Account of the White Movement and the Russian Civil War.* New York: The Viking Press, 1971.
Malet, Michael. *Nestor Makhno in the Russian Civil War.* London: Macmillan, 1982.
Mawdsley, Ewan. *The Russian Civil War.* Boston: Allen and Unwin, 1987.
Mayzel, Matitiahu. *Generals and Revolutionaries: The Russian General Staff during the Revolution; A Study in the Transformation of Military Elite.* Osnabrück: Biblio, 1979.
Mazepa, I. *Ukraïna v ohni i buri revoliutsiï, 1917–1921.* 3 vols. Munich: Prometei, 1950–1.
McKay, John P. *Pioneers for Profit: Foreign Entrepreneurship and Russian Industrialization, 1885–1913.* Chicago: Chicago University Press, 1970.
Mel'gunov, S. P. *Grazhdanskaiia voina v osveshchenii P. N. Miliukova.* Paris: Rapid-Imprimerie, 1929.
———. *Legenda o separatnom mire.* Paris: privately printed, 1957.
———. *Na putiakh k dvortsovomu perevorotu.* Paris: Rodnik, 1931.
———. *N. V. Chaikovskii v gody grazhdanskoi voiny: Materialy dlia istorii russkoi obshchestvennosti, 1917–1925 gg.* Paris: Librairie "La Source," 1929.
Miliukov, P. N. *Beloe dvizhenie.* Paris: Respublikansko-demokraticheskoe ob"edinenie, 1929.
———. *Istoriia vtoroi russkoi revoliutsii.* 3 vols. Sofia: Rossiisko-bolgarskoe knigoizdatel'stvo, 1921–4.
———. *Russia Today and Tomorrow.* New York: Macmillan, 1922.
Naumenko, V. G. *Iz nedavnago proshlago Kubani.* Belgrade: n.p., 193?
Palij, Michael. *The Anarchism of Nestor Makhno, 1918–1921: An Aspect of the Ukrainian Revolution.* Seattle: University of Washington Press, 1976.
Pidhainy, Oleh S. *The Formation of the Ukrainian Republic.* Toronto: New Review Books, 1966.
Pipes, Richard. *The Formation of the Soviet Union: Communism and Nationalism, 1917–1923.* Cambridge: Harvard University Press, 1954.
———. *Struve: Liberal on the Right, 1905–1944.* Cambridge: Harvard University Press, 1980.

Pokrovskii, G. K. *Denikinshchina: God politiki i ekonomiki na Kubani, 1918–1919 gg.* Berlin: Z. I. Grzhebin, 1923.

Rabinowitch, Alexander. *The Bolsheviks Come to Power: The Revolution of 1917 in Petrograd.* New York: W. W. Norton, 1976.

———. *Prelude to Revolution: The Petrograd Bolsheviks and the July 1917 Uprising.* Bloomington: Indiana University Press, 1968.

Radkey, Oliver H. *The Election to the Russian Constituent Assembly of 1917.* Cambridge: Harvard University Press, 1950.

———. *The Sickle Under the Hammer: The Russian Socialist Revolutionaries in the Early Months of Soviet Rule.* New York: Columbia University Press, 1963.

———. *The Unknown Civil War in Soviet Russia: A Study of the Green Movement in the Tambov Region, 1920–1921.* Stanford: Hoover Institution Press, 1976.

Reshetar, Jr., John S. *The Ukrainian Revolution, 1917–1920: A Study in Nationalism.* Princeton: Princeton University Press, 1952. Reprint, New York: Arno Press, 1972.

Rosenberg, William G. *A. I. Denikin and the Anti–Bolshevik Movement in South Russia.* Amherst: Amherst College Press, Amherst College Honors Thesis, No. 7, 1961.

———. *Liberals in the Russian Revolution: The Constitutional Democratic Party, 1917–1921.* Princeton: Princeton University Press, 1974.

Ross, Nikolai. *Vrangel' v Krymu.* Frankfurt am Main: Posev, 1982.

Savchenko, F. *Zaborona ukraïnstva 1876 r.: Do istoriï hromads'kykh rukhiv na Ukraïni 1860–1870-kh r.r..* Kyiv: Derzhavne vydavnytstvo Ukraïny, 1930. Reprint, Munich: Wilhelm Fink, 1970.

Savinkov, B. V. *Bor'ba s bol'shevikami.* Warsaw: Russkii politicheskii komitet, 1920.

———. *K delu Kornilova.* Paris: Union, 1919.

———. *Za rodinu i svobodu: Na puti k "tret'ei" Rossii; sbornik statei.* Warsaw: Russkii politicheskii komitet, 1920.

Schorske, Carl E. *Fin-de-Siècle Vienna: Politics and Culture.* New York: Vintage Books, 1981.

Semennikov, V. P. *Politika Romanovykh nakanune revoliutsii (ot Antanty k Germanii po novym dokumentam).* Moscow: Gosizdat, 1926.

———. *Romanovy i germanskie vliianiia vo vremia Mirovoi voiny.* Leningrad: Krasnaia gazeta, 1929.

Senn, Alfred E. *The Russian Revolution in Switzerland, 1914–1917.* Madison: University of Wisconsin Press, 1971.

Shoulgin, Alexander [Shul'hyn, Oleksander]. *The Problems of the Ukraine.* London: The Ukrainian Press Bureau, 1919.

Shul'gin, V. V. *Chto nam v nikh ne nravitsia.* Paris: Russia Minor, 1929.

———. *Ukrainstvuiushchiia i my.* Belgrade: N. Z. Rybinskii, 1939.

Silverlight, John. *The Victors' Dilemma: Allied Intervention in the Russian Civil War.* New York: Weybright and Talley, 1970.

Skaba, A. D. *Parizhskaia mirnaia konferentsiia i inostrannaia interventsiia v strane sovetov (ianvar' i iun' 1919).* Kyiv: Naukova dumka, 1971.

———, et al, eds. *Ukraïns'ka RSR v period hromadianskoï viiny, 1917–1920 rr.* 3 vols. Kyiv: Vydavnytstvo politychnoï literatury Ukraïny, 1968.

Skobtsov, D. E. *Tri goda revoliutsii i grazhdanskoi voiny na Kubani.* Paris: n. p., n. d.

Spirin, L. M. *Klassy i partii v grazhdanskoi voine v Rossii (1917–1920).* Moscow: Mysl', 1968.

Struve, P. *Patriotika: Politika, kul'tura, religiia, sotsializm; sbornik statei za piat' let, 1905–1910 gg.* St. Petersburg: D. E. Zhukovskii, 1911.

Suliatyts'kyi, P. *Narysy z istoriï revoliutsii na Kubani (III 1917–VI 1918).* Prague: Ukraïns'kyi instytut hromadoznavstva v Prazi, 1925.

Suprunenko, N. I. *Ocherki istorii grazhdanskoi voiny i inostrannoi voennoi interventsii na Ukraine.* Moscow: Nauka, 1966.

Thaden, Edward C. *Conservative Nationalism in Nineteenth-Century Russia.* Seattle: University of Washington Press, 1964.

Timberlake, Charles E., ed. *Essays on Russian Liberalism.* Columbia: University of Missouri Press, 1972.

Thompson, John M. *Russia, Bolshevism, and the Versailles Peace.* Princeton: Princeton University Press, 1966.

Udovychenko, Oleksander. *Ukraïna u viini za derzhavnist': Istoriia orhanizatsiï i boiovykh dii Ukraïns'kykh Zbroinykh Syl, 1917–1921.* Winnipeg: Dmytro Mykytiuk, 1954.

Val', E. G. *K istorii belago dvizheniia: Deiatel'nost' general-adiutanta Shcherbacheva.* Tallinn: the author, 1935.

———. *Prichiny raspadeniia Rossiskoi imperii i neudachi russkago natsional'nago dvizheniia.* 4 vols. in one. Tallinn: the author, 1938.

Vladimirova, V. *Kontrrevoliutsia v 1917 godu (kornilovshchina).* Moscow: Krasnaia nov', 1924.

Vynnychenko, V. *Vidrodzhennia natsiï (Istoriia ukraïns'koï revolutsiï [marets' 1917 r.–hruden' 1919 r.])* 3 vols. Vienna: Dzvin, 1920.

Wade, Rex A. *The Russian Search for Peace, February–October, 1917.* Stanford: Stanford University Press, 1969.

Walicki, Andrzej. *Legal Philosophies of Russian Liberalism.* Oxford: Clarendon Press, 1987.

Walkin, Jacob. *The Rise of Democracy in Pre-Revolutionary Russia: Political and Social Institutions under the Last Three Czars.* New York: Praeger, 1962.

Wandycz, Piotr S. *France and Her Eastern Allies, 1919–1925: French-Czechoslovak-Polish Relations from the Paris Peace Conference to Locarno.* Minneapolis: University of Minnesota Press, 1962.

———. *Soviet-Polish Relations, 1917–1921.* Cambridge: Harvard University Press, 1969.
Warth, Robert D. *The Allies and the Russian Revolution from the Fall of the Monarchy to the Peace of Brest-Litovsk.* Durham: Duke University Press, 1954.
Wheeler-Bennett, John. *Brest-Litovsk: The Forgotten Peace, March 1918.* London: Macmillan, 1938.
Wierzchowski, Mirosław. *Sprawy Polski w III i IV Dumie Państwowej.* Warsaw: Panstwowe Wydawnictwo Naukowe, 1966.
Wildman, Allan K. *The End of the Russian Imperial Army: The Old Army and the Soldiers' Revolt (March–April 1917).* Princeton: Princeton University Press, 1980.
Xydias, Jean. *L'intervention française en Russie, 1918–1919: Souvenirs d'un témoin.* Paris: Editions de France, 1927.
Zaionchkovskii, P. A. *Voennye reformy 1860–1870 godov v Rossii.* Moscow: Izdatel'stvo Moskovskogo universiteta, 1952.
Zaitsov, A. A. *1918 god: Ocherki po istorii russkoi grazhdanskoi voiny.* Paris: n. p., 1934.
Zaslavskii, D. O. *Rytsar' chernoi sotni V. V. Shul'gin.* Leningrad: Byloe, 1925.

Articles

Alekseev, M. V. "Iz dnevnika generala Alekseeva." *Russkii istoricheskii arkhiv* (Prague) 1 (1929): 15–56.
Andriewsky, Olga. "*Medved' iz berlogi:* Vladimir Jabotinsky and the Ukrainian Question, 1904–1914." *Harvard Ukrainian Studies* 14, no. 3/4 (1990), 249–67.
Anin, David S. "The February Revolution: Was the Collapse Inevitable?" *Soviet Studies* 18 (1967): 435–57.
Arslanian, Artin H., and Robert L. Nichols. "Nationalism and the Russian Civil War: The Case of Volunteer Army-Armenian Relations, 1918–1920." *Soviet Studies* 31 (1979): 559–73.
Ascher, Abraham. "The Kornilov Affair." *Russian Review* 27, no. 3 (October 1953), 235–52.
Astrakhan, Kh. M. "Istoriia burzhuaznykh i melkoburzhuaznykh partii Rossii v 1917 g. v noveishei sovetskoi literature." *Voprosy istorii,* 1975, no. 2, 30–44.
Astrov, N. I. "Iasskoe soveshchanie." *Golos minuvshego na chuzhoi storone* 3 (1925): 39–76.
Benediktov, M. "P. N. Miliukov i natsional'nyi vopros." In *P. N. Miliukov: Sbornik materialov,* 207–11. Edited by S. A. Smirnov et al. Paris, 1929.
Borschak, Elie. "La paix ukrainienne de Brest-Litovsk." *Le Monde Slave,* 1929, no. 4, 33–62; no. 7, 63–84; no. 8, 199–225.

Boyd, John R. "The Origins of Order No. 1." *Soviet Studies* 19 (1968): 359–72.
Carley, Michael Jabara. "The Politics of Anti-Bolshevism: The French Government and the Russo-Polish War, December 1919–May 1920." *Historical Journal*, March 1976, 163–89.
Cheriachukin, V. A. "Donskaia delegatsiia na Ukrainu i Berlin v 1918–1919 gg." *Donskaia letopis'* (Belgrade) 2 (1924): 163–231.
Chubinskii, M. P. "Na Donu." *Donskaia letopis'* 3: 268–309.
Conolly, Violet. "The 'Nationalities Question' in the Last Phase of Tsardom." In *Russia Enters the Twentieth Century: 1894–1917*, 152–81. Edited by Erwin Oberlaender et al. New York: Schocken Books, 1971.
Denikin, A. I. "Otvet." *Illiustrirovanaia Rossiia* (Paris), 1930, nos. 22–4.
Dumova, Natalia G. "Maloizvestnye materialy po istorii kornilovshchiny." *Voprosy istorii*, 1968, no. 11, 69–93.
———. "Iz istorii Kadetskoi partii v 1917 g." *Istoricheskie zapiski* 90 (1972): 109–59.
Dziewanowski, M. K. "Piłsudski's Federal Policy, 1919–1920." *Journal of Central European Affairs* 10, no. 2 (July 1950), 113–23; no. 3 (October 1950), 271–87.
Feldman, Robert S. "The Russian General Staff and the June 1917 Offensive." *Soviet Studies* 19 (1968): 526–43.
Filimonov, A. P. "Kubantsy." In *Beloe delo: Letopis' beloi bor'by*, vol. 2, 62–107. Edited by A. A. von Lampe. Berlin: Russkoe natsional'noe knigoizdatel'stvo, 1927.
———. "Razgrom Kubanskoi Rady." *Arkhiv russkoi revoliutsii* (Berlin) 5 (1922): 322–9.
Galuzo, P. "Iz istorii natsional'noi politiki Vremennogo Pravitel'stva (Ukraina, Finlandiia, Khiva)." *Krasnyi arkhiv* 30 (1928): 46–79.
Grave, B., ed. "Kadety v 1905–1906 gg." *Krasnyi arkhiv* 46 (1931): 38–68; 47–8 (1931): 111–13.
Grigor'ev [Genker]. "Tatarskii vopros v Krymu." In *Antanta i Vrangel': Sbornik statei*, 232–8. Moscow: Gosizdat, 1923.
Gurko, V. I. "Iz Petrograda cherez Moskvu, Parizh i London v Odessu, 1917–1918 gg." *Arkhiv russkoi revoliutsii* 15 (1924): 5–84.
Hamm, Michael F. "Liberal Politics in Wartime Russia: An Analysis of the Progressive Bloc." *Slavic Review* 33, no. 3 (September 1974), 453–68.
Ivanov, G. P. "Osvobozhdenie Novocherkasska i Krug Spaseniia Dona." *Donskaia letopis'* 3: 59–60, 323–6.
Kakliugin, K. P. "Donskoi ataman P. N. Krasnov i ego vremia." *Donskaia letopis'* 3: 68–163.
———. "Voiskovoi ataman A. M. Kaledin i ego vremia." *Donskaia letopis'* 2: 108–70.
Karpovich, M. M. "General Denikin." *Novyi zhurnal* (New York) 17 (1947): 320–1.

Kenez, Peter. "The Ideology of the White Movement." *Soviet Studies* 32 (1980): 58–83.

———. "The Relations between the Volunteer Army and Georgia, 1918–1920: A Case Study in Disunity." *Slavonic and East European Review,* July 1970, 403–23.

Krasnov, V. M. "Iz vospominanii o 1917–1920 gg." *Arkhiv russkoi revoliutsii* 8 (1923): 110–65; 9 (1923): 106–66.

———. "Vsevelikoe Voisko Donskoe." *Arkhiv russkoi revoliutsii* 5 (1922): 190–321.

Lapin, N., "Progressivnyi blok v 1915–1917 gg." *Krasnyi arkhiv* 50–1 (1932): 117–60.

Laverychev, V. I. "Russkie monopolisty i zagovor Kornilova." *Voprosy istorii,* 1964, no. 4, 32–41.

Lednitskii [Lednicki], A. "P. N. Miliukov i pol'skii vopros." In *P. N. Miliukov: Sbornik materialov,* 212–17. Edited by S. A. Smirnov et al. Paris, 1929.

Maiborodov, V. "S frantsuzami." *Arkhiv russkoi revoliutsii* 16 (1925): 100–61.

McNeal, Robert H. "The Conference of Jassy: An Early Fiasco of the Anti-Bolshevik Movement." In *Essays in Russian and Soviet History,* 221–36. Edited by J. S. Curtiss. New York: Columbia University Press, 1963.

Mel'gunov, S. P. "Rossiiskaia kontrrevoliutsiia." *Znamia Rossii* (Prague), February–March 1935.

"N. S. Riabovol." *Vol'noe kazachestvo,* August 1936, 11–13.

Obolenskii, V. A. "Krym pri Vrangele." *Na chuzhoi storone* 9 (1925): 5–56.

"Ocherki generala Denikina." *Na chuzhoi storone* 5 (1924): 300–8.

Riha, Thomas. "Miliukov and the Progressive Bloc in 1915: A Study in Last Chance Politics." *Journal of Modern History* 32, no. 1 (March 1960), 16–24.

Shafir, Ia. "Orlovshchina." In *Antanta i Vrangel': Sbornik statei.* Moscow: Gosizdat, 1923.

Shemet, S. "Do istoriï Ukraïnskoï demokratychno-khliborobs'koï partii." *Khliborobs'ka Ukraïna* (Vienna) 1: 67–79.

Shul'gin, V. V. "Glavy iz knigi 'Gody.'" *Istoriia SSSR,* 1967, no. 1, 123–44.

Smith, Jr., C. J. "Miliukov and the Russian National Question." *Harvard Slavic Studies* 4 (1957): 395–419.

Strakhovsky, Leonid I. "Was there a Kornilof Affair?—A Reappraisal of the Evidence." *Slavonic and East European Review* 35 (1955): 372–95.

Struve, P. B. "Chto takoe Rossiia." *Russkaia mysl',* January 1911, 175–8.

———. "Obshcherusskaia kul'tura i ukrainskii partikularizm: Otvet ukrainstvu." *Russkaia mysl',* January 1912, 65–86.

Treadgold, Donald W. "The Ideology of the White Movement: Wrangel's 'Leftist Policy from Rightist Hands.'" *Harvard Slavic Studies* 4 (1957): 481–98.

Trubetskoi, E. N. "Iz putevykh zametok bezhentsa." *Arkhiv russkoi revoliutsii* 18 (1926): 137–207.

Ukrainets [Bohdan Kistiakovs'kyi]. "K voprosu o samostoiatel'noi ukrainskoi kul'ture." *Russkaia mysl',* May 1911, 131–46.

Ukraintsev, N. "A Document in the Kornilov Affair." *Soviet Studies*, 25 (1973): 283–98.

Valentinov, A. a. "Krymskaia epopeia." *Arkhiv russkoi revoliutsii* 5 (1922): 5–100.

Vendziagol'skii, K. "Savinkov." *Novyi zhurnal*, no. 70 (1962), 142–83.

Wade, Rex A. "Why October? The Search for Peace in 1917." *Soviet Studies* 20 (1968): 143–9.

Wandycz, Piotr S. "Secret Soviet-Polish Peace Talks in 1919." *Slavic Review* 24, no. 3 (September 1965): 425–49.

White, James D. "The Kornilov Affair—A Study in Counter-Revolution." *Soviet Studies* 20 (1968): 187–205.

Zhabotinskii, V. I. "Pis'ma o natsional'nostiakh i oblastiakh: Evreistvo i ego nastroeniia." *Russkaia mysl',* January 1911, 95–114.

Index

Afanas'ev, Georgii, 75, 76
Ageev, P. M., 133
Aleksander I, 91
Alekseev, Gen. Mikhail V., 2, 3, 4, 6, 8n, 9n, 18, 35–43, 52, 54n, 57, 58, 61n, 66, 67, 68, 70, 72, 120, 147, 167
All-Cossack Congress, 36n
All-Russian Church Council, 78n
All-Russian Constituent Assembly, 11, 14, 16, 39, 41, 42, 52, 58, 61, 67, 82, 102, 104
All-Russian Cossack Congress, 37
All-Russian National Assembly, 78
All-Ukrainian Workers' Congress, 20
Allworth, Edward, xv, 12n, 16n
Analov, F., 107n
Andriewsky, Olga, 28n
Andriievs'kyi, Opanas, 77n, 106
Arkhangelsk government, 97, 99, 104
Armenia, 38n, 104, 144n, 150
Army of the UNR, *see* Ukrainian People's Republic (UNR) Army
Arslanian, A. H., 119n, 144n
Ascher, Abraham, 7n
Astrakhan Cossacks, 150
Astrov, Nikolai I., 70, 88, 131, 170, 172
Avksent'ev, Nikolai D., 105
Azbuka, 66, 68n, 84, 85
Azerbaijan, 38n, 144

Bagge, John Picton, 47
Bakhmeteff, Boris A., 98
Barclay, Sir George, 74n, 89

Beaupoil de Saint-Aulaire, de, 47, 74n, 84
Belarus, 14, 49, 73, 115, 117
Beletskii, A. S., 39n
Belgium, 26
Berger, Johann Nepomouk, 27
Berk, Michael, 95n
Bernatskii, Mikhail V., 149
Berthelot, Gen. Henri, 83, 93, 107, 112
Bessarabia, 91
Bezkrovnyi, Kuz'ma Ia., 63
Bilimovich, Andrei, 121
Biskups'kyi, Gen., 109–10
Black Sea Cossacks, 36
Black Sea Fleet, 38
Bobrinskii, Count Aleksei, 53
Bobrinskii, Count Vladimir, 78n
Bolbochan, Col. Petro, 106
Bolsheviks, xiii, xiv, 7, 8, 10, 13n, 14, 19, 20, 21, 22, 25, 26, 36n, 41, 43, 44, 45, 47, 57, 58, 60, 62, 64n, 99, 113, 116, 118, 125, 126, 128, 131, 134, 137, 139, 142, 150, 152, 154, 155, 161, 166, 167, 168, 174
Borius, Gen. Albert, 107, 108
Borot'ba, 46
Borschak, Elie, 22n, 26n
Bratianu, Ion, 91
Bredov, Gen. N., 129
Brest-Litovsk negotiations and treaty, 24, 25, 26n, 55, 59, 60, 62n, 71n, 90, 95, 111
Brinkley, George A., 119n, 138n, 173n
Browder, Robert P., 4n, 7n, 11n, 14n, 15n, 16n

Brusilov, Aleksei A., 3n, 18
Bubnov, A. D., 145
Bunyan, James, 20n, 25n, 26n, 47n, 69n
Bych, Luka O., 36n, 37, 57, 65n, 115

Carley, Michael Jabara, 153n
Caucasia, 46, 96, 119; see also Northern Caucasia and Transcaucasia
Caucasian Savage Division, 18
Central Executive Committee (Soviet), 4
Central Powers, 3, 11n, 20, 24, 26, 27, 38, 43, 47, 50, 55, 59, 72, 74n, 83, 167
Central Rada, 14, 15, 19–26, 32, 36n, 37, 38, 43–7, 50–1, 120, 122
Chaikovskii, Nikolai V., 96, 97
Chebyshev, N. N., 131
Chelishev, Viktor N., 131
Chelnokov, Mikhail V., 131
Cheriachukin, A. V., xv, 61, 63, 68n, 115
Chernogorchevich, A. D., 72n
Chernov, Viktor, 46n
Chkheidze, Nikolai S., 5, 104
Choulguine, Alexandre, 22n; see also Shul'hyn, Oleksander
Churchill, Winston, 130
Clemenceau, Georges, 93, 95, 112, 128
Committee of the Caucasian Mountain Peoples, 63
Communist International, 159
Comte de Martel, Damien Charles, 156
Congress of Nationalities, 16n
Constitutional Democratic party, see Kadet party

Constitution of 1906, 1n
Constitution of the Volunteer Army, 68–9
Cossack Southeastern Union, 46
Council of Members of the Legislative Houses, 53
Council of Nationalities, 16n
Council of People's Commissars, 21, 25, 26
Council of (Russia's) State Unity, 78, 79, 80, 85, 110, 111, 169
Council on Foreign Affairs, 94
Crimea, 145, 155
Curzon Line, 135
Curzon, Lord George, 147

d'Anselme, Gen. Philippe Henri, 108, 112, 115
Dagestan Cossacks, 46n
Dashkevych-Horbats'kyi, Volodyslav, 85, 91
Demidov, Ivan P., 43
Denikin, Gen. Anton I., xiv, xv, 2, 3n, 4n, 5n, 6, 8, 9n, 10, 17n, 18, 19, 36n, 39, 40n, 41, 52, 53n, 54, 55, 57, 58–66, 67, 68, 70–81, 83, 87n, 88n, 94n, 96, 97, 99, 100, 107, 108, 111, 112, 116, 117, 118, 119, 120–54, 156–7, 160, 163–4, 166, 168n, 169, 170, 171, 173–5
Denikin, K. V., xv
Denikin's Special Council, see Special Council
d'Esperey, Franchet, 93, 107
Deviatka, 39n
Diderikhs, Lieut. Gen. M. K., 37
Directory, see Ukrainian People's Republic (UNR) Directory
Dnieper River, 150, 154
Dobrynin, V., 36n, 42n

Dolenha, Sviatoslav, 77*n*
Dolgorukov, Prince Pavel, 79, 80
Dol'nyts'kyi, Myron, 135*n*
Don Cossacks, 16*n*, 25, 26, 35, 36–37, 40*n*, 46–7, 61, 62, 74, 94, 147, 150, 158
Don Krug, 35*n*, 46, 61, 115, 133
Don region, xiv, 25, 27, 35–9, 42, 43, 46, 47, 58, 61–4, 72, 73, 75, 77, 96, 104, 115, 133, 150
Doroshenko, Dmytro, 18*n*, 21*n*, 23*n*, 45*n*, 47*n*, 51*n*, 52*n*, 63, 64*n*, 65, 72*n*, 73*n*, 74*n*, 75, 76*n*, 77*n*, 78*n*, 79*n*, 85*n*
Dragomirov, Abram M., 68, 69, 70, 77, 140
Dratsenko, P., xv
Drozdovskii, Mikhail G., 61
Dukhonin, Nikolai N., 46
Duma Committee, 66
Duma, State, 1, 2, 3*n*, 4*n*, 13, 53, 78*n*
Dumova, A., 7*n*, 13*n*, 15*n*

Efimovskii, E., 121
Ekaterinodar, 36*n*, 57–8, 63*n*, 65, 66, 68, 70, 71, 72, 75, 83, 91, 92, 94, 95, 100, 102–3, 108, 109, 117, 121, 125, 127, 131, 133, 135, 167, 171
Entente, 3, 8, 9, 10, 21–3, 26, 39, 43, 47, 48, 49, 53, 67, 72, 74, 75, 77, 81, 83–100, 102, 106, 107, 108, 111, 112, 118, 121, 127, 132, 133, 137, 138, 143, 144, 146–7, 151, 157, 168
Entente Military Command, 74*n*
Erlich, Lieut., 83
Estonia, 38*n*
Evert, Aleksei E., 3*n*

Fedenko, Panas, 45*n*

Federalist League, 104
Fedorov, Mikhail M., 39*n*, 86, 131
Fedyshyn, Oleh S., 51*n*
Filimonov, A. P., 36*n*
Finland, 12, 14, 38*n*, 42, 73, 98, 102
Finns, 13, 16, 29, 103
First All-Ukrainian Military Congress, 19
First All-Ukrainian Workers' Congress, 20
First Universal, 37
Fischer, George, 15*n*
Fisher, Harold, 26*n*, 47*n*
Fitzwilliams, Maj., 23
Foch, Marshal Ferdinand, 153, 161
Footman, David, 62*n*, 96*n*
France, 22, 23, 47–9, 55, 70, 81, 83, 84–5, 93, 96, 103, 108–18, 127, 128, 135, 138, 146, 148, 152, 154, 161
Free Cossacks, 51*n*
Freydenberg, Col. Henri, 108, 112, 113, 115, 116, 118

Galicia, 87, 128–9, 134–44, 152
Galuzo, P., 11*n*, 14*n*
General Secretariat of the Central Rada, 14, 21, 22, 24, 26, 45–8
General Staff of the Russian Army, 1, 3, 5
General Staff of the Volunteer Army, 40, 57, 66
General Ukrainian Naval Council, 38*n*
George, Lloyd, 138
Georgia, 38*n*, 73, 94, 144
Gerbel', Sergei N., 75
German Military Command, 50, 51, 62, 71*n*
Germany, 7*n*, 10, 11*n*, 27, 49, 50–2, 55, 61–8, 71*n*, 74*n*, 82, 87, 90, 93, 94, 165, 166–8

Gerua, Gen. A., 129, 134
Giers, N. N., 162
Glinka, Grigorii V., 151, 160
Gogol Union of Little Russians, 44
Gol'denveizer, A. A., 44, 51n
Golovine, N. N., 17n, 64n
Gorlov, Capt. V. M., 160
Great Britain, 47–8, 55, 81, 83, 93, 119, 127, 128, 130, 138, 146, 147, 148, 151
"Great Russia," 49–50, 84
Grishin-Al'mazov, Gen., 107, 108n, 109, 114
Guchkov, Aleksandr I., 3n
Gurko, Vasilii I., 71, 92
Gutnik, Sergei M., 53

Halip, Artem, 115, 136, 137
Hamm, Michael F., 1n
Henno, Emile, 49, 81, 84–5, 88–9, 91, 92, 105–8, 118
Herder, Johann G., 31
Heroys, Gen., 130
Hrekov, Gen. Oleksander, 108, 110, 117n
Hrushevs'kyi, Mykhailo, 22

Il'in, N. S., 84
Iudenich, Gen. Nikolai, 159
Ivanov, G. P., 61
Ivanov, N., 7n
Izvol'skii, Aleksandr P., 97

Jadwin, Edgar, 130
Jassy Conference, 84, 85, 88–93, 94, 108n, 110
Jews, 13, 45, 87, 113, 114, 171
Juzwenko, Adolf, 42n

Kadet party (People's Freedom party), 8, 12, 13, 14–15, 16, 35, 36, 39, 40n, 48, 51n, 52, 53, 63, 64n, 66, 68, 69, 70, 71, 72, 73, 82, 85, 86–7, 89, 94, 101, 103, 105, 111, 118, 124, 131, 141, 143, 148, 164, 166, 169, 170, 172, 173, 174
Kadygrobov, V. A., 121
Kakliugin, K. P., 35n, 36n, 62n
Kaledin, Aleksei M., 8, 35n, 36, 42, 46, 47, 61
Kalmyk Cossacks, 46n
Kamianets-Podilskyi, 51n, 116, 128
Kaplin, P. M., 63
Kapustians'kyi, M., 129n
Karnicki, Gen. Aleksander, 135
Katkov, George, 2n, 7n
Kazanovich, B., 58n
Keller, Count Fedor, 3n, 78, 79
Kenez, Peter, 144n
Kennan, George, 23n
Kerensky, Alexander F., 4n, 6n, 7n, 9n, 14n, 15n, 16, 18n, 21n, 40n, 105
Keyes, Gen., 130
Kharkiv region, 67
Khrystiuk, Pavlo, 16n, 18n, 19n, 23n, 24n, 25n, 26n, 37n, 106n, 116n
Kievlianin, 44
Kirei, Gen., 157
Kistiakovs'kyi, Bohdan, 28n, 32–3
Kistiakovs'kyi, Ihor O., 78n
Koenker, Diane P., xi
Kokoshkin, F. F., 13n
Kolchak, Adm. Aleksandr V., xv, 95, 97, 102, 103, 132, 133, 160
Konovalets', Colonel Evhen, 117n
Kornilov, Gen. Lavr G., 7–10, 18, 19, 35, 39–43, 57–8, 72, 147
Korolenko, Vladimir, 140
Korostovets', Ivan, 74n

Kotliarevskii, Sergei A., 71*n*
Krasnov, Petr N., 61, 62, 63, 64, 69, 73, 74, 77
Kravs, Gen. Antin, 129
Krivoshein, Aleksandr V., 52, 78*n*, 86, 151, 158, 160
Krupenskii, A. I., 121
Krymov, Gen. Aleksandr M., 5, 8
Kuban Cossacks, 36, 40*n*, 42, 46, 57, 62–4, 68, 69, 94, 147, 150, 158
Kuban campaigns, 43, 57, 58, 61, 62*n*, 65, 68*n*, 72
Kuban Rada and government, 36, 37, 46, 57, 62, 63, 64, 68, 69, 115, 117, 133*n*, 150
Kuban region, 40*n*, 42, 43, 57, 63, 64, 65, 66, 68, 69, 73, 77, 104, 115

Lampe, A. A. von, 36*n*
Lapin, N., 1*n*
Latvia, 38*n*
Laverychev, V. I., 7*n*
Laws for the Provisional State Structure of Ukraine, 51
Lednitskii, A., 11*n*
Left Center, 52
Lehovich, Dimitry V., 71*n*
Lenin, V. I., 7, 13*n*, 25, 37
Leontovitsch, Viktor, 15*n*
Levashov, S. V., 110
Levyts'kyi, Osyp, 135*n*
Liapunov, M., 121
Lisovoi, Ia. M., 61*n*
Lithuania, 38*n*
Little Rada, 24
"Little Russia," 49–50, 67
Lomnovskii, Gen., 75, 76, 79, 80
Lopukhovskii, Col., 75
Losskii, N. O., 72*n*

Lotots'kyi, O., 12*n*, 136*n*
Lukomskii, A. S., 3, 8, 46, 59, 68, 69, 145
L'vov, Prince Georgii E., 16, 19, 97, 103
Lynnychenko, Ivan A., 121
Lyzohub, Fedir A., 51*n*

Maiborodov, V., 114*n*
Mai-Maevskii, Gen., 122, 141
Makarenko, Andrii, 77*n*, 106
Makhno, Nestor, 157
Makhrov, Gen. Petr S., 145*n*, 146*n*, 147, 149–50, 151*n*, 159–63
Maklakov, Vasilii A., 48, 95–8, 100, 101–5, 130, 131, 133, 134*n*, 144, 152, 153*n*, 162, 171*n*, 172, 174
Malinin, I. I., 124
Mangin, Gen. Charles, 148, 153, 154
Manifesto of the Volunteer Army, 40–3, 70
Manilov, V., 45
March Revolution, 1, 3, 10, 41, 42, 70
Margolin, Arnold D., 47*n*, 99*n*, 104, 105, 106*n*, 113, 114, 115, 116, 128*n*, 131
Margulies, M. S., 53*n*, 65*n*, 70*n*, 91*n*, 93*n*, 103, 104, 107*n*, 108*n*, 109*n*, 110–11, 114
Markov, Sergei L., 8, 39*n*, 58
Mawdsley, Ewan, 142*n*
Mazepa, Isaak, 128*n*, 129, 130*n*, 152*n*
Mazzini, Giuseppe, 31*n*
McCully, Newton H., 148
McNeal, Robert H., 92*n*
Mel'gunov, S. P., 2, 3*n*, 9*n*, 97*n*
Meller-Zakomels'kii, V. V., 110*n*

Merezhkovskii, Dmitrii, 159
Miliukov, Pavel N., xv, 1, 2, 6,
    11n, 12, 30n, 39, 40, 42, 52n,
    59, 64n, 71, 75n, 85n, 86–7, 88,
    89, 90–3, 97n, 169n, 171n
Millerand, Alexandre, 155
Miller, Gen. Evgenii K., 162
Monarchist bloc, 66, 75n, 77, 79,
    80, 81, 145, 146, 169, 171
Mustafa (Kipchak *murza*), 156
Mykytiuk, Dmytro, 135n

Nakhichevanskii, Khan, 3n
Natiiv, Gen. O., 65
National Center, 44n, 52–4, 67, 70,
    78, 79, 80, 82, 85, 87, 95, 109,
    111–12, 113, 118, 168, 169,
    171, 172
Naumenko, V. G., 57n
Nazaruk, Osyp, 109n
Neniukov, Adm., 145
Nepenin, Gen., 130
Neratov, A. A., 149
Nesterovich-Berg, M. A., 8n
New Russia, 67
Nichols, Robert L., 119n, 144n
Nikolaevich, Nikolai, 3n
Nikolaevsky, B. I., xv
Nol'de, Baron B., 13n, 71n
Non-party Bloc of Russian Voters,
    44, 53, 140
Northern Caucasia, 36n, 46, 107,
    119, 122
Noulens, Joseph, 22
Novgorodtsev, Pavel I., 121, 124
Novikov, Col., 89
Novocherkassk, 37, 38, 39, 43, 45,
    47, 57, 58, 61, 62, 68n

Obolenskii, V. A., 146, 147n, 149,
    151n

Odessa, 106–18, 127, 132
Odinets, Dmitrii, 45, 159, 160
Officers' Union, 6, 7
Omel'chenko, Hryhorii V., 63
Omelianovych-Pavlenko, Gen.
    Mykhailo, 130, 136, 139, 158
Omsk, 95, 96, 97, 99
Orlov, Capt., 145

Panina Sofia V., xv, 70, 71, 172
Paris Peace Conference, xv, 94, 95,
    98, 104, 116, 128, 170
Pavlov, E. V., 62n
Pélissier, Jean, 22, 137
People's Freedom party, *see* Kadet
    party
Percy, Gen. J. S. J., 151
Perlik, D. D., 156
Pétain, Gen. Philippe, 128, 129
Petliura, Symon, 77n, 81, 101, 106,
    107, 110, 112, 117, 125, 127,
    128, 130–8, 141, 142, 152, 153,
    ·160, 161
Petrunkevich, I. I., 174n
Petrushevych, Evhen, 128
Pichon, Stephen, 84n, 116
Pilsudski, Józef, 128, 160
Piontkovskii, S. A., 35n, 157n
Pipes, Richard, 12n, 25n, 28n
Poklevskii-Kozel, Stanislav, 84, 85,
    87, 108
Pokrovskii, G. K., 36n, 69n
Poland, x, 11, 12, 13, 42, 71n, 73,
    90, 98, 121, 128, 130, 131,
    134–5, 136, 138, 144, 148,
    152–64
Poles, 13, 29, 60, 128, 130, 134,
    152, 153, 154, 159, 160, 161, 168
Polish Riflemen's Brigade, 18
Political Council, 40, 43, 66, 68n,
    120

Poole, Gen. Frederick C., 83
Popular Socialists, 52, 93
Progressive Bloc, 1, 3, 12, 66
Protofis, 53, 54, 73, 81
Provisional Commission (on the Nationality Question), 121
Provisional Government, 3–5, 6, 7, 11, 13, 14–17, 18, 20, 21, 22, 35–36n, 37, 39, 42n, 44–5, 46, 48, 51n, 61n, 69, 71n, 82, 97, 99, 139, 174, 175
Putilov, Aleksei I., 8

Radkey, Oliver, 46n, 68n
Raeff, Marc, 12n
Rakovskii, G. N., 140n
Red Army, 25, 80, 142, 149, 159, 162
Reshetar, Jr., John S., 26n
Revolution of 1905, 27
Riabovol, Mykola S., 36n, 57n, 63
Riasnianskii, O., 64, 75n
Right-Bank Ukraine, 125, 128
Right Center, 52
Riha, Thomas, 1n
Robeck, Adm. Sir John de, 148
Rodichev, Fedor I., 6, 131
Romania, 91, 138
Romanovskii, Gen. Ivan P., 8, 9, 39n, 57, 146
Rosenberg, William G., x, xi, 15n, 70
Rossiia, 113
Rozwadowski, Gen. Tadeusz, 160, 161
Russian army, 2–7, 17–19, 21, 25, 38n, 46n, 60, 72
Russian High Command, 2, 7, 17–19
Russian National Union, 44
Russian Political Conference, 97–8, 99n, 136, 162
Russian Political Council (in Paris), 98–101, 102, 104; *see also* Special Council
Russian Political Council (in Warsaw), 159–60, 162
Russian Provisional Committee, 85
Russian Socialist Revolutionaries, 13n, 39, 40, 46n, 52, 62n, 116, 105
Russian Third Army, 159–60, 161, 162
Russkaia mysl', 33
Ruzskii, Nikolai V., 3n

Sakharov, Vladimir V., 3n
Sakhno-Ustymovych, Mykola, 50, 51
Sapieha, Eustachy, 160
Savchenko, F., 14n
Savenko, Anatolii I., 67, 114, 121, 140
Savinkov, Boris V., 39, 97, 136, 159–62
Sazonov, Sergei D., 49n, 84n, 87, 94, 95, 97, 100, 103
Schorske, Carl E., 27n
Sergeev, A. A., 4n
Shafir, Ia. 145n
Shakhin-Girei, Sultan, 63
Shatilov, Gen. Pavel, 145, 158
Shavel'skii, Georgii, 146n
Shcherbachev, Gen. Dmitrii G., xv, 18, 24, 83–4, 93, 153
Shemet, Serhii, 51n
Shevchenko, Taras, 12
Shingarev, Andrei, 6, 39
Shlashchev, Iakov A., 145, 146
Shlashchev-Krymskii, Ia. A., 145n
Shliapnikov, A. G., 4n
Shlikhter, A. G., 107n

Shul'gin, Vasilii V., 1*n*, 3*n*, 44*n*, 49, 53, 59, 66–9, 84–8, 92, 94, 107, 108, 109, 112, 113, 114, 120, 121, 134, 140, 171
Shul'gin, Vitalii Ia., 44
Shul'hyn, Oleksander, 23, 74*n*
Shura, 14
Shvets, Fedir, 77*n*, 106
Siberia, xi, xv, 46, 73, 95, 104
Sich Riflemen, 117*n*
Skaba, A. D., 125*n*
Skobtsov, D. E., 36*n*, 63
Skoropads'kyi, Hetman Pavlo and his government, 18, 50, 51, 53, 54, 57, 63, 64*n*, 66, 69, 73–82, 85, 87, 88, 90, 91, 106, 117, 120, 168, 169
Skoropads'kyi, Ivan, 51*n*
Smith, Jr., C. R. 11*n*
Socialist Federalists, *see* Ukrainian Socialist Federalist party
Socialist Revolutionaries, *see* Russian Socialist Revolutionaries *and* Ukrainian Party of Socialist Revolutionaries
Sokolov, Konstantin N., 39*n*, 64*n*, 65*n*, 68, 69*n*, 70, 71, 171
Southeastern Union (Cossacks), 46
South Russians (Iugorossy), 44
Special Council of the VA, 68–71, 77, 99–100, 101, 102, 118, 120, 123, 124, 139, 141, 143, 170, 171, 172, 174; *see also* Political Council
Stankevich, V. B., 5*n*
State Council, 53, 78*n*, 88
Stepankivs'kyi, V. Ia., 30*n*
Stepanov, Vasilii A., 39*n*, 68, 70, 71, 101, 121, 171, 172
Strakhovsky, Leonid, 7*n*
Struve, Petr B., 15*n*, 28–30, 32, 39*n*, 97, 149, 155, 158, 162, 166*n*, 167, 169*n*, 171, 172
Stryzhevs'kyi, Col., 129
Suny, Ronald Grigor, xi
Suvorin, Boris, 37*n*
Svatkovskii, V., 30*n*
Svechin, Gen. Mikhail A., 61, 62*n*, 64*n*

Tabouis, Georges Marie, 22, 23, 26, 47, 48, 84
Tahanrih district, 62, 64*n*
Tatar National Congress, 156
Tatars, 156–7
Tatishchev, B. A., 149
Terek Cossacks, 46*n*, 150
Third All-Ukrainian Military Congress, 20
Third Cavalry Corps, 5
Third Universal, 20, 21, 45, 46*n*
Thompson, John M., 94
Titov, A. A., 86, 89
Transcaucasia, 64*n*, 94, 119, 144, 156
Troinitskii, N. A., 12*n*
Trotsky, Leon, 25, 60, 142
Trubetskoi, Prince Evgenii N., 79*n*, 153, 154
Trubetskoi, Prince Grigorii N., 39*n*, 71*n*
Tsaritsyn, 62, 64, 65, 122
Tsereteli, Iraklii, 104
Tyshkevych, Count Mykhailo, 136

Udovychenko, Oleksander, 152*n*, 155*n*
Ukrainian Academy of Sciences, 51*n*
Ukrainian Central Rada, *see* Central Rada
Ukrainian Democratic Agrarian party, 50

Ukrainian Galician Army (UHA), 128, 134–7
Ukrainian General Staff, 129, 130, 136
Ukrainian Military Command, 162
Ukrainian National Committee (Paris), 158
Ukrainian National Gallery, 51n
Ukrainian National Museum, 51n
Ukrainian National Union, 73, 77n, 87, 89, 90, 92, 116
Ukrainian Party of Socialist Revolutionaries (UPSR), 19, 21, 24, 39, 46, 52, 116, 126, 137
Ukrainian People's Hromada, 50
Ukrainian People's Republic (UNR), 19–21, 23, 24–5, 26, 27, 45, 48, 50, 62n
Ukrainian People's Republic (UNR) Army, 23, 64n, 65, 74, 77, 81, 105, 106, 107, 108, 110, 116, 117, 125, 127, 128, 129, 133–4, 136, 137, 139, 153, 162
Ukrainian People's Republic (UNR) Directory, 77, 79, 90, 91, 101, 106, 107–18, 120, 125–32, 134, 136, 137, 139, 142, 143, 152, 157, 160–3
Ukrainian People's Republic (UNR) government, 23–7, 43, 46, 47, 48, 116
Ukrainian Social Democrats, 24, 46, 116
Ukrainian Socialist Federalist party, 24, 51n
Ukrainian State Archives, 51n
Ukraintsev, N., 7n
Union for the Salvation of the Motherland, 35
Union of Agrarians, 73
Union of Military Duty, 5

Union of Regeneration, 70, 79, 80, 85, 95, 109
Union of the Honor of the Motherland, 5
Union of the Russian People, 85
Union of Volunteers for National Defense, 5
United States, 47, 48, 74n, 130, 148
Ural Cossacks, 46n

Val', E. G., 83n
Valentinov, A. A., 151n
Velikaia Rossiia, 169
Vendziagol'skii, K., 39n, 41n, 43n; *see also* Wendziagolski, K.
Vinaver, Maksim M., 95n
Vishniak, Mark, 105
Vynnychenko, Volodymyr, 22, 24, 47n, 77n, 106, 107, 114n
Vyshnegradskii, Aleksandr I., 8
Vyshnevs'kyi, Archbishop Ahapit, 141

Walicki, Andrzej, 32n
Walkin, Jacob, 15n
Wandycz, Piotr S., 135n
Wendziagolski, K., 39, 41, 43, 120
Western Ukrainian People's Republic (ZUNR), 128
Wheeler-Bennet, J. W., 59n
White, James D., 7n
Wildman, Allan K., 4n, 17n
Woodward, E. L., 138
Wrangel, Gen. Petr N., 2n, 122, 145–64, 175

Xydias, Jean, 114n

Zaionchkovskii, P. A., 17n
Zaitsov, A. A., 64n

Zalizniak, M., 13n
Zaslavskii, D. O., 3n
Zbruch River, 152
Zhabotinskii, Vladimir I., 28, 33